Shania Twain
Still The One

Shania Twain
Still The One

JIM BROWN

QUARRY
MUSIC
BOOKS

The publisher acknowledges the support
of the Government of Canada,
Book Publishing Industry Development Program,
Department of Canadian Heritage.

Order No. QP 00815
ISBN 1-55082-269-1

Editorial development, design, type, and imaging
by Quarry Press Inc., Kingston, Ontario, Canada.

Published by Quarry Press Inc.,
PO Box 1061, Kingston,
Ontario K7L 4Y5 Canada
www.quarrypress.com.

Distributors:
General Distribution Services
325 Humber College Blvd,
Etobicoke, ON M9W 7C3,
Canada

Music Sales Corporation
257 Park Avenue South, New York, NY 10010
USA

Music Sales Limited
8/9 Frith St, London W10 3JB England

Music Sales Pty. Limited
120 Rothschild St., Rosebery, Sydney, NSW 2018
Australia

Printed in the United States of America by
Vicks Lithograph and Printing Corporation

CONTENTS

A
New Standard
for
Country Music

1

THE SHANIA STORM

WHEN SHANIA TWAIN FIRST APPEARED IN NASHVILLE, a poor girl from way the heck up there somewhere in Canada, she was not immediately recognized as a messenger from the Great White North, a commoner in the court of country Kings and Queens who was not afraid to speak her mind, not intimidated by the courtiers on Music Row. Steadfast in her prerogative to express a woman's point of view in her country music, Shania ascended the throne. By the time she'd taken her message to the whole world and come home to her husband Mutt Lange on the Swiss shores of Lake Geneva, filmmaker Luc Besson had completed *The Messenger*, his feature film version of the life of St. Joan, starring Milla Jovovich.

A timely re-telling of the inspiring yet tragic tale of the world's prototypical feminist, the first of ten indictments read to Joan d'Arc before she is burned at the stake in Besson's film is the transgression of wearing male apparel and cutting her hair short in the fashion worn by 15th-century men. While Shania would be the first to say she is no Joan, her declaration of a woman's right to have a little fun begins with forgetting that she is "a lady" and wearing both "men's shirts" *and* "short skirts." Similar to Luc Besson's contemporary Joan d'Arc, John Madden's Academy Award winning *Shakespeare in Love* portrays the first (fictional) appearance of a woman on the Elizabethan stage, the mysterious woman of Shakespeare's sonnets who presumes to play the role of Juliet, which, until then, had, oddly enough, been a role for a young man. Gwyneth Paltrow's portrayal of this young woman who must disguise herself as a man to play a woman's role suggests just how far women have come since Elizabeth I was a queen. While Shania has no inclination to suffering a fate as tragic as Juliet who challenged the patriarchal old world system by wanting to marry into the wrong family, the marriage of her "country" with Mutt's "pop" has been met with opposition.

Shania doesn't want to be a man, but she's determined not to be reined in by politically-correct behavior, free to color her hair, free to "feel the way I feel," determined to "feel like a woman." These lyrics from *Man! I Feel Like A Woman!* prompted male reviewers to say she was vacuous, style with no substance. They just didn't get it. Women got the picture, though, especially feminists who realized immediately this was a challenge to the party line adopted during the women's liberation years. Women who wore suits to challenge men's power had often became cold and severe, and, in their pursuit of power, they often sacrificed their femininity.

Shania was now suggesting the time had come to drop these antagonistic postures, just as she'd suggested in *Whose Bed Have Your Boots Been Under* and *Any Man Of Mine* that it was time for country music to drop the cheatin' and hurtin' lyrics and lifestyle. While both attitudes had once inspired country women singers, the time had come for a new standard. Phrased positively, Shania Twain's cornball, hokey lyrics did have a deeper meaning, though her message from the North was seldom acknowledged among her critics. And while her fans found her lyrics to be good medicine when they sang along, she presumed to be no Doctor Ruth, no fortune teller or psychotherapist. There were no hidden agendas here. She was not about to start a movement or run for political office. She just wanted people to give themselves a chance to be happy — to set themselves free from the cares and concerns and restraints that held them prisoner. Her fans empowered her to make COME ON OVER, she acknowledges, and on tour, she paid them back in spades.

Shania has rocked her country all over the world, having as much fun as she can, singing silly lyrics like "You're a rocket scientist . . . That don't impress me much . . ." and "Honey, I'm home and I had a hard day. Pour me a cold one and by the way . . . Rub my feet, gimme something to eat . . ." Her audiences have been large, loud, rowdy, and proud to be there together with *their* Shania. In the face of these massed celebrations, opposition from the country music establishment has melted away. During her Come On Over tour, *Country Weekly* received so many letters supporting Shania and denouncing a put-down letter they had printed that the publishers championed Shania with yet another cover story. "I'm sick and tired of seeing readers trash Shania," wrote Melissa Trask of Clearwater, Florida. "Just because she has a body worth showing off or doesn't wear a cowboy hat doesn't mean she isn't country. I think they are all jealous and should get over it." Her fans were surprisingly articulate when it came to telling it like it is. "This 'holier than thou' attitude toward Shania is so hypocritical," John Sifford of Fort Collins, Colorado, wrote. "She is a bright, spirited, and gifted artist who has lived a fairly conservative personal life. She doesn't dress like they did back in the '50s, but her music is powerful, unique, energetic, and fun. Her fans come from all walks of life; from four-year-old kids to teenagers, to old guys like myself. After nearly 50 years of listening to country music, Shania is my all-time favorite." In a fan club newsletter, eight-year-old Michael Waring of Springdale, Arizona paid tribute to his Shania with a poem: "Listen to the thunder, way up in the North land / A beautiful songwriter and a rockin' Country band / Music that is as pure as any Daisy or Rose / It's the Shania Storm, the one everyone knows." With fans like Melissa and John and Michael, Shania could hold her head high above the controversies about her native heritage, country music pedigree, and vamp image that swirled among her many navel-gazing critics.

What worked best for Shania was to accentuate the positive in her songs. When she sang, "Love gets me every time. My heart changed my mind. I gol' darn gone and done it . . ." people felt good, gol' darn it! When she sang, "You're still the one that I love . . ." her fans felt how grateful she was for the love of her husband. If she was "so glad we made it," so were they. And when she finished off with "Look how far we've come my baby . . ." she was still the one her fans loved. Look how far they had come together. They could feel it being there with her. Singing along with Shania, they felt they were part of her love.

2
SHOW US YOUR SHANIA

L ANA FLOEN HAD EIGHT YEARS OF EXPERIENCE SINGING with her husband, keyboard player Keith Floen, in their Calgary-based country band Kickstart before she got lucky. Lana was one of the first 50 callers to Calgary's Country 105 FM who qualified as contestants in the "Sing at Shania" contest in May 1998. Competing at Dusty's Saloon, Lana next became one of ten semi-finalists, winning for her rendition of Shania's *(If You're Not In It For Love) I'm Outta Here*. As the final night of competition neared, Lana had moments of doubt as to whether she really wanted to keep on going. Stage fright was an affliction that would sometimes come over her. She would sometimes forget her lyrics. The largest audience she had ever entertained was 6,000 celebrant Calgarians during Stampede Week at the Fracmaster Breakfast. But her family and friends were behind her now, urging her on. All of the finalists were required to deliver their best effort singing to a track of Shania's first hit, *What Made You Say That*. Lana practiced it every day. She was nervous, but her kids, Kylah, 8, and Jason, 14, told her she could do it. No problem, mom.

Calgary, the Stampede City . . . where stetsons and western boots are regularly worn by oil company execs, politicians, weekend cowgirls, country boys, and ranchers . . . and where, when they are not competing in rodeo events, professional rodeo riders prefer sneakers and baseball caps to the C&W costumery . . . is the real capital city of country music in Canada. Not Toronto, where various attempts to establish a "Nashville North" identity haven't taken hold. Country music is the music you hear in Alberta truck stops, not muzak, pop, or hip hop. Calgary is home to the studios of CMT Canada and the Canadian Country Music Hall of Fame, a city where two-steppers and line-dancers work out on the dance floors of large Texas-style night clubs like Ranchman's, Cowboys, and Longriders, and where the NHL hockey arena is named the Saddledome. Canadian country musicians and recording artists from the Maritimes (like Hank Snow and Anne Murray) through the Ottawa Valley and the farming belt of southern Ontario, across the vast expanse of the Canadian prairie and the Rocky Mountains down the Fraser Valley on the West Coast all converge on Calgary for the Stampede in July and Canadian Country Music Week in September. When touring country superstars like Garth Brooks bring their shows to Canada, they often stage two or three shows in Calgary simply because they sell more tickets there than anywhere else north of the 49th Parallel. Shania was scheduled to perform two shows at the Saddledome.

Lana Floen did win that final night at Cowboy's, and right then and there, she was being interviewed by the dailies and the entertainment magazines. Her phone was ringing off the wall. What had she gotten herself into? But she had plenty of family support. Lots of friends' support. "We all went out for brunch," she remembers. "It was really neat. It was quite an experience."

Before she knew it, June 6th had rolled around. "I went to sound check and got to listen to Shania," she remembers. "I got to rehearse the song with her bass player, Andy. He was great, telling me just to relax when I went out there. He was a nice fella. He told me to enjoy the experience. Get out there and do your thing. Look around. Look around at all the people. Just enjoy it."

Lana's husband was on the road at the time, so after this rehearsal, she and her sister, Cindy, went over to Dusty's where this madness had all started and had dinner with some friends and family. Back at the Saddledome, they took their place among the 19,000 fans who were arriving. Cindy was thrilled to see that she and Lana had seats in the front row. As the songs *It Takes Two* and *Black Eyes, Blue Tears* went by, Lana did her best to keep herself calm, which was difficult because Shania had everyone pumped. When the high-school choir began filing onto the stage for *God Bless The Child*, someone tapped Lana on the shoulder and led her to an area near the side of the stage.

Although Lana had not met with Shania at all that day, she could remember the time, two years earlier, during the the 1996 Canadian Country Music Awards show, when Keith had been one of the studio musicians who had backed Shania — Keith had introduced her to Shania. Lana still had the photo Keith had taken of her and Shania. That was a comforting memory. She remembered Andy's words, too, and began to breathe deeply and slowly, calming herself, and began to look at all the people. They were having a great time! Miraculously, she felt a total calm come over her. This was going to be just fine.

As the choir began filing off the stage, a stagehand with a flashlight came up to Lana and led her to another level. She was handed a microphone and given her final instructions. When Shania announced Lana's name, she stepped forward to center stage. Shania asked her a couple of questions, and they got comfortable with the audience together. When the band started the song, Lana could feel the music throbbing through the soles of her shoes. "It was awesome," she remembers, "and the audience — when I first got out there — they were applauding, but then there was a quiet lull as they waited to see if I could actually sing. I got about three words into it — and they just went absolutely crazy. It was *awesome!*"

Lana sang the lead vocal, with Shania handling the backup, which, when Lana thought about it later, was really something — Shania Twain was *her* backup singer, even if it was just for one song. Just for one sweet blessed moment in time. When the song ended, "I just wanted to get off the stage," Lana recalls. "I knew she had a show to do. But Shania said, 'Wait, wait . . . that was excellent! Next time, if I'm in town and I've got laryngitis, I'll just call Lana and she'll fill in for me.' "

The fans loved them both, hooting and hollering all over again as Lana made her exit. Backstage, Lana was interviewed by a reporter from *The Calgary Sun,* and by the time she came back into the theater, the show had ended. People from the sky-boxes were beginning to stream down from above. Someone she knew caught sight of her and a chant went up. "They were chanting, 'Lana! Lana!'" she recalls. "I was all goosebumps and tears. Someone said, 'There she is!' And people were trying to touch me . . . a little girl grabbed at my coat." Outside the Saddledome, as she and Cindy were walking down the stairs toward the taxi cabs waiting on the street below, there were more people who showed their appreciation. She spoke with a man and a woman and their little girl and signed autographs, scribbling her name nervously across the souvenir programs.

Singing with Shania that night had restored Lana Floen's confidence and reaffirmed her resolve to perform and record. "I've always wanted to do this. My whole life," she told me. "I just felt, once I had got up with Shania, that this is what I want. I can do this. It just confirmed that for me. It was wonderful! I still get very nervous before I go up, but it's under control these days. We're just working on our CD, right now. My husband and I write together. At this point we're shopping around for a studio and a record deal. We've been working with Rick Hutt who produced Beverley Mahood and quite a few people." Lana and Keith haven't decided on a title for their album, yet, but they just might call their CD: "Go For It!"

"I didn't know if I really wanted to do it," Tianna Lefebvre admitted later, remembering how she had very nearly not entered the "Show Us Your Shania" contest at all. "Like, I didn't think they'd pick *me*, anyway." Tianna's boyfriend, Mike Sanyshyn, an accomplished studio musician who has toured with several Canadian country stars and had even been considered for Shania's touring group during the auditions, told her to do it anyway. Send in her tape.

Tianna was not a teenage sensation or a lucky amateur, like some of the girls were in other cities; she was already in her 20s and had recorded a five-song CD and one of her cuts had been played on the radio. The winner of the Vancouver version of the "Show Us Your Shania" contest would sing *What Made You Say That* with Twain at GM Place, the home of the NBA Grizzlies and the NHL Canucks. A week before the concert, Tianna and the other finalists competed at a local TV station. The Morning Show team from JR Country FM, Clay St. Thomas and Tamara Stanners, were there, too, broadcasting the competition live over the radio. Tianna was still convinced that they would pick one of the other singers, but after she sang *What Made You Say That* on the VTV *Breakfast Show*, it was her name that show host Linda Freedman announced would be joining Shania Twain in the big arena show.

"As soon as it happened," Tianna remembers, "everyone was phoning. The phone was down. Nobody could get through. There was flowers . . . people sent me flowers. There was people phoning for interviews. Namwa Delaney from VTV came to my home in White Rock the night of the show and did another interview. It was neat." That quickly, after she had almost not entered at all, Tianna had become part of Shaniamania.

The night of the arena show at GM Place, Tianna was scheduled to run through the song with Shania during sound check but there wasn't time, but just before Shania went on, she met with Tianna. Someone snapped a photo of the two of them together. When the star recognized Tianna's boyfriend, Mike Sanyshyn, it broke the ice.

"She said, like, 'Hi, Mike, how are you?'" Tianna remembers. "It was cool. And she said that she'd heard my tape. She had okayed it. She was very real. Very personable. You know, like, a lot of stars might not have listened to it."

Tianna waited in the wings until it was time for her to go on. Shania was out there on the lip of the stage, wearing shiny black skin-tight, patent-leather pants, a white halter top, a leopard jacket. She was awesome. For a brief frightened millisecond Tianna felt like fleeing, then Shania was telling the audience that she wanted them to meet someone special — me, Tianna thought. Me! Someone was pushing her forward. Shania had her firmly by the hand. Tianna felt a spark, a sudden transfer of energy, and she knew there was going to be no problem.

Tianna would later tell interviewers, "She was squeezing my hand. I remember how tightly she held it. And then she introduced me and said I was going to sing. And she gave me a huge hug. She was great! She made me feel really comfortable, actually. It was a great experience." For months afterward people would come up to her and say, "You're the girl who sang with Shania!" A few months later, Tianna met with Tony Rudner, her producer, who told her she really needed to get a full album out there. She could sing much better now than when she'd recorded that first five-song CD. Those cuts had really only been demos. Now, running through some of the songs that she and Tony had selected, she could hear that Tony was right. Perhaps some of Shania's magic would rub off on her when she went into the studio to record. Perhaps it already had.

Bobbi Smith was 12 years old when she sang with Shania during her second visit to Vancouver on April 4th, 1999. To many people, Bobbi was a novelty act. A kid who could sing like an angel. But she was determined to erase that perception, to prove that there was more to her than merely her young age. As one of the finalists in the "Show Us Your Shania" contest the previous year, Bobbi had competed with four adults on the VTV *Breakfast Show* in Vancouver. She hadn't won that day, but later in the year she had cut a record, a song called *Sweetwater* written for her by Doug & The Slugs' guitarist, Al Rodger. At 11 years old, she was still singing to her tracks when she performed at the 1998 BCCMA Awards show in Vancouver, but she had already begun to work with bands. That summer, she sang the national anthem at the opening ceremonies of Mountainfest in Merritt. Then, on Saturday, on the huge Mountainfest stage, she opened for Travis Tritt, performing her set backed by some musicians from nearby Lynden, Washington. Vancouver *Province* reporter John P. McLaughlin gave her a terrific review. She was on her way!

When Shania came back to Vancouver, Bobbi won the "Under 12 Twain" contest, competing with four 12-and-under finalists at CJJR, the local country station, where her performance was broadcast live on the radio. Bobbi had an edge over some of the other under-12s. Ever since she had turned 10, she had been picking up backing track tapes from Peter and Smokey at the Power Plant, the recording studio on the old EXPO site where you could "make your own record" singing to star tracks. She already had tons of tapes of Shania. She could sing *Any Man Of Mine, Whose Bed Have Your Boots Been Under, (If You're Not In It For Love) I'm Outta Here* . . . So, *What Made You Say That* was easy. No problem.

At 10, she'd been fine with singing karaoke country. With a band people took her more seriously. People were saying she looked like LeAnn Rimes, which was cool. Of course, most 12-year-olds hadn't opened for Travis Tritt. Now, she had a chance to sing *with* Shania Twain! She had also begun to define her image. Bobbi's mom, Karen Smith, remembers that one afternoon when Bobbi was watching "small but good" Olympic champion skater Tara Lipinski, Bobbi had said, "I could be 'little but loud.'" For a while, it became her manifesto.

Little but loud Bobbi Smith breezed through the competition at JR Country FM. Next thing you know, she was in a silver limo gliding over the 2nd Narrows Bridge from Lynn Valley into Vancouver and pulling up at GM Place. Things were kinda moving quick and slow at the same time, she recalls. *That* was different. But she could handle it. She would get used to it. She would be cool. Her mom and dad and grandfather, Barry, and grandma, Audrey, her vocal coach, Monique Lefevre, and her auntie Velma were all there with her in the limo. They were all pretty excited.

At sound check, Andy, Shania's bass player, ran through the song with Bobbi, playing an acoustic guitar while she sang. His eyes got real big, she noticed, when he heard her first notes. He was impressed. Which was good. People were always surprised when they first heard her sing. She was so small, they said, but she had a real big voice. She felt happy, and the swirly energy with all the people coming and going and talking together backstage was good, too. There was a meet-and-greet with Shania. Tons of people, now. Tons of food, but she wasn't hungry at all. Everyone was buzzed just being there. Her manager, Pat Roberts, was up from Seattle, so she was in good hands.

Then, she and her mom, Karen, went out front and took their seats in the front row as the show was about to begin. For a while, it all went by like a dream. Leahy, the openers, were fun. Different. Then Shania appeared, a jungle cat in skin-tight leopard skin pants and turtle-neck top, the bared muscles of her tummy and lower back rippling as she paced back and forth across the stage and leapt onto the T-shaped catwalk directly above where Bobbi sat. Shania wasn't wearing heels or boots, but her gray hi-tech runners were wedged like heels, and the way they gripped was super, way better than stacked pumps would grip.

When they came out to take Bobbi backstage, the butterflies set in. Pat was there and he got a smile out of her. She felt herself loosening up, and then the kids from her high-school choir came into the green room all chattering away. They were buzzed, too. Ready or not, they trouped out on their way to sing *God Bless The Child* with Shania. Bobbi knew that Shania did that at all of her concerts. It was kinda settling to see them. Bobbi had a whole pack of her own people in the audience, not just her folks, *lots* of people who had paid scalper's rates for their tickets and weren't sitting anywhere near the front row. They had all told her that they would be there for her. And she knew she looked good in her black velour jumpsuit and platform pumps. The boa arm-bands were kinda appropriate, too. When the choir came back *they* were *really* buzzed. They'd pulled it off! They were done. For a moment, Bobbi imagined herself afterwards, sweating and happy that she had gone and done it.

When it was time, Bobbi was pumped, way pumped, numb, almost. Her legs were all pins and needles like when you sit cramped and lose your feeling in one of your limbs. Her legs were falling asleep. She had to walk it off. Pat helped her. He didn't want her to freak, she could see that. Then she was onstage walking toward Shania and the bright glare of stage lights, and the band hit into the song. She did good. So good, that — and she couldn't *believe* this — Shania's eyes got big when she heard Bobbi's first notes, just like Andy's had. Real big. Shania was surprised, and she missed one of her harmony lines before she got it together. Shania was just like everybody else — she couldn't believe that such a big voice could come out of such a small person.

The days that followed kept on getting sweeter and sweeter. Bobbi began recording in earnest, working with award-winning producer Tony Rudner. Tony was almost her next-door neighbor, so that worked out fine. She performed at Countryfest 1999 before an audience of 20,000 along with the Dirt Band, Brad Paisley, John Berry, and Deana Carter in Portland, Oregon. She opened for Chris LeDoux in Montana and Julian Austin at the Williams Lake Stampede. One week she worked with the musicians from Randy Travis's band who were so smooth and *so* professional. During rehearsal, they got her to do a different arrangement of *Walkin' After Midnight*. And they were impressed when she got it on the first run-through!

A single from the sessions with Tony Rudner was mailed to radio in the Northwest and all across Canada. The song was *Sorry* and for 18 glorious weeks it was on the Canadian country charts. In the fall of 1999, Bobbi recorded some more tracks, including *Close My Eyes*, a song written by Lisa Brokop, this time working with Tom McKillip, Lisa's musical director, as her producer. The material that she tracked on the sessions with Tony Rudner and Tom McKillip was very good, written by some of Nashville's best, like Cyril Rawson, Sherrié Austin, LuAnn Reid, and Greg Barnhill.

When Bobbi's debut album I CAN'T HELP MYSELF was released, the lead single, *Up*, zoomed up the Canadian charts, climbing in leaps and bounds. Bobbi's bio, printed in black and white, had only one highlighted item among her many accomplishments. That item was her performance singing onstage with Shania Twain at GM Place. For Bobbi, singing with Shania was her highlight of highlights. She was proud of that moment and determined to someday be the singer with the star billing. To be the next Shania, if she could. Singing was what she loved to do. Most kids her age spent a lot of time watching TV. She hated TV. She would rather be singing or listening to music on the radio.

Bobbi's brother, Brody, was special, too. He'd played Pugsley in *The New Adams Family* TV series when he was eight. Now, he was being offered movie roles. Karen Smith was proud of her children's accomplishments, but for a while there when she'd been taking Brody to his TV studio tapings all week long and Bobbi to her weekend gigs, Karen had barely had a life of her own. She had quit her job as a hair stylist and pitched in. Taping 65 episodes of a TV series in 18 months was some kind of Guinness Book of Records accomplishment, though, and it had burned Brody and Karen out. She and her husband Gordy were glad that the intensity had tapered off some. Of course, the $51,000 that Bobbi's album cost to record and manufacture meant that budget balancing was required until Bobbi got onto a few more tours and Gordy was able to sell those records at her shows. Like many mothers of child prodigies, Karen Smith bubbles over with enthusiasm when she's telling stories such as how Bobbi first got started singing country, glued to CMT, imitating Reba's every move, watching Reba and not *Mr. Dressup* like so many other three-year-olds did. Singing with Shania had also made a big impression. Bobbi had begun to wear runners during her shows, making Shania moves on stage. "She can kick as high as Britney!" Karen says proudly. "She's a mini-Shania!" That summer at Mountainfest 2000, she was slotted for a nine o'clock show right before Brooks & Dunn.

Choosing to sing a duet with an aspiring young female vocalist in every city on her tour was one of many special moments that Shania Twain designed into her shows. Helping others was second nature to her. She'd always done it when she could. And she always had time to spend with the physically and mentally challenged fans who came to her concerts. She *was* a generous spirit. She had created her own charity, donating the proceeds from the royalties from her song *God Bless The Child* and a percentage of her show revenue to help feed kids whose parents were financially challenged. During the tour itself, special promotions, such as the online ticket auction organized by the Ottawa Centre for Research, raised thousands of dollars in support of school breakfast programs.

Although some detractors have painted negative portraits of her, the truth is that Shania Twain cares. She has become an inspiration for many people, including one young boy, Alexander McDonald, who came out of a coma while listening to her music. She met with the three-year-old recovery patient, who called her 'Nia, in 1997. She also met with Kristy Plotsky, a survivor of a heart transplant who had written Shania an inspiring letter, and hundreds of similarly inspired patients who had recovered. In fact, there have been times when she has been an inspiration simply through people discovering her music videos on CMT. When leukemia patient Merle Terlesky spent three weeks confined to his hospital room in Vancouver General recovering from a bone marrow transplant, *Province* staff writer Brandie Weikle reported that "an angel in tight jeans paid him a visit."

"I started clicking onto CMT and saw lots of Twain," Terlesky told Weikle. "It just kind of cheered me up." Being confined to bed in the hospital meant that he missed out when tickets for her concert went on sale, so Terlesky entered contests in hope of winning a ticket. He even considered exploring the scalper option. However, with his limited disability pension, he couldn't afford to go that route. Desperate, the former paramedic wrote a letter to Shania herself. "I thought the letter would just disappear into the wind," he told Weikle.

Wrong. Universal Music rep Alfie Williams credits Twain herself with reading Merle's letter and instructing her people to make sure that the bone-marrow-transplant patient was given two tickets to her show and a backstage pass. She wanted to meet him.

"I was bouncing off the walls," Terlesky relates. "I was very touched . . . I have absolutely no idea what I am going to say when I meet her." This example of Shania Twain's generosity of spirit moved Alfie Williams to declare, "It's quite amazing that a woman of that popularity still hasn't lost touch."

The singers who got to perform with Shania felt equally blessed. Of course, welcoming teenaged sensations up to sing with you was an honored tradition in country music. The fans loved it when you did it. And they often showered equal enthusiasm on the child prodigies themselves. Tanya Tucker had scrambled up onto stages with Ernest Tubb and Mel Tillis when she was knee high to a grasshopper. Shania had done it herself with several Canadian country stars when she had been a kid. Now that she was touring again, after a few years spent forging a career in Nashville, and a few more making hundreds of personal appearances to promote her breakthrough album THE WOMAN IN ME, it was her turn. Her fans had turned out in droves at malls when she was merely on hand to sign a few autographs. She owed them for that support. It was payback time. Time to help others a bit.

The way that Shania set the contests up, the local radio stations screened the applicants and promoted her tour at the same time. It worked well for the radio people, too. And it involved each local community. Shania's originality and her generosity was appreciated by people at all levels of the country music business. CJJR FM deejay Tamara Stanners, one of the people who became involved in the Vancouver promotion, was aware of the controversy that followed Shania around, but saw Twain's most important influence as being crucial to the emergence of a new individuality in country that was sorely needed in 1998. "The big thing for me this year was the Dixie Chicks," Tamara told Vancouver *Province* journalist John McLaughlin. "They gave me faith and hope that there's a future for country because it scares me sometimes the way Nashville makes everything sound so similar. People criticize Shania for not being country enough, but I think she gave people the freedom to expand and I think the Dixie Chicks grabbed that. I want country music from the heart. Garth showed everybody how important marketing is in country music, and I think everybody followed his lead a little too well, took it too far, and forgot what the music is all about."

Shania had helped refocus peoples' interest back onto the music. Before the tour had begun, she had told *Country Song Roundup*'s Janet E. Williams, "I'm proud that the music is strong enough and succeeding without tour support. Most people tour to support the stuff on their album and that's where a lot of their sales come from. So I am blown away by it and I can't believe it and it is happening so fast. How can you have a number one album and not be touring with it? I don't know! I am just so thrilled with it. There is no formula . . . Nobody knows the answers to what does and doesn't work. I think that people are the only ones who do. You just have to give it your best shot and let them decide."

When she first began to tour, Shania was also proud that her show employed the latest technology — huge video and exploding pyrotechnic displays — all working along with her fun-loving approach to performance, but she cautioned journalists not to be blinded by the smoke and mirrors. "We're offering the best in lighting and sound," she told *Country Weekly*'s Deborah Barnes, "but the music will always be first. It's funny, but my performance style and communication hasn't changed since I was a teenager . . . I started singing without my guitar and moving around the stage and interacting with the fans in clubs. I was always a communicative performer, so I've just taken that to a bigger stage."

What her concerts revealed was that Shania had a far wider appeal than mere record sales figures had shown. As the audiences were seen arriving at her concerts, they were discovered to be a river of grannies, granddads, moms, pops, teenagers, and four- and five-year-olds. Everyone knew her songs and everyone was eager to participate when she drew them into the action on numbers like *Honey, I'm Home*. Her music had not simply crossed over. Her music had hit a universal harmonic. Country fans, Metallica fans, it didn't matter. They were all Shaniamaniacs, many of them dressed up Shania style, many waving banners that declared, "We love you Shania!" and "Shania Rocks The Country!"

"You would not *believe* the number of kids," Shania proudly told Deborah Barnes. "Two-year-old kids know all the words. It blows my mind. I bring them up on stage and it's unbelievable."

3
ON THE ROAD WITH SHANIA

B Y 1998, SETTING UP A NORTH AMERICAN TOUR was a complex task. When you were done planning and ready to hit the road, a convoy of trucks would be lined up, loaded with stage machinery, speaker cabinets, mixing boards, sound and lighting gear, and video equipment for the big projection screens. Your crew would include more than 25 technicians who would be greeted by 40 local stagehands when the trucks and buses pulled up to a venue.

Terry Gray, stage manager/production manager of the Merritt Mountain Music Festival (Mountainfest), has experienced the development of stage shows from the days when he and Dan Cowan first toured with Canadian rock star Jerry Doucette who hit big with *Mama Let Him Play* in the late 1970s. Cowan has gone on to work with the Canadian production company House of Blues, the successor to Universal Concerts, as their West Coast rep. Cowan often calls up his old pal, Terry, when he has a show coming to town. Having Terry's experienced presence available means that some of the headaches Dan faces on a day-to-day basis will go away more quickly. Terry had gotten the call when Celine Dion's tour came west; he also got the call to help out with Shania's tour.

"I had some time off during the time Shania was here," Terry remembers. "And I was interested in seeing her show, and being part of it, because I'm interested in production. Sound and lights and staging and all of that, that's where my interests lie. I'm interested in seeing what us Canadians are doing in comparison with what's going on out in the international scene. I was totally blown away by the production of Celine Dion's show. When she left here, everything that was in that show was Canadian, and it made you feel proud that *that* was going out to the rest of the world."

Terry Gray had special reasons for wanting to assist in the production of Twain's show. "I like her as an artist," he told me. "She's a *woman*! She sings about being a woman. I like that. It's great music." Terry was also interested because local musician Cory Churko was working in Shania's band. "Cory was a member of the Underground Outlaws here for many years," Terry remembers, "and it was great to see him get a break. Of course, I'm always interested in the set-up. I want to be there when they load in."

Terry told me that there were at least eight trucks loaded with equipment and eight or more tour buses. Shania's bus, however, was not brought directly to the GM Place compound. "Shania doesn't like to stay right next to the venue," says Terry. "She likes to be somewhere outside of the city. She stayed out near . . . Horseshoe Bay . . . somewhere." And the production company protected her privacy.

"They have this incredible video production that travels with them," Terry says with enthusiasm. "They set up what is basically a movie studio backstage so that they can produce a video as she is performing. And they could play all the footage that was inserted, the bits and pieces that were part of the production, onto the video screens that the audience saw during the show."

Each afternoon, the video technicians would play the footage of the previous night as they were cuing up their system. Naturally, Terry was glued to their every move, helping out when his assistance was needed here and there. "Shania would come in," he remembers, "being the street person, not the rock star, and come in there and want to see what the show had looked like, the previous show. She was really hot on Leahy, their support act. She really liked what they did and she wanted to see their footage. It was always really good. She was also there to get the artist's perspective — watching herself, doing a critique of herself, looking to see what she could do to make things better."

Per usual, Shania's warm personal manner won Terry over right away. He was impressed with her interest in the show production and her drive to want to make things better. Up close and personal, however, he had to readjust his image of her. "I was really surprised," he says, "to see what a tiny person she is. I don't know what I expected. She's tiny — but she's cute as a button. We're used to seeing her in her videos where she is bigger than life with the angles of the shots and so on." At five-foot-four, in loose-fitting shirt and jeans, her mane of auburn hair tucked beneath a baseball cap, and wearing the comfy Luc Bergen flat shoes she prefers when she's not entertaining, Shania does, as Terry suggests, become just another person who has walked in off the street. Just acting naturally becomes her ready-made camouflage. Shania has told interviewers that she and Mutt sometimes slip through crowded theater lobbies to take in the latest feature film. Together, they've become pretty good at blending in.

"Still," Terry says, "in street clothes, just hangin' around in there watching things, she was cute as a button!" It seems to be his favorite description of her. He is a huge supporter. "I'm glad that she's doing as well as she is," he says. "She's got a great talent. She's got a great band. They sound really good, and we should all be proud that she's a Canadian."

One of the moments Terry remembers with fondness, from Twain's two separate Vancouver stop-overs, is the time he drove Shania to the Robson Street boutiques where she wanted to do a little shopping. Once she realized that he proceeded with caution, was level-headed, and wasn't hitting on her or her friends, he became the one she asked for if she needed a driver.

"One of the other neat things that happened," Terry remembers with a wry smile, "is that I managed to get a tour jacket. I had asked to get a tour laminate (a laminated All Access pass), because that is one of the few things that I collect at the productions I work on . . . I've got *way* too many t-shirts. I had asked one of the guys who I had done some running for if I could have a laminate, and he gave me this jacket. It was from some special promotion they did somewhere. It was nice of him to give it."

In September 1998, I spoke with Cory Churko in Calgary right after Shania's sound check and rehearsal for the CTV Canadian Country Music Awards show at the Jubilee Auditorium. Cory was upbeat and cheerful about the positive way things were being handled during the tour. As a member of Shania's band, one of the three fiddle players on the show, he'd fit right into the production, especially since the players were included in the way the choreography was blocked out. Musically, the band was required to duplicate much of what had been played on the studio sessions and mixed into the cuts on the album. But the band had its own toughness, too. Shania's live performance band took each studio track that one step further into the real world. So, it was cool that management respected their input.

"We're taken care of really well," Churko told John McLaughlin. "We just kinda show up and make sure we're good and rested for the show. We roll into town on the bus and all our luggage is taken care of . . . The stress is pretty minimal. If we're flying and we're going for a long way, we'll go executive class. The short ones — it's coach. Sometimes we have private charters, we get a little jet. Those are always fun. You drive right up to the door, you don't have to put your seat belt on, and you can stand up when the plane's taking off."

A few years ago band players often pursued a relentless routine of party-down madness — groping groupies and raising hell — when they were out on the road. Churko alludes to less spectacular and far healthier pursuits on the Shania Twain tour. One night in Saskatoon, the band and the crew had gone skating and a fun-time hockey match had broken out just like the spontaneous shinny games that took place on frozen ponds all across the Canadian prairies every weekend during the winter. Other times they would go swing-dancing. One thing was for sure, they all had to be in great shape. Shania — their fearless leader — there wasn't a gram of fat on *her*, and she moved about the stage with tireless energy.

There had been a few incidents, however, where physical stamina alone wasn't enough to prevent some near disasters. "I fell off the back of a stage one night in the States somewhere," Churko told McLaughlin. "It was really funny but I . . . could have done some damage. Shania walked onto one of the treadmills backwards once and went flying. She actually bounced when she hit."

When I spoke to Dan Cowan, he was wary at first. There had been far too much mud slung at Shania, and Dan didn't want to see any more flying from my pen. Once he recognized that I was writing a tribute rather than an exposé, Dan turned me on to Shawn Sakamoto of Gold & Gold Productions. Shawn had been the guy most thoroughly involved in Shania's swings through western Canada. I already knew that Shawn was a second generation production company person who was following in his father's footsteps. Shawn's dad, Ron Sakamoto, is known throughout Canada as a capable guy, acknowledged by the industry for his longstanding track record.

"With Shania's production people," Shawn told me, "they are all out of Bruce Springsteen's or Billy Joel's traveling entourage, it seemed like, when I was working with them, and they're the best in the business. They just go out of their way to make sure that they do a show every day that physically can be done without a lot of last minute wondering if the show is going to go up or down. They don't paint themselves into a corner by attempting to do things that are technically impossible to do within the buildings they are playing.

"Because Shania wants to play everywhere, they have to have a package that can play everywhere. Shania's people are simply the best at doing that. It's the lowest stress day. All you have to do is be sure that everything that we talk about, in the months prior as we are advancing the show, is possible."

Once again, I had to assure Shawn of my intentions because he held a fierce loyalty to Shania Twain. He simply did not want any ill to befall her through anything that he said.

"The way that these people go about doing their business," he confided, "you'd never know that there's that much work going on in the building. They're just that good. I've worked with guys that have one semi-truck — that you have to work a hundred times harder on — than these guys showing up with their eight or ten trucks."

As Terry Gray had suggested, there were even more buses than trucks. "George Travis, their production manager," Shawn explained, "is very good to his crews. They don't stack their buses full. A bus that holds 13 people, they put six or eight people per bus, because everybody is living on that bus. They put their lighting crew on one bus. They put their sound crew on a bus. The video guys are on a bus. The musicians are on a bus. Shania has her own bus. It just makes living on the road a lot easier for those folks. . . . I would have *loved* to have been a musician on that tour! Shania treats all of her people so well that it's unbelievable. She does a lottery every day for all of them. They have their names in a bingo bag. She pulls out a name a day and they get a cash incentive. I think it's a few hundred bucks . . . You just never hear about those things happening on the road with anybody else. With some crews, usually, a crew guy won't even think about the artist, you know . . . They're just doing their gig type of thing, or, they'll have a negative spin on the artist because they might not like their job or whatever is happening at home and they blame it on their work . . . or whatever. You won't find one person in the Shania Twain crew or entourage that has one bad experience or negative thing to say. You just won't. It's unbelievable."

"We put a dinner together for them in Kamloops," Shawn recalls. "They were dancing until three or four in the morning. Shania was dancing with everybody. She'll dance with one guy till that guy wears out. Then she'll dance with somebody else . . . and she never breaks a sweat! I don't know how she does it. It's a really great organization. She just takes the time to make sure that everybody's happy.

"There's concerns that Shania has every day about how she wants thing to run," he volunteered. "They go through a whole production-development cycle that happens prior to us. All of that is coordinated as part of the marketing plan with the record company and everyone. So, by the time it comes to me, what I get is a multiple page production rider and contractually we agree that everything that's in that booklet can happen the day of the show in the building that we put her in. We go about making sure that, what the vision is, is the reality the day of the show.

"Now, with some artists, the vision can be so grandiose that there is no common mind found, the day of the show . . . we just know that things aren't going to be the way they are expecting them, and that they are expecting to do something that just can't happen. With Shania, they are so good, and all these people have been to these buildings so many times before, they know what they're doing. These guys could do this with their eyes closed.

"In Kamloops, for example, all we did was we didn't hang up as many P.A. cabinets, because we didn't need as much sound coverage. Short of that, they got the 100 percent full-on show. Basically, this show was built to fit between the dashers of a hockey arena. So, we know that we have 210 feet by 85 feet to work with including our floor seating. Next time she comes through, it'll be a whole new ball game — in a stadium configuration. Then, it'll be more along the lines of what you've seen in the recent videos.

"If you notice Shania's show, she doesn't have a whole lot of production up there. If you look at Vince Gill — the last tour, he had his big garage set. It made it a real homey feeling, like they were just playing in a garage band. Or, you take a look at Brooks & Dunn — they've got everything. They're comin' in, they're bringing Nashville to you! That's what you get out of their show. With Shania, there's nothing on the stage. *She's* on the stage. And all the lights are up ... and everything's up. Everyone from 360 degrees can see what she is doing. Everyone can be a part of the show from that perspective. Let's face it, that's all she needs. You just put her on a stage . . . You could put her on the stage at the Jubilee Auditorium with no microphone at all . . . and she could sing like a canary, and you'd have a full house. She wants that, eh?

"I tell you what, it's just so wonderful to work with her. It really is. A lot of times, you do a lot of big shows, and you just don't say that. All you've got to say is, 'Thank god it's over.' It's not like that with Shania. It's just so wonderful to work with her and her people."

When I mention that I had interviewed Bobbi Smith, Shawn remarks, "I actually saw Bobbi just last month in Calgary where she was doing some dates. She was doing some dates in the United States before, but — to spend one song on stage with somebody who is just so awesome — the magic has to come through! There are only a couple of artists that have won my respect the way that Shania has. One of them would be Harry Belafonte, who, at the age of 71, spent two hours after his show back of the Jubilee in Calgary — the last time I worked with him — talking to a lady who ran a children's home. She was in her 70s as well. And he took the time to talk with her. He took down the kids' names. He took down her name. It was a good two hours. He was supposed to be long gone. We were done loading out the Jubilee and he was still out there talking to her. It's very rarely that you meet something that Royalty *should* be. But Harry Belafonte is like a King. And Shania Twain, when you work with her, she is every bit a lady — she is the Queen of Canada, as far as I'm concerned."

Some country stars have buses of their own, decorated with customized paint jobs that emphasize the artist's logo or depict their name in stylized lettering. This bus thing has become a some sort of weird Nashvillian status symbol which began back in the late 1940s with traveling bands like Ernest Tubb & His Texas Troubadours, though most of the stars in those days still traveled in big old Cadillacs, Lincolns, and Chryslers pulling trailers piled high with luggage and equipment. Hank Snow drove a top-of-the-line Buick, which pulled a house trailer for his family, and his crew drove a van that housed a grandstand-sized tent and his horse Shawnee. George Jones' first band bus was far from luxurious, a rusted old hulk with chairs and bunks that weren't fastened down, but when George got together with Tammy Wynette, their modern bus bore the banner, "Mr & Mrs Country Music." When Tammy divorced Jones, the first change she made was to have the bus banner repainted. As the years went by, acquiring a bus became a symbol that announced you had truly become a Nashville star. Traveling by bus was the way to go, especially when people began to tear out some of the seats and install a few bunks. Waylon Jennings developed the concept some when he customized his Silver Eagle and made it one of the first fully equipped recreational vehicles to hit the highway. These stars proudly exhibited the many luxury features they had installed — mirrored bedroom suites, fully-equipped wet bars, big screen TV sets — each newly installed feature designed to help the stars get through the boring hours while their Silver Eagles rolled down the more than 100,000 miles of roadway per year that many of the top acts traveled.

Shania had traveled by car and cube van back in the days when she had been singing in bands in Ontario, riding with the guys, helping set up gear, then she had shared a rented bus with Toby Keith and John Brannen in 1993 during their "Triple-Play Tour." During the last flurry of promotional appearances before she began rehearsals for her first major tour, interviewers were curious — Did she have a bus now? What was it like? What luxuries was she having installed?

"I'm designing it right now," Shania told *Today's Country* radio show host Greg Shannon. "I'm having a lot of fun. Nothing really fancy, I'm pretty simple about stuff like that. It's not going to be elaborate. I'm a bit frugal as far as having all the latest things goes. I want a good stereo. No carpets, because I'm taking Tim with me and I don't want all that dog hair and all that . . ." Tim, Shania's specially trained German Shepherd, was both a companion and a bodyguard, a practical solution to mounting the sort of security that celebrities needed to have on a 24-hour-a-day basis in the 1990s.

The space aboard her bus would be practical, too. She wanted to be able to feel at home on the road, to cook meals, so the kitchen was fully fitted out.

"Nothing really extravagant, actually," Shania described her home on wheels. "My bus probably won't be considered all that exciting. I'm going to take my horse with me. I'm gonna pull him along. He's a good traveler. He's traveled most of his life. He's a retired show horse, so now he's going to travel just for fun." When she hit the road, her horse Dancer, like Hank's Shawnee, would travel in its own trailer. Daily rides would become key to her road resilience. "I definitely have to take my horse with me," she told James Muretich during another interview. "So, I'm probably going to be pulling a trailer behind the bus. I gotta have my horse. Otherwise I'd go crazy . . ."

4
SHANIA IN PERSON

EVERYTHING I READ AND HEARD ABOUT SHANIA while researching this book confirmed my initial impressions when I first interviewed her in 1995 during the promotion of her break-out THE WOMEN IN ME album. Ken Ashdown, the local Mercury Records rep, gave me a call and asked if I was interested in meeting with Shania. I told Ken that I didn't have the CD. "No problem," he said, "I'll express courier you the CD and promo pak. Would you like to have breakfast with my artist?"

Before I left the office at six, the CD arrived and I just took the courier package along without opening it, drove home, and ate dinner. Shania Twain had put one album out, but nobody had sent me a copy. Though Larry Delaney, publisher of *Country Music News*, had raved about it in a cover story I read, I wasn't sure I'd even heard a single cut on the local country stations. Maybe a song called *Dance With The One That Brought You*.

I opened up the package, stuck THE WOMAN IN ME CD on the stereo, and flipped through the promo pak. Hummm, I thought, Shania is a looker. They've got her pictured here in full-color Vogue fashions as well as the more usual cow-girl get-up. There was even a picture of the singer with a horse. By this time, the music had gotten to me. Hot damn, I thought, this is something new. It's like Garth, only exciting, like he was on his first records. As I familiarized myself with the Shania Twain story from the artist bio, I began to realize that Shania's producer and husband Mutt Lange had created a whole new kind of country music that was lush and glitzy pop but at the same time never really veered from its country roots.

The following morning, the tires of my vehicle humming over the paved surface of Lion's Gate Bridge, I reviewed the Shania Twain story in my head, recreating it from my memories of the bio. Shania (pronounced Shu-Nye-Uh) was Ojibway for "On My Way." Twain had been brought up poor in rural Ontario. An entertainer from age eight, her parents had wakened her up 'round about midnight to take her into the local watering-holes after last call and before closing time so that she could sing. It was a source of income for the family. So, she'd been in the music business just about all of her life. When her parents' lives were tragically terminated in a car accident, Shania was already touring with her own band, but came back home to raise her brothers and sisters before heading to Nashville to become a star.

She'd had over-the-phone songwriting sessions with Lange before meeting him, then worked with him, and finally married the lucky guy. It sounded like a page torn out of the Patsy Cline song book, only with a happy ending. Little did I know at that time that THE WOMAN IN ME would go on to sell more than 12 million copies in the United States alone. Little did I know that Shania Twain's navel would soon be as famous as the great pyramid at Giza. But I did wonder just what Shania Twain would be like in person.

The hotel was one of those elegant ones. I was told I was expected, then led through a quiet restaurant to a table set for two. The tablecloth and napkins were color-coordinated. The silverware had been polished till it gleamed. When Ken Ashdown arrived and introduced me to Shania Twain, she was just another person. No big hair. No gobs of makeup. Dressed simply in soft hues. Her eyes did light up when I told her how good I thought her music was. They got real big. I realized then that Shania Twain was just another country girl who'd made it big in Music City, U.S.A. Right away, she wanted to know: What did I hear as the next single?

Ken Ashdown went off somewhere to make arrangements for the media party, which was to be held at the Press Club a few hours later in the day. Boy, I thought, I'm getting the royal treatment. Here I am alone with country's next superstar. I don't know why I thought that, but there was something about Shania Twain, a quiet confidence that told me that the music was no fluke, and that if anybody could out-Garth Garth, it would be this woman sitting across from me nibbling at her toast. Nor did I know then that during Twain's first meeting with Mercury Nashville president, Luke Lewis, Shania had declared that "she wanted to be as big as Garth" or that record exec Lewis had "looked into her eyes and knew that she could do it." I didn't learn that until I read a cover story in the January 1999 issue of *Cosmopolitan* magazine written by Trish Deitch Rohrer that featured the Timmins, Ontario singer as the magazine's "Fun, Fearless Female of the Year."

When Shania and I finished our munching and had our coffees topped up, I pulled out my trusty Sony Walkman and we began to talk on the record. "Your story," I began, "is kinda like the ultimate Cinderella story, the ultimate country music scenario, now that you've met the love of your life, your dream producer and co-writer, and gotten married to him. Especially, since your new CD seems to be one of the best releases to come out in a while."

Shania Twain's answer to my leading statement was confident and articulate. She even qualified my modifying phrases. "It is a Cinderella story," she said. "Not rags to riches, I'm not rich, yet. But certainly rags to something."

I could tell that Shania was skilled at these interviews. She had thought everything through beforehand. I tried a question: "When you were only eight years old you were singing . . . did they have to stand you up on a chair so the audience could see you?"

That got a smile. "The guitar was bigger than me. I wish they would have made those half-width size guitars when I was 8, 9, 10, 11, and 12. I was so small that they couldn't lie flat on me. They were sticking out, like that . . . because I couldn't get my arm around them. I've been doing it for a very, very long time. I'm 29 years old, now, and it has been 21 years that I've been singing professionally."

Good, I thought, the story just sort of rolls off her lips, all I have to do is guide this. I asked what were the stars on the radio who had inspired her.

"I listened to all kinds of music. We had a multi-format station happening in our home town. I heard everything through radio, but at home it was always country. And I only sang country music as a child. I had other influences. I was really enamored with the Carpenters. Their harmonies . . . were so beautiful . . . I learned so much, at a very young age from groups like that. Karen's voice is just like silk. It is so gorgeous! There were many influences along the way. I think Dolly Parton is the one from the beginning, right up until now, who has been the one. Dolly has done everything. She's an exceptional writer. She's an actor. She's a great personality. She's everything!"

If I had seen some of the videos that would soon be made, I would have made a reference to how Shania has become a music video star, acting in her own mini-movies. What I did say was more conversational. "I like Dolly, too. And one of the reasons I like her is her versatility. She's equally effective doing a simple acoustic bluegrass tune, like on the TRIO album, as she is in the larger country pop productions like *Islands In The Stream*. There's some splendid acoustic stuff on your new CD, as well."

Another smile.

"I'm very comfortable with that. I'm not a great guitar player. I never spent very much time perfecting my skills on guitar. I'm a singer-songwriter. I use my guitar as an instrument to write. But I never performed without my guitar until I was at least 16, and when I first put it down, it was so awkward without it. I think any singer-songwriter is comfortable doing an acoustic-type thing. They are used to just sitting and singing with the guitar. It is one of my favorite things to do."

"Let's talk about the album itself," I said. "Your husband, co-writer, and producer has not come up with a pop album here. It is very country!"

"Yes! A lot of people are pleasantly surprised. Maybe they were even expecting it to be over-produced . . . or too rock. I think what he has done, through this CD, is created a new standard for country music. What people don't realize is, of course — yes, as far as Def Leppard is concerned, he is a major contributor to that success, of course, yes! But to go from Def Leppard to Billy Ocean to Michael Bolton . . . they are worlds apart."

I wanted a clarification here, and said, "You are saying that he brings out the best in everyone he deals with?"

"He enhances the artist's music," she said. "A lot of the success of this album has to do with the writing and what he has done with the sound of it. Right from the beginning, he said, 'We need to go into your catalog. I want to know what you write, what you've been writing, then we'll go from there. You be the basis to the creativity of this album. Because it needs to be you not me.' And so that's what we did. Ten out of the 12 songs on this album are songs that I was writing before I even met Mutt. It feels very good. Like *Whose Bed Have Your Boots Been Under*."

"My favorite song is the second to last cut, *No One Needs To Know*."

Shania surprised me by snapping her fingers to establish a rhythm as she began to sing:

Am I dreamin' or stupid
I think I've been hit by Cupid
But no one needs to know right now . . .

Boy, Shania's mind is as clear as a bell, I thought.

"Working with a producer who can get the right vocal out of you makes the difference between an average album and a killer one . . ."

"Yes. Mutt's always been great at that with everyone he's worked with. I think that the advantage that we have together is that we love each other."

There it was in a nutshell. Shania Twain's THE WOMAN IN ME was music fostered by love and crafted by skilled hands. I put away my machine and we made small talk until Ken Ashdown returned. Later that day, I attended the Press Club meet-and-greet session and was knocked out by the extravagant spread of food and wine. There was sushi and quiche, for gosh sakes, exotic cheeses and fruit, everything gourmet and as tasty as Shania's entrance, this time looking like a million bucks and wearing a smile a mile and a half wide.

Shania Twain and Mutt Lange set new standards for country, confirmed with the release of her third album, COME ON OVER, the best-selling album by a woman in the history of country. Shania's is a Cinderella story, alright, and although she had told me in 1995 that she wasn't rich "yet," she surely is now. The January 1999 cover story of *People* magazine portrayed Shania Twain collaged together with the pop divas she had out-drawn during the past 12 months — Mariah, Whitney, Jewel, Celine, and Madonna. Here, for all the world to see, Shania Twain was recognized as the premier woman singer in the world.

Shania live in 1993 promoting her first album (top) and signing autographs during FanFest at Canada's Wonderland, August 1995.

Live on stage in Vancouver.

The
Canadian
in
Shania Twain

1

ON THE BORDER

S HANIA TWAIN WAS BORN EILEEN REGINA EDWARDS on August 28, 1965
in Windsor, Ontario, the second of three daughters born to Clarence
and Sharon Edwards. There, at the southern tip of Canada, across the
river from Detroit, Sharon Edwards' favorite music was country & western —
Patsy Cline, Hank Williams, and Buck Owens — but long before Sharon's
daughter Eileen headed to Nashville to forge a career writing and singing a style
that can now be described only as 'Shania' music, she would be drawn to the
Beatles and Little Stevie Wonder, Brenda Lee and Dolly Parton, the Supremes
and Marvin Gaye, Joni Mitchell and Buffy Sainte-Marie — a complex mix of
rock, pop, folk, dance, and country music that influenced her mature masterpieces.

Windsor and Detroit have a lot in common. Car manufacturing is the pri-
mary industry in both cities, and while Detroit has often been the end of American migrations — slaves traveling along the underground railroad from the
South through Detroit to Canada, displaced sharecroppers migrating North during the Depression looking for work on the assembly lines, and so-called draft
dodgers fleeing across the border during the Vietnam War — Windsor has been
the gateway for Canadians seeking fame and fortune in Chicago, Cleveland . . .
and Nashville. For Michelle Wright, the Canadian country female artist from
neighboring Chatham who immediately preceded Eileen Twain in her pilgrim-
age to Nashville, being raised in this cultural melting pot of southern Ontario
meant being able to listen to country on CHAM Hamilton, one of the top
country AM stations in the nation, and Motown on Detroit stations. Nearly
everyone in Canada who loved country music tuned their radios to *Don Messer's
Jubilee* and sat back to listen to the down-east sounds of Messer's fiddle-playing
and the vocalizing of Charlie Chamberlain and Marg Osborne. From Motor
City, the R&B grooves of Motown artists like the Supremes, the Miracles, the
Temptations, the Four Tops, Marvin Gaye, Mary Wells, and Stevie Wonder
were broadcast across the border. Just as Delta blues players had influenced

honky-tonking hillbilly singers like Hank Williams and Memphis rockabilly artists like Elvis Presley and Carl Perkins in the '50s, Motown influenced several country singers who were raised in southern Ontario in the '60s and '70s. Michelle Wright would call her unique brand of country "cruise music."

Arkansas rockabilly legend Ronnie Hawkins came to Canada during this time with Levon Helm in tow as the drummer for his band, The Hawks. Performing in clubs along the Yonge Street strip in Toronto, the Hawk forged a unique lineup of Canadian musicians — Robbie Robertson, Rick Danko, Richard Manuel, Garth Hudson — who along with Levon Helm became known as the Band. They would back Bob Dylan when he went electric, before recording the remarkable MUSIC FROM BIG PINK album at their communal home in West Saugerties, New York, a rich blend of country, rockabilly, rock & roll, rhythm & blues, even cajun music.

Along the other fabled musical strip in Toronto, Yorkville Ave, folk acts like Gordon Lightfoot, Neil Young, Joni Mitchell, and native singer-songwriter Buffy Sainte-Marie were making their big-town debuts. Born on the Cree Indian Piapot Reserve in the Qu'Appelle Valley in Saskatchewan and raised in Maine, Buffy Sainte-Marie, like Ian & Sylvia, tekked to Greenwich Village in the early '60s where she had hung out with Bob Dylan and caught the attention of Vanguard Records' Maynard Solomon. Solomon later described her singing style as having "a hint of blues-inflection, a trace of Indian song, a touch of Parisian chanson, an echo of beat, a bit of weird, but no where a direct or crucial influence," as Nicholas Jennings reports in his book *After the Goldrush*. Buffy was an original. When she put fellow Canadian Leonard Cohen's poem *God Is Afoot, Love Is Alive* to music, her recording became an eerie, echoing, tape-looped anthem providing both solace and inspiration. *Universal Soldier*, her song made popular by Donovan, was inspired by the sight of wounded and heavily bandaged soldiers as they were coming off a flight in the San Francisco airport. "All these soldiers came in pushing their friends in wheelchairs and on guerney stretchers," she later told Nicolas Jennings, "at a time when the newspapers were still insisting there was no war going on in Vietnam. But here was proof. These guys were bandaged up and looking real bad. It started me wondering exactly who was responsible for war." A Canadian-born songwriter became one of the first to write a popular protest song about the conflict in southeast Asia. Her songs would also become hits for Glen Campbell (*Universal Soldier*), Elvis (*Until It's Time For You To Go*), and Jennifer Warnes & Joe Cocker (*Up Where We Belong*).

While Sharon Edwards was carrying her second child, Eileen, a wannabe folksinger from Saskatchewan by the name of Joan Anderson — who had come east to Toronto to see Buffy Sainte-Marie at the Mariposa Folk Festival and stayed the winter in the city's trendy Yorkville district where she worked as a sales clerk in a department store — was entertaining her first Ontario audiences at small folk clubs like the Penny Farthing. Anderson was also with child. She gave birth in February 1965 to a girl, whom she named Kelley, but through the poverty of her circumstances was forced to give up for adoption, a decision that would haunt her throughout her life until she was reunited with Kelley in 1997.

While Sharon Edwards was coming to term, Joan began to make some song-writing breakthroughs, although her efforts to get gigs at better clubs in Toronto like Bernie Fiedler's Riverboat were less successful, and, by a simple twist of fate, Joan Anderson moved even closer to the Edwards' household when she met and married Chuck Mitchell, a Detroit folksinger, and took up residence with Mitchell on the campus of Wayne University in Detroit, directly across the river from Windsor. Their crash-pad existence proved a challenge, but Joan, now Joni, met Gordon Lightfoot, Buffy Sainte-Marie, Tom Rush, and Eric Anderson there. During one overnighter, visiting songwriter Anderson taught Joni some of the unusual open-tunings that would become key to her songwriting and perfor-mance style. After a gig with Chuck Mitchell in Winnipeg, Joni met Neil Young. She played him her song *Both Sides Now*, which, she told Neil was her song about coming of age. Young responded by playing her his own coming-of-age song, *Sugar Mountain*. Before she returned to Detroit, Joni crafted an answer song to Young's which she called *The Circle Game*.

During the final weeks of Sharon Edwards' pregnancy, the Byrds' jingle-jangly rendition of Dylan's *Mr. Tambourine Man* became the number one song in North America. The Beatle's *Ticket To Ride* was dropping from the Top 10 to make room for *Help*, the title track from the Fab Four's second feature film. It was a unique and pivotal moment for popular music.

As Nicholas Jennings remarks in his book *After The Gold Rush*, "a revolu-tion was underway. Led by the twin, transatlantic forces of Dylan and the Beatles, musicians everywhere began to aspire to more literate lyrics and more experimental sounds. The once-gaping chasm between folk groups and rock bands was blurring. Musicians moved freely from bars to coffeehouses and switched comfortably from rock and R&B to folk and blues."

While folksingers like Mitchell and Young, along with rock singers like John Kay of Steppenwolf and David Clayton Thomas of Blood Sweat & Tears, would travel south to California or New York to pursue their careers, American enter-tainers would travel north to Canada. Although not a draft dodger, one of the young Americans who relocated to Canada at the time of the Vietnam War was Detroit-born and raised Gilda Radner, who would discover a professional theater career in the Canadian cast of *Godspell*. "In 1969, while National Guardsmen lined the streets of Ann Arbor," Gilda remembered in her autobiography *It's Always Something*, "and the air was filled with pepper gas, young people were moving to Canada, angry over American political policies and resisting the draft. I moved, too, but because I fell in love with a Canadian sculptor." After two years in *Godspell*, Gilda became a member of the Toronto cast of Second City Theater, and, because the improv troupe was linked to a similar Chicago-based cast, she met Canadian actors like Ottawa-born Dan Ackroyd and Chicago actors like John Belushi and Bill Murray, all of whom were conscripted by Canadian producer Lorne Michaels for his "Not Ready For Prime Time Players" featured in New York on *Saturday Night Live*. When joined by the likes of Great White North SCTV comedians Rick Moranis, Dave Thomas, John Candy, Catherine O'Hara, Eugene Levy, and Martin Short, this cast of Canadian actors set new standards for prime-time TV comedy in North America.

It was a fortuitous moment in time for a songwriter to be born. The year Shania was born the Beatles were heard everywhere, displacing Elvis on albums playing on home hi-fi consoles and through the tinny speakers of hand-held transistor radios. Along with the Beatles and other British Invasion bands like the Stones, the Kinks, the Animals, and Herman's Hermits came the folk-rock sounds of Bob Dylan, Donovan, the Byrds, and The Mamas & The Papas. On the television, the world mourned the death of President John F. Kennedy and followed the Peace marches of soon-to-be-assassinated Martin Luther King, but the beat went on despite these tragedies, and the dawning of the age of Aquarius brought a new concern for the rights of women and ethnic minorities. All signs promised a better world for everyone, but especially for women, and country women for a while caught the feminist fever. Loretta Lynn recorded *Don't Come Home A-Drinkin' With Lovin' On Your Mind*, a ground-breaking message song sung from a woman's point of view. This coalminer's daughter would later become even more committed to women's rights issues in the '70s. Loretta continued to break new ground in songs like *The Pill*, dealing with contraception and abortion issues, and then in her autobiography, *Coalminer's Daughter*, where she became the first hillbilly woman to speak frankly about her lack of sex education and the double-standards applied to men and women when it came to fidelity in marriage. For many years after, mainstream country would remain a brooding genre where love was most often reduced to stolen pleasure or heart-break depicted in cheatin' and hurtin' songs.

Early in her career, Shania would tell interviewers that all she had wanted to be was "Stevie Wonder's backup singer." She wistfully daydreamed in her song *When* that the 1950s and '60s times could return: "I'd love to wake up smiling — full of the joys of spring / And hear on CNN that Elvis lives again /And that John's back with the Beatles." Shania was a child of the love generation. She would later tell an Australian radio show host that it is important to "love who you are." When she set out to rock her country all over the world, the Beatles and the love generation would be included not only in the lyrics of her songs but also in the spirit of her live shows. Beatlemania had become Shaniamania. Shania was everywhere. On TV videos and specials. On country and pop radio. On the covers of magazines ranging from *Cosmopolitan* through *Rolling Stone* to the tabloids in the racks as people stood in line at supermarket check-outs. Children and grandchildren of the '60s generation were singing Shania's songs like *Honey, I'm Home* and *Don't Be Stupid (You Know I Love You)*. They sang, "So, you're a rocket scientist . . . that don't impress me much" just as their parents had sung "She loves you, yeah, yeah, yeah," back in the '60s.

In Windsor, baby Eileen emerged into this world blessed by this convergence of musical styles. Thirty-three years later, she would do some converging of her own when her song *You're Still The One*, which she wrote for her husband Mutt Lange, bridged the gap between country and pop. With *You're Still The One*, she rose to the very top rung of the pop music ladder, and with the release of THE WOMAN IN ME, Shania opened the doors for other country women like Faith Hill, Trisha Yearwood, and Martina McBride to crossover with their country pop. Faith and Shania have a lot in common, besides their musical style. They share the experience of being adopted.

Eileen Twain's family didn't reside there near the border in southern Ontario for very long after she was born. Her mother, Sharon, would remember the music, however, and, when one of her offspring displayed an ability to sing, Sharon who would become obsessed with seeing her daughter become a country star. Sharon would soon pluck her three-year-old daughter Eileen from her seat at a local eatery and set her on a counter top so that she could be seen while she gave her first ever concert . . . a brief, impromptu performance which drew a smattering of applause from the people eating there. Before that spontaneous event would take place, Sharon, Jill, and baby Eileen would experience some turbulent times.

Clarence and Sharon were not getting along all that well during those years, and, when a third child, Carrie-Ann, was born, the marriage was on its last legs. When Clarence abandoned them, Sharon didn't hang around pining away for his return for very long. She didn't want any more inappropriate treatment than she had already received. She took her three daughters and moved on before things got even worse than they already were. Eileen was two years old at the time of the split-up in 1968. She had no memories of her birth-father to take with her, none that she would retain, and he wouldn't come up significantly again in her life for many years.

Years later, when Clarence's name did come up, his relatives would speak out against Shania, but Clarence himself would refuse to make statements to the press and would merely be quoted by a local bartender and by relatives who chose antagonism to color the memory and cover up the fact that Clarence had not supported his offspring, not made the regular child-support payments that could have made his presence in his daughters' lives more welcome.

By the time that Eileen was three years old, Sharon had begun to live with Jerry Twain, an Ojibwa lumberjack and prospector who worked at various jobs in the logging and mining industries in northern Ontario. By the time Eileen turned six, Sharon had secured her divorce from Clarence and married Jerry Twain. The newly-wed couple lived in Timmins, Sudbury, and then in South Porcupine, before settling down back in Timmins, 657 miles northwest of Eileen's birthplace in Windsor and 500 miles from Toronto. In this remote mining community, far from the corporate headquarters of the chartered banks, television networks, and major label record companies in Toronto, and even further from the bustling commercial shipping activity on the Great Lakes and the newly completed St. Lawrence Seaway, country music would often be the only music young Eileen heard. It was her parents' favorite music.

The marriage was a good one. The love between Sharon and Jerry brought stability to the lives of Sharon's three daughters, and in time, two brothers came along, Mark and Darryl. Jerry Twain's work was seasonal, however, and there were times when there were few groceries to put on the table. Although these lean times were a challenge, the Twains did make it through the tough times to the years when Jerry was able to secure lucrative contracts in the burgeoning tree-planting industry. They survived these lean years by pulling together as a family unit. And they got help from Jerry's native band members who shared the meat from community moose hunts with the Twains.

Clarence was mostly out of the picture. "We maybe saw him three times," Carrie-Ann later told a reporter from *People* magazine. "We hardly know him,"

Shania told an interviewer from the same magazine. "My dad's side of the family (she was referring to Jerry Twain) was the side we grew up with. So, it was the Indians that really were our family."

When Jerry married Sharon, he adopted Jill, Eileen, and Carrie-Ann. As his adopted children, the three young girls became members of his native band, the Temagami Anishnawbe Bear Island First Nation. At this time, Eileen, along with her sisters, gained First Nations status. Various sources have said that Clarence had mixed blood, as well, but that his aboriginal or Métis ancestry was consistently denied by his family who were derived from French and Irish ancestry. Sharon came from Irish stock. If this were to be true, all of the children could also be looked at as either aboriginals, adopted aboriginals, or Métis. None of this would ever have mattered had not some antagonistic journalists later taken issue with Shania's references to her Ojibway heritage. As far as Shania is concerned, she was raised native. She is proud of her heritage. She is also proud of both her father and mother, grateful they cared enough about her to instil a strong set of character-building moral values which served her well long after they passed away and she was left to raise her two younger brothers and her sister Carrie-Ann.

2
SHANIA'S
NATIVE HERITAGE

THERE WERE TIMES WHILE SHANIA WAS GROWING UP that her First Nations status was not always a benefit. According to the brief biographical sketch provided by aboriginal author Barbara Hager in her book *Honour Song*, Shania quickly learned what it was like to be identified as an aboriginal. "They were often the only aboriginal family in their neighborhood," Hager wrote. "Growing up, she and her siblings often encountered racial intolerance, and she remembers having to stick up for her brothers and herself." Shania also endured the usual racial slurs, and at one time the indignity of one set of white parents refusing to let their son date her. But perhaps more disturbing is the treatment Shania has received from some quarters of the fifth estate concerning her native ancestry.

In 1995, Shania told Barbara Hager, "I grew up in a Native family, and have always considered myself Native. We didn't think in terms of a step-father, half-brothers . . . We were all just family." Her comments were soon misconstrued. The first such report came from the town of Timmins itself when in 1996 the local newspaper, *The Timmins Daily Press*, which ironically had the contract to publish Shania's official newsletter, ran an article with the sensational headline, "Shania Confesses She Might Not Be Native," largely based on second-hand comments attributed to her birth-father, Clarence Edwards, third parties and his relatives. (Shania revoked the paper's right to have anything to do with her fan club.) Eighty-three-year-old Regina Nutbrown, Shania's biological grandmother, was reported to have said, "All she talks about is this Indian man but what about her real father? What about us? It's terrible what she's doing . . . I hate those lies." Despite the dubious nature of this article, the national and international press seized upon the story. In his book *Three Chords and the Truth*, Laurence Leamer, for example, claimed that Shania had deliberately misinformed the public about her native background and up-bringing in Timmins.

"Jerry Twain was the man who brought Shania up," Leamer wrote, "and whom she learned to consider her father, and he was the reason she claimed to have Indian blood." That is not what Shania had said: she had said that she "grew up in a Native family," not that she had "Indian blood." There *is* a difference. And while Leamer is correct in citing an *Esquire* magazine article as being incorrect by reporting that Shania "grew up in the tiny Ojibwa Indian community of Timmins," for the city was indeed once a thriving mining community, he was off-base when he concluded that Shania must be lying about the poverty her family endured and the backwoods life they enjoyed snaring rabbits for the cooking pot and eating moose meat. Leamer said that Shania had a "virtual past." Among other allegations that Laurence Leamer dug up for his attack on Shania Twain were statements made by Robert Kasner, the son of Shania's first manager, Mary Bailey, who told Leamer that he resented the attention his mother paid to Eileen's career and the money she spent on it.

"The whole thing is a big deal in my home town," Shania told the *Los Angeles Daily News*, "because the Twain family have never met the Edwards family. My little brother just goes, 'Who's Clarence Edwards?' It's ridiculous to have this family try to claim me back. Our struggle since our parents died was to stay grounded and anchored as a family. . . . It's kind of late to try to claim me. . . . I warned my family that fame brings some weird stuff. I told them there would be times when they'll just have to laugh at something they've read or heard. They have a sense of humor about it. They're not glory seekers. My grandmother didn't ask for tabloid people to hound her. . . ." In an interview with *Rolling Stone* reporter Erik Hedegaard, Shania defended herself, saying, "Well, I want to set that guy (Leamer) straight. Because you know what? The reality, if anything, is that I'm easy on the subject. The only reason I talk about it at all is because I have this charity (the Kids Cafe / Second Harvest Food Bank, which provides meals for underprivileged children) and I want to make people aware of it . . . It's all very true. Like, as if I'd make any of it up for commercial gain! I have not fabricated anything in my life."

When Eileen Twain recorded *Half-Breed* with guitarist Paul Sabu and producer Harry Hindes in 1989, she was picking up on Cher's rocking 1973 number one rendition of the song. Cher had brought a new dimension to the lyrics. Sung from a woman's point of view, the plight of the song's protagonist gains emotional force. Cher's version of *Half-Breed* made the tortured-and-torn-between-two-worlds aspect of the lyrics more poignant. Eileen Twain's 1989 version is a heavy metal production, at least as raucous as Pat Benatar and

Alannah Myles' records, although it adds little in interpretation to what Cher had already done very well. No doubt, Eileen could identify with the lyrics, and once Nashville and Timmins began to question her heritage, she seemed to be caught in a dilemma similar to the young woman in *Half-Breed*.

The appealing ideal of a beautiful Native woman suffering as a result of her exposure to 'white men's ways' had been introduced to the songwriting community in Nashville during the '60s by Canadian poet, novelist, and singer-songwriter Leonard Cohen. Before he moved to Nashville in 1968, Cohen's pornographic novel *Beautiful Losers* had begun to create waves. The book was first published in a hardbound edition in April 1965, four months before Eileen Regina Edwards' birth. The plot-line plunges the reader into the soul-searching existence of a young Montrealer distraught by the suicide of his wife, Edith, and both tyrannized and captivated by Edith's lover, "F," a boastful bisexual predator who abuses occult knowledge for selfish reasons. The troubled protagonist becomes fascinated by the life of a 17th-century Iroquois martyr, Catherine Tekakwitha, and resolves to research her true history. The Iroquois maiden's beatification began when she was converted to Christianity by Jesuits and then took an Oath of Virginity. Wracked with guilt at the cannibalism, enslavement (of young braves and maidens from other tribes within the five tribes of the Iroquois nation), and sexual promiscuity practiced by her Mohawk people, Catherine begins a program of sexual abstinence, fasting, and self-immolation. Before she succumbs, Jesuit priests perform the holy sacrament. Soon after that, a pattern of miracles began to affect the lives of the people living in New France. The miracles continued whenever someone in dire straits spontaneously sent their prayers to her. By the time of Cohen's boyhood days in Montreal, St. Catherine Street had been dedicated to Tekakwitha's memory and small plaster statuettes were being manufactured of her in the manner of the usual Catholic relics. She had become far more than merely the first Iroquois virgin.

Cohen's telling of the story of the first Native North American saint is often bizarre, yet contains several eerie parallels to the life of Shania Twain. Catherine Tekakwitha was born in 1656 and began life in a tiny village on the banks of the Mohawk River. Both of her parents and all of the members of her immediate family were killed in a Plague that swept through the village when she was only four years old. She herself bore the effects of the crippling disease for 20 more years until her death. For several years, she could not brave full sunlight. She knew the pangs of hunger well.

As young Catherine grew into her womanhood she became attracted to the preachings of Jesuit priests who were there in her area to convert "heathens." Even though she was very young, she saw baptism as a way of avoiding the brutal existence and practices of her people. Once baptized, she displayed a fanatic adherence to Christian ideals. She sewed thorns into her bedding, engaged a friend, Mary Therese — who had succumbed to cannibalism during one long unsuccessful hunting expedition but felt terribly guilty about her actions — to share and take turns applying tree branch whippings, and experimented with self-inflicted pain by placing burning logs against her legs. These preoccupations, and the fact that she had been disfigured by the Plague that took her parents' lives, guaranteed her continued virginity, which in itself was a miraculous feat given that this had never happened to any member of the five tribes before this. Every young girl was either taken in slavery or taken in marriage. Oddly, as her ordeal continued to the death, Catherine seemed to become better looking despite her wasted condition, and, at the moment of death, is said to have turned both white and beautiful. She is known as the Lily of the Shores of the Mohawk River.

In the experimental prose of the controversial novel, Cohen's work paralleled Beat author William Burroughs' *Naked Lunch*. By the time that the novel had appeared in a more affordable paperback edition, a powerful visual image from Cohen's debut Columbia Records album *The Songs Of Leonard Cohen* put a picture to the strange tale. This romanticized painting of a young Native woman in a classic Joan of Arc pose, engulfed by crimson flames, was chosen as the back cover art of the debut album. Her beatific demeanor in the face of unbearable pain and suffering seemed appropriate to illustrate the dark, brooding, tortured-yet-transcendent lyrics of Cohen's songs on the record.

Cohen had recorded that album in New York working with legendary producers John Hammond and John Simon. Already a ladies man, his songs *Suzanne* and *So Long, Marianne* became identified with the Leonard Cohen mystique. Many fans also identified these mysterious lovers with both Catherine Tekakwitha and with the burning woman depicted on the cover art. Everyone, who saw the cover art and heard the strange new music, was affected. Buffy Sainte-Marie wrote of Cohen's work in *Sing Out* magazine that his unorthodox songwriting style "lifted you off familiar ground. It's like losing track of time."

Although Cohen never cut a "country" record on Music Row during his two-year tenure in Tennessee, he met and recorded with musicians like Charlie Daniels there. Daniels would tour with him in Europe in the '70s. Cohen's influence in Nashville was felt throughout the songwriting community. He was this little Jewish poet from Montreal who attracted gorgeous women in the same way flypaper attracts flys. They were drawn to him by an irresistible force. He was one strange dude but his angst-ridden themes and even stranger music probed more deeply than the usual cheatin', hurtin' song. They were food for thought.

Leonard Cohen has played a unique role in the emancipation of women in music. For example, he often praised women and saw them as "mankind's salvation." Long before the women's revolution in music in the '90s, Cohen told an interviewer for the *New York Times*, "I wish women would hurry up and take over. It's going to happen, so, let's get it over with . . . then we can finally recognize that women are the minds and the force that holds everything together." His songs empowered recording artists like Judy Collins with singular material like *Suzanne, Sisters Of Mercy, Priests,* and *Hey, That's No Way To Say Goodbye*. Cohen's rare gift for poetry was not matched by an equal talent for singing, but his songs were often performed and recorded by women. When sung by the likes of Joan Baez, the final lines of *Suzanne* provided an eerie moment for those who had read about Catherine Tekakwitha.

In 1968, Cohen, disenchanted by his experience working with New York producers, who, he felt, overproduced his simple compositions, chose to record his second album in Nashville in the Columbia studios on 16th Avenue, where producer Bob Johnson had previously worked with Dylan on the BLONDE ON BLONDE album. Like many songwriters who move to Nashville, Cohen settled down to a rural existence in nearby Franklin, Tennessee, where he rode horses, took up firing guns at targets with a passion, and prepared his songs for the recording studio. His singular presence there, long before Eileen Twain moved to Tennessee, coupled with the reading of his novel, contributed to the idea of an Indian maiden who sang country music. However, when 'Indian maiden' Buffy Sainte Marie showed up around this time in Nashville to record among other songs, Cohen's *God Is Afoot, Love Is Alive*, she was not seen as a country artist, perhaps because of her political activism.

Before this, the subject of Indian maidens in country songs had been limited to the lyrics sung by male vocalists like Hank Thompson, whose *Squaws Along The Yukon (Are Good Enough For Me)*, a number 2 hit in 1958 on country & western charts, was little more than racial bigotry dressed up in the lyrics of a novelty song. The Hollywood film *Rose Marie*, which told the story of a red-coated Mountie's romance with a young Native woman, had possessed more dignity, and had found a far larger audience when it was shown in theaters in the '40s, even though by today's standards the depiction of the situation leaves much to be desired. Nelson Eddy and Ginette MacDonald's vocalizing came from the tradition of light opera and the Broadway musical. Yodeling guitar slinger Slim Whitman recorded country versions of *Rose Marie* and *Indian Love Call*. They were both number 2 charters during the '50s. Hank Williams' contribution to the mythmaking comes in his song *Kaw-Liga,* where a wooden Indian on the street outside a shop falls in love with an "Indian maiden in the antique store." Johnny Preston's 1959 hit *Running Bear* features a doomed romance between a brave named Running Bear and a maiden by the name of Little White Dove.

Rattlesnake Annie made her Nashville debut with the Junior Opry in the '50s, but remained a fringe performer, more popular in Europe than on Top 40 country radio in the U.S., even though she penned *Texas Lullabye* with David Allen Coe and hung out with Willie Nelson who shared her love of traditional country. To accentuate her Cherokee heritage, she wore her trademark snake rattle as an ear ornament. Loretta Lynn was one-quarter Cherokee, but this was not played up by the Wilburn Brothers who developed her, by Decca Records, or by Loretta herself, and is not mentioned with regard to her sister Crystal Gayle in the promotional material issued by her labels. Native heritage was not perceived as a particular advantage by all Nashville industry people during the '60s, especially when a person wasn't actually raised Native.

Marvin Rainwater, born Marvin Karlton Percy in 1925 in Wichita, Kansas, was one-quarter Cherokee, which gave credence to his 1959 MGM release *Half-Breed*, a song written by John D. Loudermilk which actually spelt out the dilemma in red and white terms, but stalled at number 16 and failed to improve on the MGM artist's debut number 3 release *Gonna Find Me A Bluebird. Half-Breed* was the last Marvin Rainwater single released by MGM and future efforts for Warner Bros. and other labels failed to make the Top 20. During Rainwater's days at MGM he regularly entertained in full feathered headdress and fringed buckskin regalia. Having adopted his mother's family name, Marvin Percy proudly utilized his Native heritage to full advantage in the country & western world. Loudermilk's *Half-Breed* had far more impact for Cher in 1973. The lyrics were more believable when sung by a woman as dynamic as Cher, a forceful example of a woman whose rights were doubly compromised: "My father married a Cherokee. My mother's people were ashamed of me. The Indians said that I was white by law. The white man always called me Indian squaw. Half-breed! Is all I ever heard. Half-breed! How I learned to hate the word. Half-breed! She's no good, that one. Words that were used against me since the day I was born . . ."

In Nashville, Leonard Cohen explored his fantasy of being both a cowboy and a country & western singer, although the recordings he made with Bob Johnson at the Columbia studios were stark, acoustic, folk-pop records. At this time, he met Kris Kristofferson, who was impressed with *Bird On A Wire*. Kristofferson, although a Rhodes scholar, worked at the time as a janitor at Columbia Records. And he would be the songwriter who befriended the beautiful Sammi Smith and the first beneficiary of the potential of an Indian girl singer recording a country song for the cowboy music market. In 1971, Sammi Smith crossed over big time with her recording of Kristofferson's *Help Me Make It Through The Night*, a number one gold record on the Mega Records label on the country charts, and a number 8 hit on the pop chart. Although Mega didn't hype her as an Indian maiden at the time, when she moved to Electra in the '80s, she chose to champion her Apache heritage and toured with an all-Native band, Apache Spirit.

Sammi was born Jewel Fay Smith in Orange, California, and arrived in Nashville in 1967. She was possessed of a rare beauty and could move audiences to tears with her songs, but found herself working with a label that had been created as a tax dodge, was mandated to lose money, and though her hit turned this focus around, the Mega executives showed little further vision and failed to capitalize on her potential. Sammi married Willie Nelson's Family Band guitarist, Jody Payne, and wrote *Sand-Colored Angels* for Conway Twitty and *Cedartown Georgia* for Waylon Jennings, but her own singles failed to recapture the magic of the CMA Single of the Year that she'd been handed when she befriended a janitor working in the Columbia Records building in 1970.

Nashville-born Rita Coolidge championed her mixed white and Cherokee heritage, wearing her long, dark hair in braids and adorning her arms, ears, and neck with silver and turquoise jewelry. She made many friends in the rock & roll world during early tours as a backup singer with Delaney & Bonnie & Friends and Joe Cocker. Leon Russell dedicated his song *Delta Lady* to her. Steven Stills wrote several songs to her, including *Cherokee*, *The Raven*, and *Sugar Babe*. This involvement led her toward a fusion of R&B, rock, and country. Her musical history veered further from Nashville when she began singing backup vocals for the likes of Stills, Eric Clapton, and Dave Mason. She met and married Kris Kristofferson in the early '70s, but recorded in L.A. rather than in Nashville. She had many successful singles and albums but charted only once in the country Top 40. Her rare beauty and powerful vocals on cuts like Jackie Wilson's *Higher & Higher* might have caused some wishful thinking on Music Row, but she never was theirs to groom.

With Sammi Smith's limited success, the quest for an Indian maiden country singer in Nashville seemed to have run its course. The possibility that this young woman, when she came along, would be Canadian like Leonard Cohen who had sanctified Catherine Tekakwitha with his novel, now seems most peculiar. Shania would not exactly become a martyr, but for a while she was persistently persecuted for proclaiming her Native heritage, and her perseverance in the face of this extreme criticism proved she was a woman of character, whether she had Indian blood in her veins or not. Her Native upbringing served her well when dealing with opposition from cynical critics and industry insiders. She held no one, not even her first producers, ransom over the events she experienced during her rise to country superstardom. If not for her parents' strong sense of willpower, which they passed on to her, she might have succumbed to the opposition and become a tortured woman burnt to a crisp by a cynical press.

Because her biological father denied his Native heritage, or because he never had it — as his relatives maintain to this day — Shania Twain was to be revealed as not being a legitimate Native singer by blood, even though she fit the bill as far as someone who had been raised Native. She had not fully explained the situation to people at that time. Because of the controversy that erupted, the bio that the publicity people at Mercury Records put together for her debut SHANIA TWAIN album seemed to be fabricated to make some mileage out of her Native ancestry, an aim that also *seemed* designed to make commercial profit from that image. No matter how loud she protested, she seemed to be a fake. It was a cruel twist of fate.

As recently as 1999, Michael McCall, author of *Shania Twain: An Intimate Portrait of a Country Music Diva*, still insisted that Shania's bio was fake. "Little of the outrageous tale she told," McCall declared, "was true." While Laurence Leamer and others like Michael McCall accused Shania of fabricating a life to enhance her mystique, other respected journalists came to her defense. Nashville *Tennessean* reporter Robert K. Oermann got to the root of the matter by calling Shania. "It's difficult to be called a liar," Shania told Oermann. "Jerry Twain is my father. He raised me. It's very frustrating for me to be denied the only ancestry I've ever known. As the adopted daughter of my father, Jerry, I became legally registered as 50 percent North American Indian. Being raised by a full-blooded Indian and being part of his family and their culture from such a young age is all I've ever known. There's a harsh reality there that I wouldn't want to go into detail on. He (Clarence Edwards) caused my mother a lot of pain. And you have to understand. He did leave us. My mother had good cause to not have him be the man who raised us. I always knew of the existence of Clarence Edwards. But I don't ever remember him being there in our house. I didn't even know what he looked like until I was a teenager. My oldest sister Jill has memories of him and is terrified of the fact that this man could ever be part of our lives again." Shania explained that her mother's brother, her Uncle Don (Morrison), was "angry that they're trying to re-enter our lives with so much aggression and so much bitterness. Uncle Don told me that there's Indian in the Edwards' side of the family, as well. The grandmother was called an Indian princess. I grew up with the impression that there was Indian heritage in that family, too." Between the lines, Oermann further filled in the situation. "Twain said she scarcely knows Nutbrown or anyone connected with her mother's first marriage. And she says Edwards abused her mother and deserted the family, after which her mother married Jerry Twain."

While Shania may not have been aware of the history of Indian maidens in North American literature and music, she *was* aware of the power that singing *Half-Breed* could bring to a performance and included the song in her shows during the 1980s. She certainly wanted to make as strong an impression as she could, and she did have her First Nations status. Nobody could take that away from her. She was a beautiful, mysterious presence in her fur parka on the cover of SHANIA TWAIN. When she was crucified by critics who leapt at the her-itage issue during the promotion of THE WOMAN IN ME, she unknowingly ful-filled the prophesy hinted at on the cover of Leonard Cohen's first album, reliving the vilification of an assertive woman, a modern-day Joan of Arc or Catherine Tekakwitha, in the country music business.

3
RAGS TO...SOMETHING

MOST COUNTRY WOMEN ARTISTS HAVE ENDURED POVERTY as children, drawing inspiration from these tough times for their music. In her autobiography *Dolly: My Life and Other Unfinished Business*, Dolly tells of the times she was so poor and hungry right there in Nashville, before she secured a recording contract with Fred Foster at Monument Records, that she resorted to haunting the corridors of hotels and eating the leftovers on the room-service trays set outside the rooms. Loretta Lynn and June Carter Cash both devote whole chapters of their autobiographies to describing the poverty of their childhood days in the hills and hollers of east Tennessee. As Shania spoke of her lean years when the only food to be had was a mustard sandwich, she was honoring an old country music tradition. She was also telling the truth.

International interviewers were especially curious about her childhood lifestyle roughing it in the bush. One Australian journalist listened patiently to Shania's stories about snaring rabbits and shooting partridges, then asked, "You took these home and ate them . . .?" She told others about the .22 calibre rifle she used to shoot those animals.

Both Jerry Twain and his father maintained a trap-line, as did many men in the northern Canadian wilderness at that time, before concerned animal rights activists had begun their lobby against leg-hold traps and the sale of animal pelts. Those pelts were, at the time, valuable, and a source of income. The animal flesh was nourishing. When Jerry found that Eileen loved to accompany him on his trips into the forest, he encouraged her interest. She was, all commentators agree, more of a tomboy at that time than the typical young North American girl. Jerry's parents taught her to track and to trap, snaring small game like rabbits for the cooking pot. My own father took me along when he went out hunting ducks, grouse, and deer, though I didn't take to shooting things as enthusiastically as my older brother did. For Dad, this was part of my education. Learning to shoot, skin, and butcher a deer was something I might need to do someday, he believed. Like my own father, Jerry Twain would shoot game animals to feed his family. Venison and moose meat was a regular meal for many rural families at that time, although, nowadays, it is looked upon by city-folk as a delicacy.

"We camped out a lot when I was growing up," Shania told Barbara Hager. "Not in campgrounds but out in the bush, or near an uninhabited lake that my father knew about. We would just sleep in the back of the truck or pitch a canvas tent somewhere."

From personal experience, I know Shania's descriptions of her childhood and family life to be typical of many less fortunate Canadian families who struggled with minimum incomes rather than go on the dole. Like many Canadian families, regardless of their ancestral background, the Twains often went on fishing and hunting trips and lived outdoors for days at a time. In the case of my own family in the West Kootenay region of southern British Columbia, my father packed a large canvas tarp in the family car along with the fishing gear and blankets, and that tarp served as either a ground sheet when the weather was good or as a shelter when it rained. Sometimes, we built a fire at Queen's Bay Point near the water gauge tower on Kootenay Lake, at the exposed front of a small cave, making use of the projecting rockface as a home away from home. Other times we rented one of the small log cabins that some people had built on the lakeshore of several of the smaller mountain lakes in the area, where there would be a small wharf and a dozen or so rowboats for rent. Fishing was good in those days: we caught so many fish — rainbow trout, arctic Char, and land-locked Kokanee salmon — that we ate little else during summer months. Little else except the eggs laid by the chickens we raised in a small shed in the backyard of our house in Nelson, the unsold day-old bread and pastry that my father, a baker by trade, brought home from his job, and the vegetables we grew in our garden. Nicknamed "Pontiac" after the great chief of the Ottawa, my father knew all the prime game trails and roamed the hills during hunting season. Before he grew older and the quotas on all fish and wildlife were severely limited, our family rarely ate store-bought meats. In August, our family would make a trip to the high meadows where the huckleberries and Saskatoon berries grew large and juicy and delicious and pick buckets full to make into jams and jellies. There was ample food for a family foraging off the land or fishing the waterways or harvesting their garden. This was an accepted way of life for Canadian families before the advent of an urban fast-food culture in the 1970s and '80s.

"We would go for days with just bread and sugar and milk," Shania explained without complaining. This, too, was something that other Canadians ate at that time. Cubed pieces of white bread with white sugar and hot milk was my own father's favorite breakfast cereal. We kids ate it often, as well as oatmeal porridge other mornings and sometimes even the luxury of a store-bought cereal, and we did so most probably because the bread was there and Kellogg's Corn Flakes cost money that could be put to better uses.

In the 1970s, stumpage fees paid by logging companies were diverted from government coffers and handed out to contractors who took up the task of replanting after the logging had been done. This was in keeping with a growing awareness of a need to replenish the resource that had for so long merely been harvested and clearcut, as if it were inexhaustible. Jerry Twain, as a Native with First Nations status, was eligible for a small business loan to start up his tree-planting enterprise. To independent contractors like Jerry Twain, the daily and monthly quotas set out in the contracts he signed meant his crews would be living outdoors for weeks at a time, although crew members would often head for town on weekends. It was the same out West where many of my friends worked as tree-planters. Several were contractors. All of these people lived outdoors in tents or makeshift shelters. RVs were far too expensive a luxury for most seasonal laborers, although camper trucks soon became the most usual domicile for tree-planters.

Seasonal workers everywhere exist in life's margins, learning to make do with what is available. This is the crux of the stories Shania has told about her childhood. Her family was making do with what they had. When she mentions that her school lunches were meager when measured against the goodies wrapped in her classmates' lunch pails, she is explaining who she is and where she came from, not complaining or seeking sympathy.

Back in 1995 Shania had told me that her life was "a Cinderella story. Not rags to riches. I'm not rich, yet. But certainly rags to something." In Shania's case, her step-father had not turned out to be evil as in many fairy tales, but a loving father who adopted her willingly and taught her his Native heritage lovingly. While her mother urged her to become a performer, setting her up on the counter of that restaurant where she gave her first "concert" when she was only three, Jerry first taught her how to play the guitar. The guitar they had was too big for her at first to get her arms around, but as she grew she got quite good at playing it as accompaniment for her songs.

Making plans for her daughter's music career was sometimes the only activity that would cheer up Shania's mother, relieving her from the depression that accompanied their family poverty. Eileen soon found herself singing in radio stations, TV studios, community centers, senior citizens homes, and wherever else Sharon could get her booked. When Eileen was eight, her parents would waken her around midnight and, after the bar inside the Mattagami Hotel had stopped serving alcoholic beverages, she would be allowed to come in and sing with the band. She got good tips and sometimes as much as a $25 fee for singing. That helped put groceries on the table. Several video tapes were made of her singing at this time, and strangely — in the video footage preserved for the VH1 Special *Behind The Music* — she bears a haunting resemblance to a young Patsy Cline. To Mary Bailey, her first professional manager, she was a lot like a young Tanya Tucker. At one time, she teamed up with family friend Lawrence Martin as a duo for talent contests. Martin, an aboriginal country artist, told *People* magazine that "Sharon was like her manager. She'd fight for Eileen."

One route to recognition for a young singer in Canada at the time was to enter talent contests. These contests were a favorite with the fans who turned out in droves to witness amateurs competing to see who could sing *Crazy* or some other Top 40 cover song better than everybody else. *Crazy* seemed to be a fixture for female vocalists vying to be the next Patsy Cline or Tammy Wynette. At first, the prizes were money or having a 45 rpm record produced in a local studio and mailed to radio. After a while, the contests got more elaborate with entire packages and full 10-song albums being offered to the national winner of a contest pitting regional winners against each other. Terri Clark is one star who had her beginnings winning a talent contest, judged by Dick Damron, whose post-award advice to her boosted her career. Record producers Gary Buck and R. Harlan Smith are two of the most dedicated developers of Canadian country talent. But with a few exceptions like Terri Clark, the stars have seldom come from the ranks of contest winners; in fact, some Canadian country music industry people believe that winning a talent contest can be as much a curse as it is a blessing.

For years, Sharon Twain had entered her daughter in regional talent contests in Ontario only to see one or another of the contestants get the nod from the judges. "Mom was the one who wanted me to be a singer — a country singer," Shania later told Larry Delaney. "She got me singing, and by the time I was ten years old I was performing to audiences with my uncles and dad's cousin supporting me in a family band. I played guitar back then, too." As Shania recalls, her parents drove "all over Northern Ontario and to far-off Toronto for formal singing lessons, shows, and talent contests. . . . But," Shania told Delaney with a sigh, "I never won a talent contest in Ontario. Mom was *so* discouraged. She couldn't understand why her little girl never was able to win a contest. She always came away disappointed. Then, when I was still in my early teens, Mom took me to out British Columbia to enter a contest there. I won in three separate categories of the contest. It was wonderful . . . and it sure made Mom happy!"

The Canadian west coast was 3,000 miles away from Timmins, so traveling there represented a huge effort on Sharon Twain's part, an effort similar to the time that Wilbur and Belinda Rimes took *their* daughter, LeAnn, to New York when she was still a pre-teen to compete in auditions for a role as Little Orphan Annie in *Annie 2*. Sharon appears to have had every bit as much sense about how to promote her daughter. Shania insists that as a child she would have been content to play with her Barbie dolls and sing her songs up in her room. She had to be pushed into performing, constantly encouraged. She didn't think much of the smelly, smokey barrooms her parents took her to, either, or the drunken crowds that she would entertain. What did excite her was the 20 to 25 dollars she would get paid for doing it. At first, she had a passion to sing and write but not much inclination to get up before crowds. She was actually quite shy.

In 1993, for Shania's first-ever cover story in a national magazine, *Country Music News* editor Larry Delaney wrote, "By the late '70s and early '80s, Shania was close to being a 'teenage country sensation,' and, through her mother's ongoing efforts, was able to land guest appearances on several of Canada's top TV series of the time." Following her appearances on those shows, Shania, still Eileen at the time, toured with several bands, although she had begun to sing pop songs because that was where the money was at. She was, after all, dependent upon her music for her income. However, Delaney adds, "that did not sit well with mom at the time."

Eileen was a somewhat rough and ready tomboy young teenager whose front teeth were prominent, and when she developed noticeable breasts at an early age, she would confine them under thick layers of clothing to de-emphasize their size. She wasn't much interested in having boys come on to her, she was too wrapped up in her music. Her guitar playing in those video-taped vignettes, whether she is singing a current Top 40 country song, a Hank Williams classic like *Kaw-Liga* or *I'm So Lonesome I Could Cry*, or Dolly Parton's *Coat Of Many Colors*, is surprisingly strident, and her picked notes, strummed chords, and tempo changes are evidence that the music lessons the family scrimped for were paying off.

Yet at 13, when kids like LeAnn Rimes and Celine Dion burst upon the international scene, Eileen Twain still was a backwoods kid with a huge heart and tons of potential. During her high-school years, she worked diligently to improve herself, but she would never forget those after-midnight times when she rubbed the sleep from her eyes and traipsed into those smokey bars to perform for the drunk and rowdy crowds. Years later, she would tell *People* magazine that she sometimes had disturbed dreams of her parents waking her years after they had passed away. In one dream, they were video-taping her as she lay half-awake in bed. "Mom, what's going on?" she cried out in her dream. "Did you forget? They're filming you today," her mother — still in the dream sequence — answered. "Pondering the dream, Twain suggests, 'sometimes you feel your career overruns your personal life.'"

Back in the 1970s when her mom would wake her up, whispering, "Eileen, you have to get up . . ." the eight-year-old must have been having more pleasant dreams, imagining the day she would be a star in Nashville. While Sharon was determined that her daughter would become a country star, Eileen's fancy soon turned to rock and pop while she was in high school singing and playing in several bands. "I was, during my teen years, doing whatever the clubs hired us to do," she told the producers of her VH1 Special. "If they were hiring rock bands, I would be in a rock band. If they were hiring Top 40 bands that summer, I would be in a Top 40 band that summer . . . whatever paid the bills." When she could put words to it, she knew she wanted to be an international star. She wanted to record whatever music would become most popular. She was no country purist, although it would have pleased Sharon if her daughter had been. At times, she merely made the pragmatic decision and lent her skills to whatever would pay the bills.

Eileen Twain's first job that entailed adult responsibilities, other than her ongoing efforts to make it in the music business and a part-time job at a MacDonalds franchise, was working as a fore-woman for her father's tree-planting crews. "She supervised the 13-person tree-planting crew — all Cree and Ojibway from Manitoulin Island, Moose Factory, Moosonee, and other Northern Ontario communities," Barbara Hager reports. Shania began to work on these projects when she was in high school, and continued to plant trees after she had left home. She would return to Timmins from Toronto, where she worked in various bar bands, to help out, salting a few dollars away for the long, cold winter months when pay from her music gigs was not always sufficient to keep the wolf from the door. "We worked the forests," Shania later told Larry Delaney at *Country Music News*, "planting trees in reforestation projects from spring to fall of each year. We did it for years as a family unit. Then, when the cold weather came, I'd go back to singing." She learned how to wield an axe and thought nothing of firing up a chainsaw, activities that teach a person to pay attention to what they are doing and a respect for life and limb.

Eileen did her job well. Her sister Carrie-Ann remembers the time that Eileen was her boss and patiently showed her how to use her trowel, inserting the nursery-grown baby tree in the soil and tamping it down. She also remembers how the work was tough, physically. As she explained in the VH1 profile of Shania, "the bugs, and the smell, and the heat, and you had to wear a hard-hat, and you had to wear jeans. Shania was already out there and she was going to teach me, and she made me do it. She showed me how to do it and told me, 'You're going to make it through the day.' " Toting your bag of silvicultured trees, a heavy weight, was a challenge to all tree-planters. The only saving grace came from the fact that each time you planted one, the bag grew lighter. In order to reach quotas agreed upon in the contracts, the work went on from dawn till dusk.

But Shania always came back to singing. At the age of 17, Eileen cut free from her mom's apron strings and took the big step, moving to Toronto on her own where she got into rock and pop bands full-time while hanging around the big city recording scene.

"My sister was old enough and had a grip on what she wanted to do and where she was going," Carrie-Ann said in the VH1 special. "So, I think my mom was just happy that she had decided to choose and stay with that path, that musical path."

During these formative years, Eileen opened for a variety of touring acts that included both the Tex-Mex country of Freddy Fender and the brash arena rock of Canadian bands like Trooper. Adopting another persona, she donned evening gowns and sang in Toronto nightclubs, performing concerts with artists as removed from the rock and country worlds as Bernadette Peters and the Toronto Symphony.

Eileen's first recording experiences took place in Toronto studios with producers like Stan Campbell, whom she met when she taped her first *Opry North* radio show at CFGM in Toronto. An early duet with Tim Denis, *Heavy On The Sunshine*, was an album-cut pressed onto vinyl on Denis' self-titled album in 1985. She also sang backup vocals on Kelita Haverland's 1986 album TOO HOT TO HANDLE, which was produced by Tony Migliore, and she was heard on the radio on a daily basis for the first time when Kelita's single *Too Hot To Handle* from that album was playlisted on Canadian country stations.

Kelita had a background in theater and was the closest thing Canadian country audiences had to their own Minnie Pearl in those days. Her stage shows were often spiced with vignettes featuring characters she would play, complete with convincing costumes, like the gossipy Sophelia Flannigan and Honky

Tonk Queen Dixie Lee. Ironically, Haverland's songwriting was influenced by the tragic deaths of her own parents and older brother, a situation that would soon come to pass for her backup singer, Eileen, although Eileen's brother would survive the tragic logging road accident.

Years later, one of these Toronto sessions, ten rock demos Eileen had recorded for producer Harry Hinde, would come back to haunt her. Those early tracks showed that she could sing, but they also pointed out that, as a producer, Hinde was heavy-handed and lacked originality. The overall poverty of imagination in the production would be used against her by her detractors, even though some of the original material she had co-written with guitarist Paul Sabu showed flashes of the potential that would spark her later songwriting. For nearly a decade, those Toronto tracks were out of sight out of mind, stored in a tape vault. They were not the tracks that convinced the Mercury Nashville executives to sign her to a record deal, but they were a valuable learning experience both for the time spent singing vocals in a recording booth and as a testing ground for her songwriting. She kept at the writing, and the mere fact that she could do it would interest the Mercury executives.

Eileen's parents had both been strong role models. Photos of the couple show them to be stalwart, caring parents. Shania has spoken of her father's ability to hold things together in their worst moments of poverty through his sense of humor. One of the few descriptions that we have of Sharon also comes from Shania. As she told James Dickerson, author of *Women On Top: The Quiet Revolution That's Rocking the American Music Industry*, "she (Sharon) couldn't sing a note, but she was a wonderful, wonderful lady. Everywhere she walked, she was definitely going somewhere. She was certainly not the sort of person to kinda saunter around."

Her daughter's life in the big city and her pursuit of rock and pop goals disturbed Sharon. Sharon had gotten to know Canadian country recording artist Mary Bailey during the taping of Eileen's *Opry North* show. While the CFGM Toronto crew were taping the syndicated radio show, the two women had talked and become friends. Sharon now appealed to Mary in hope of turning Eileen back to her country roots.

Toronto-born Mary Bailey was 29 years old when she began her recording career on RCA Canada in 1976. She had come back to her music after a few years working for the Sarah Coventry Fine Fashion Jewellery Company and she kick-started her country career in earnest with a string of Cancountry releases. For a while, she became a regular on the Ontario touring circuit. The title song from her first album, MYSTERY LADY, became her signature tune, and during the 1980s Mary was known as the "Mystery Lady" of Canadian country music. In the early years of the decade, Mary also charted briefly in the United States with *Too Much, Too Little, Too Late*, one of few Canadian women who had any radio success at all south of the border at this time. By the late 1980s, Mary's radio presence had begun to wane. However, her years of experience dealing with industry people in both Toronto and Nashville would serve her well when she became Eileen's manager. She would have a couple of stabs at it before finally getting her client signed to a record deal in Nashville.

Mary Bailey first heard Eileen sing in the 1970s. "She was this little girl," Mary would recall, "who got up on stage with her guitar and blew me away!" At a show in Sudbury where they were both among the opening acts for a touring Nashville star, Eileen's rendition of Hank Williams' *I'm So Lonely I Could Cry* actually brought tears to Bailey's eyes. By the mid-1980s, they had run into each other several times. Not long before she died, Sharon encouraged Eileen to secure Mary Bailey as her manager.

"Shania's parents were killed," Larry Delaney reported in *Country Music News*, "in a head-on collision with a fully-loaded logging transport on a highway near Wawa, Ontario, on November 1st, 1987." On the night of November 1st, Eileen was in her Toronto apartment when she got a call from her sister Carrie-Ann. A friend took the call and handed her the phone, as she recalls in *Behind the Scenes*. "I knew that something was very wrong. My heart was just jumping out of my chest. I was freaking before I even got on the phone." As she took the receiver and put it to her ear, she could hear voices in the background. "My other sister (Jill) was telling my brother — he had just walked in the door, and it was such a scene. My other brother was in the accident. He lived, thank God. We were such a young family. My parents were only 40 and 42 at the time."

As the details unfolded, she learned that her parents' Chevy Suburban had been hit head-on by a logging truck that had hurtled toward them in the way those massive vehicles do on the remote logging roads that are often company owned and scheduled for traffic to all be going in the same direction at certain hours of the day and the reverse direction at other hours. Jerry and Sharon had all but wrapped up the tree-planting operation for the winter. "It was one of their last trips of the year that the accident happened," Shania told Delaney, "on a Sunday, not long after Sunday trucking was reintroduced to Ontario highways. It shouldn't have happened. My brothers and sisters and I took it very hard. We lost a big piece of our world."

Shania's immediate grief had been almost too much to bear, but unexpected help from a near stranger helped her make it through that first terrible night. "My heart was just . . . It was pounding as hard as it could pound," she told *Daily Mirror* reporter Nina Myskow. "I was in shock. The whole night I just cried. I was out of control. I was numb. Wow, it's really weird what comes over you and how out of control you can get. There was a girl who lived in the apartment upstairs, that I didn't really know, only passing in the hall. She made me tea for hours, and just rubbed my back, rubbed my back. That's all she did. And thank God for that. I've never seen her again, but I really needed that. At moments like that, you're just out of yourself. I managed to get to my home town for the funeral, and once I was with my family, it made it a lot easier. But we were all lost. It was a terrible time."

Jerry and Sharon had left no will and there were adult responsibilities to be taken care of. Eileen was the best equipped to take charge and she did. "My brothers were 13 and 14. My younger sister was two years younger than me. My other sister was a year older and on the verge of getting married and had a child. I was still single, with no children. I decided I was too old to just dump my brothers on a relative. I really felt like I had to keep us together. So, I put everything on hold to look after family.

"I had to learn very quickly about a lot of things. Insurance. Mortgage. Lawyers . . . a nightmare. But responsibility prevents you from wallowing in grief. I was on automatic pilot. I had to get up and move on every day. Getting through, that's what you have to hold on to. And you know what? My life prepared me for what is happening today. The whole thing is overwhelming, and very challenging, actually. So I'm grateful for all the bad things that have happened to me. Of course, if I could have my parents back, I would, in a heartbeat, change that. But yet the experience I went through, I'm glad. Without that, I'm not sure I could have coped with this. It's a crazy life. It's not normal to live like this. It may not be true for everybody. But for me, I come from a small town, I'm just a normal little person, and this is a very big deal for me. But I'm coping with it better than I would have . . . now."

Carrie-Ann admits that she hadn't realized, at the time, just how much of a sacrifice her sister had made, and was equally candid in her summation. "Someone had to do it," she told VH1. "Shania is very strong and strong-willed. I certainly didn't want to do it. I never sensed any resentment. . . . She was there the next morning and then a whole new life started for her."

4
FROM HUNTSVILLE
TO NASHVILLE

MARY BAILEY WAS THERE FOR EILEEN when the going got tough. She had made contact with a producer in Huntsville, Ontario, who operated a Las Vegas style cabaret show in a ballroom at the Deerhurst Resort. He hired Eileen on Mary's recommendation. She could now support her family without giving up her music. Three years later, when Mary agreed to act as Eileen's manager on a full-time basis and to work toward getting her a record deal in the United States, she jumped in with both feet, and, before she got her artist signed, found the resources to finance a demo session and cover other costs incurred when she and Eileen traveled to Nashville.

"After guesting several times at the Deerhurst Resort," Shania told Larry Delaney, "I was invited to perform there as a regular. I saw it as an opportunity to provide for my brothers and sisters and still maintain my music career." She sold the family home in Timmins, packed up their belongings, and rented a house in Huntsville. "I set ourselves up in a home and got everybody feeling good about themselves again. It was tough, but we survived." Shania purchased a pickup truck for transportation. When the well outside the rented house dried up, she showed that she had as much gumption as any pioneer woman when she washed their clothes in the river. "She would bring these big jugs of water from Deerhurst," Carrie-Ann told *People Weekly*. "We would all jump in her truck and go down to the river to bathe. We hated it."

Shania was not exaggerating the situation in her interviews. Cold water cabins, as these dwellings are called in rural Canada, are to be found in most provinces. Some of them even have small cisterns or water tanks, but they often do not have more than a sink and a drain. An outhouse in the summer, and a pail in the winter, which must be emptied daily, often provide basic toilet requirements. They are the sort of low-cost housing that writers like myself sometimes seek out when they are writing their early books, and I retain fond memories of just such a one-bedroom house in Silton, Saskatchewan, where I lived through one summer, fall, and winter. On Christmas day, it was 40 degrees below zero and I had to step lively when I hauled water from the public well, but there were plenty of warm feelings during the turkey dinner my partner, our daughter Anna Marie, and I shared with our neighbors that afternoon.

When Shania reminisced about those days for the VH1 cameras, she laughed nervously and spoke of "all that I put those guys through and put myself through. . . ." Three years down the road, when her youngest brother finally left the nest, she had seen enough of parenting, thank you very much. Where most young women her age were getting married and planning families, she had quite different thoughts going through her mind. "I felt like I was 45 years old at 25," she told Larry Delaney. "I had to focus my energies on my musical career if there was ever going to be one."

Her years spent there at the resort provided a full education in the art of entertaining. She sang a wide variety of material, Broadway show tunes, pop standards, and rock & roll, constantly refining her stage abilities. Although she was part of a troupe, she was the brightest star in the show, and while the star did not regularly expose her navel to the audience, the girls in the chorus line all did. Their costumes were little more than heels, thongs, cupped bras, and feather headdresses. "It was great," she said of her days at Deerhurst when she recalled those memories for VH1. "The dancers taught me how to use my space a little better. I learned how to walk up and down stairs and sing at the same time in three inch heels." By the time that someone from Nashville came around to see what all the fuss was about, she had been at Deerhurst for nearly three full seasons and had become skilled at the art of being a supper club entertainer. Her sister, Carrie-Ann, later remembered that the Deerhurst productions had been "very classy, a Vegas kind of show." Eileen had also gained show-business expertise that would prove to be invaluable while designing the stage show for her first major tour.

By 1990, Eileen already exuded both a sense of confidence and a warm sensuality many men interpreted as sexuality, a bearing she would later exploit in her videos: while men's eyeballs popped out of their sockets when she moved to her music, women admired her self-possession and moxy. And as the Deerhurst Resort's Lynn Foster later told *People* magazine, "She was gorgeous, and men saw that. She learned how to not get involved."

From her parents, Eileen had learned such pose and integrity. When I suggested that her parents' tragic death might have forced her to grow up quickly and assume an adult role, Shania was firm in stating that she believed it was her parents efforts *before* they passed away that had been most important. "My parents — in developing a career for me when I was so young — *that* actually made me grow up very quickly as well. My childhood career matured me, and, in a sense, prepared me for what was coming." No doubt, when her parents were suddenly and swiftly lifted from her life as if God had reached down and gathered them to his bosom for no apparent good reason, Eileen, then 22, was grief-stricken. She told me that her song *God Bless The Child* had originally been part of the healing process. "At the time when my parents died," she related, "what that lullabye did for me was to comfort me. It was like a bellow of sorrow . . . I would go for long walks and just sing this." The hurt that she had felt had not gone away overnight. "It's like going to war and coming back," Shania would tell Trish Deitch Rohrer for a cover story published in *Cosmopolitan* magazine in March, 1999. "Every once in a while, someone has to slap you and say, 'Hey, the war is over!'"

Shania would face another battle when tabloid-level journalists dogged her with a catalog of her brothers' escapades, impaired driving charges, and other brushes with the law. These writers saw this as Shania's failure in taking care of her brothers in the years following the tragic death of their parents. Shania has expressed her fear that Mark will likely be scarred for the rest of his life by the specter of this tragic accident, but her brothers have nevertheless gone on to careers refitting boats, working as electricians, and exploring computer related fields out west.

Once her brother Mark was out on his own, Eileen must have felt this longed-for relief from family responsibility, for she called Mary Bailey. "I told her I was ready to give it my everything," she explained to Larry Delaney. "Could she please see what might be available for me." After watching her show at Deerhurst, Bailey felt that her protegé was ready, too. Calling on her Nashville friends and connections, Bailey set about the task of enticing someone to travel to Huntsville. That person turned out to be Richard Frank, a Nashville attorney, who took time off from his busy working schedule to make the trip. He was not disappointed.

"At 11 o'clock at night," Frank later remembered for the VH1 special, "in a theater full of people who had been drinking, china clattering, silver clashing, you could have heard a pin drop as soon as she hit her first note." That rapt attention from her audience most impressed Dick Frank, although he could tell from the way Eileen handled difficult ballads like *Somewhere Over The Rainbow* that she was a terrific singer. "After what I had heard," he added, "I had no doubt that we could get a recording contract." Mary Bailey convinced Eileen that Dick Frank knew what he was talking about. At one time or another he had been involved in the careers of both the Everly Brothers and Patsy Cline. Eileen took heart. Frank would later declare that Shania was the "greatest natural talent I have ever been involved with."

"It became a chain reaction after that," Shania told Larry Delaney for her 1993 cover story in *Country Music News*. "The ball went from Mr Frank to Norro Wilson who produced a demo on me to Buddy Cannon at Mercury Records to Harold Shedd who signed me to the label." Going to Nashville with Mary Bailey was exciting, but there was a good deal of culture shock to get over. It was only the second time that Eileen had been outside of Canada. "I went to the 'states' once before on a vacation to Florida," she said during the taping of her VH1 Special. "Other than that, I had never crossed the border."

Long before Shania crossed that border, other Canadian women country singers had made their way south to Nashville, showing extraordinary courage in doing so. Not only were they women, they were foreigners among the patriotic male realm of Music Row. Shania Twain didn't simply appear out of nowhere to take the world by storm in 1995. Shania was the product of half a century of struggle and strife in the trenches for Canadian female vocalists who had a mind to take their music to an international audience.

The appalling working conditions for women artists during the '50s, '60s and '70s in the country music industry have been documented in my book *Country Women In Music*. There were insults to be borne and a social stigma to be overcome if you wanted to become a country woman singer. For many years, society often viewed women who sang country as "loose" and sometimes as outright sluts, and the business side of things was until very recently completely run by a good ole boys' club of male stars, agents, managers, promoters, and record execs who routinely took advantage of their position to exploit women in every way possible. Suffice it to say here that it was tough for women to gain recognition in the male-dominated entertainment and record selling business and that in the beginning singing 'answer songs' and duets were often the only routes to success for a 'girl singer'. For Canadian women, it was even tougher because the domestic market is much smaller than the American market.

Shania is well aware of her rich Canadian country music heritage. "I remember Gary Buck and Dallas Harms," she told me while discussing this question. "I used to be on shows as the opener for Anita Perras [CCMA Best Female Vocalist in 1986 and 1987] when I was just a kid and she was a teenager. I opened for people like Carroll Baker. Ronnie Prophet was one. Mary Bailey, my manager, was an entertainer when I was a kid."

The first Canadian woman to chart on the *Billboard* magazine country & western chart was 14-year-old Myrna Lorrie, who hit the number 6 spot in 1955 with *Are You Mine*, a duet with fellow Canuck Buddy DeVal. Myrna was rewarded for her efforts when she was named the best new C&W artist that year in Nashville. She toured with Hank Snow and other Opry stars, but *Are You Mine* was to be her only Top 40 radio hit in the United States. In the years that followed, Myrna Lorrie had considerably more success back in Canada where she won the first ever Juno Award for Best Country Female Artist and had her own TV show. In the 1960s, Lucille Starr, who had come to Hollywood as part of the Canadian Sweethearts with her singing partner Bob Regan, had an international hit when she teamed up with A&M Records producer Herb Alpert to record *The French Song*. As a solo artist, Lucille had success in Europe and Canada, but she didn't stick in the U.S. market for long. In the 1970s, Anne Murray and Carroll Baker dominated the domestic country recording scene. Murray hit big in the States, too, and went on to become one of the top all-time female achievers, selling some 30 million records in the pop and country markets. She won several CMA and Grammy awards, twice hosting the televised CMA Awards show in Nashville.

Still, the Canadian scene remained under the domination of a boys' club headed by artists like Ray Griff, Ronnie Prophet, Wilf Carter, Hank Snow, Dick Damron, Stompin' Tom Conners, and Tommy Hunter. Carter made it big in New York, then Snow's *I'm Movin' On* became a number one hit on the *Billboard* C&W charts for a record 21 weeks in 1950. He went on to become the 20th most played country artist of all time. Griff and Prophet saw success in both countries, with Prophet hosting his own TV show in Canada and operating his own theater in Branson, Missouri. Damron and Conners barnstormed their way across the frozen wastes of Canada for several decades and became Canadian legends. Tommy Hunter hosted a CBC TV show for 26 years and became as entrenched on the national network as the famed *Hockey Night In Canada* broadcast. With the advent of television, Hunter's weekly show supplanted *The Don Messer Jubilee* as the top forum for country talent in Canada. For a Canadian country artist, appearing Friday night on *The Tommy Hunter Show* was equal to an Opry appearance in the United States. Country fans from

Vancouver Island to Newfoundland regularly tuned their TV sets to the show to view Tommy's celebrated American guests and homegrown stars.

Eileen Twain's first appearance on the Hunter show came in 1984 while she was still a teenager. Her performance was reported in *Country Music News*, the first significant national press that she received. Her mother, Sharon, was still the driving force behind her career at that time, and it was Sharon who secured the booking. Eileen also appeared on the *Opry North* show and *The Mercey Brothers Show* at this time. "I remember those Tommy Hunter shows," Shania later told Larry Delaney. "He was such a tall man and he stood over me like a big tree. . . . He was such a nice and friendly man. He kept telling me there was nothing to be nervous about being in front of the TV cameras. I remember appearing on his show when Ronnie Milsap was the headliner. Glen Campbell headlined another show I taped. I can remember singing *Walk On By*. Boy, would I ever like to see tapes of those shows again!"

During the 1980s, the national Canadian Country Music Association and the various regional provincial associations had all striven to develop a Canadian "star system." Striven to produce a star as bright as Shania Twain. The goal was to see record sales for Canadian country artists that amounted to more than a hill of beans. For years, the Toronto-based subsidiaries of the U.S. major labels had operated primarily to sell the already packaged Nashville, Austin, Hollywood, and Bakersfield stars. Sure, a few Canadians were usually signed to each label. However, it was far easier for a Toronto exec to sell American product in Canada than domestic records because the marketing was already accomplished and because Canadian country radio stations endorsed the U.S. stars. Few domestic artists made it all the way to the favored number one position on the radio surveys.

To make the playing field a little less tilted, the CRTC (Canadian Radio Television & Telecommunications Commission), the government body responsible for granting licenses to radio and television stations, had put in place a "Canadian content" rule dictating that radio stations play at least 30 percent Canadian artists. Before this ruling was put in place, Canadians like Hank Snow, Myrna Lorrie, Dallas Harms, Lucille Starr, Shirley Field, The Mercey Brothers, The Rhythm Pals, Orval Prophet, and Dick Damron were already getting their share of airplay in most Canadian markets, even though many of these artists recorded their records in Nashville. Directly after the 1972 ruling, music directors had to scramble to locate enough Canadian records, and what they laid their hands on wasn't always the greatest. So, it became accepted practice that you would most often hear the Canucks, especially the independents, at 4:30 in the morning — when few listeners were even awake. Even though the Canadian product got better and better, this practice did not necessarily change at many radio stations. Consequently, most Canadian country artists had what were in those days called "turn-table hits" — they had records that charted, and they received the royalties that accrued from the airplay, but they had dismal sales figures. Sales figures for Nashville stars weren't all that much better in Canada, but these were merely added to their U.S. sales when an accountant was tallying up profits, and the success of their careers did not hinge on how many records they sold in the great white north. In this radio climate, independent Canadian record labels and their hopeful artists thrived for many years, and their independent spirit contributed to the concept that a person could become a "star" on Canadian country radio simply by issuing two or three catchy 45 rpm records. To encourage some further activity, and the development of some artists who could sell more records, the associations staged talent contests.

In the 1980s, the Canadian country scene had begun to heat up for female artists. While Anne Murray and Carroll Baker were the reigning country Queens, Sylvia Tyson, who had earlier hit big in the United States as part of the Ian & Sylvia folk act in the 1960s, moved over to country, and Myrna Lorrie made a comeback, hitting with *Blue Blue Me*, a Cancountry number one in the late '80s. Tracey Brown, the lead singer of the Family Brown, the most celebrated Canadian country group of all time, was popular north of the 49th Parallel.

By 1987, a new wave of young Canadian country women was surging to the fore, led by kd lang out west and Michelle Wright in the east. By the end of the decade, lang was the ruling Queen of Canadian Country and an international country star. Then, the controversies concerning her vegetarianism and her endorsement of the "Meat Stinks" campaign plagued her career in country, and she chose to move forward into a career in pop music. She has never looked back. In the early 1990s, Michelle Wright stepped into the breach and took her music to the North American audience via a string of hit CMT videos directed by award-winning video director Steven Goldmann. Michelle was viewed as the leader of a pack of rising Canadian female stars that included Patricia Conroy, Joan Kennedy, Kelita, Cindy Church, Lisa Brokop, Sharon Anderson, Casandra Vasik, and Anita Perras. The various degrees of success that each of these artists achieved served as enticing examples to young Eileen Twain, and with each new success story she became more and more convinced that she, too, could realize her Nashville dream.

Music Row was interested in signing girl singers from Canada, especially if they weren't as rebel-minded as kd lang. Sharon Anderson and Lori Yates were signed to Nashville labels, and, while their records did well in Canada, both artists failed to click in the United States. Michelle Wright fared better with her Arista Records debut. In 1992, Michelle made her mark on Nashville when *Take It Like A Man* burst into the Top 10. A year later, she was named Top New Female Artist by the California-based Academy of Country Music. That show was broadcast live on the NBC and Global networks to a combined audience of more than 30 million viewers. In June 1994, Michelle co-hosted the TNN/Music City News Country Awards show with Waylon Jennings and Billy Dean. But after this promising start, the 'Myrna Lorrie' syndrome set in and her star has fallen from the Nashville firmament. Her most recent U.S. Top 20 hit was *Your Love* in 1999, a collaboration with adult contemporary artist Jim Brickman.

Montreal born and raised Patricia Conroy put her country career together working in a family band in Quebec, a folk rock act in southern Ontario, and out on the Canadian west coast where she recorded her first country radio hits before signing with Warner Canada and heading to Nashville. Patricia won her first CCMA award in 1990 when she picked up the association's Vista Rising Star Award as best new artist. In 1993, she received her second CCMA, the album of the year award for BAD DAY FOR TRAINS. The next year, she was named the CCMA's Best Female Vocalist. Shortly after that she released the critically-acclaimed, ground-breaking YOU CAN'T RESIST and the chart-busting Cancountry hit *Keep Me Rockin'*. Conroy's video of that single was one of the earliest videos in which a country girl just plain wanted to have some fun, a performance video where Patricia rocked her country. In 1995, Patricia was featured on George Fox's CBC-TV Special *Time of My Life* along with three other female vocalists.

On the telephone from her home in Nashville, Conroy recently remembered that this show had come at a critical time for Canadian country women. "It was a pivotal moment for a lot of us," she told me. "I had put out a few albums and I was asked to do the show. Susan Aglukark was on the show. She was hot, hot! She was kind of the new kid on the block. And Lisa Brokop, who was making a name for herself in the states with EVERY LITTLE GIRL'S DREAM. And then there was someone by the name of Shania Twain, who really was the new kid on the block. She had just won her first CCMA awards that September. We all had great expectations for her. So, she was on the show, too. I was the veteran. It was kind of a Canadian Diva Special. Country divas. Shania was really, really friendly. I didn't get to talk to her all that much, but I sensed she was a woman of strength, which, as it turned out, she was. You need to be to make the kind of splash that she has. You don't come out of nowhere and do that, even with all the help she's had from her husband and her label, Mercury Records, here in Nashville. At that moment, women in country were really making their mark. The CBC likes mixing things up. I think they did that with the kd lang and Anne Murray TV Special earlier and they did it again with the four women in 1995. You know what? It's always a good idea. It's always a good idea to put a bunch of women together and . . . give them a show."

Motown influences, I suggested, had been a common influence on Michelle, Shania, and Patricia herself. "I'm certainly influenced by that music," she agreed, "that Motown sound and people like Stevie Wonder and Diana Ross, all of that music." The Canadian 'content' that the Canadian country women were taking to Nashville was that same dance music feel? I asked. "Exactly," she agreed, "with a real rhythmic dance-oriented feel to it, rather than just the lyric for the song being the main reason for the song."

Keep Me Rockin' had been Patricia Conroy's most influential contribution. She had recorded the track at Le Studio in Morin Heights, Quebec, not far from her home town. What had led her to take her country music in this direction? I wondered. To just let it all hang out like that? "The thread that you mentioned," she said, "and you were bang-on when you said it mentioning Michelle and myself and Shania, is that we like to get up there and rock. *Bad Day For Trains*, when I think back on it, *was* pretty daring. That sort of got me started and led me to record *Keep Me Rockin'* and the album YOU CAN'T RESIST. That whole album has a real electric rock feel to it. That wasn't really premeditated, although, because of my earlier influences, all the way from the Rolling Stones to Stevie Wonder, I really wanted to portray that as a performer.

"It didn't hurt the mix at all that Kenny Aronoff was the drummer on those sessions. He was, like, the anchor — to the whole session. And we knew it the minute we tracked the first song. Knew that this was going to be a rockin' album. That was all there was to it. I knew we had something. With *Keep Me Rockin'* we let it rock out at the end, we did that purposely. I said, 'Man, this is too hot to let it end!' I was laughing, and that's there on the track. There was chairs being kicked over in the studio. The guitarists, David Grissom and Brent Rowan, kicked over their chairs. That album is my favorite because of what happened in the studio — the combination of the people, and the kind of 'rock meets country head on' feel to this album. It was kind of ahead of its time, unfortunately."

For a while, however, Patricia's career, like Michelle Wright's, became tangled up in blue, so to speak, with the international video boycott of 1994 and early 1995 when Canadian independents were yanked from CMT in retaliation for CMT being exiled from Canada. Lisa Brokop, Terri Clark, and Shania were the Canadian artists who survived that momentary international crisis. All three signed themselves directly to a Nashville major and never had a Canadian record deal that could have held them back. Although Lisa Brokop has since been dropped from two U.S. major labels, retreating across the border where she is much loved, Terri Clark and Shania Twain have succeeded in the international arena. Terri and Shania also ran neck and neck in the competition for the top Canadian country awards throughout the latter half of the decade. Although a lot of attention has been given to Shania for her fashion 'statements', Terri Clark made her own when she donned her trademark stetson for her breakthrough videos *Better Things To Do* and *When Boy Meets Girl*. Like most of the Canuck singers, Terri is fiercely independent, although she has forged a good relationship with her Nashville label, Mercury Records. And right from those first *Billboard* hits, Terri has had a hand in writing all of her records. Having that creative input has been crucial to her continuing popularity with her fans. In April 2000, Terri told *Country Music News* reporter Phil Sweetland, "I think that the power of the word is very, very amazing and I think that you have to be careful what you say because I get letters from people who say the lyrics of a song will change their lives." All and all, a remarkable generation of Canadian country female talent.

Even more impressive was the progress that Canadian rock and pop women were having in the '90s. Jann Arden and Sarah McLachlan led the way in the early going. Alanis Morissette and Celine Dion became huge international stars before the decade ended. Along the way, they were joined by Holly Cole and Diana Krall with their jazz approach to pop. Then Shania arrived to complete an era that had begun 40 years earlier with pioneers Buffy Sainte-Marie, Joni Mitchell, and Anne Murray, then continued by domestic rock stars like Shari Ulrich, Sass Jordan, Jane Siberry, Luba, and Alannah Myles until kd lang's rebellious Canadian angel with a lariat arrival on the international scene. Like kd, Shani Twain would crossover from country to pop, and like kd, she would break all the Nashville rules.

Years before in Nashville, both Anne Murray and Olivia Newton-John had broken out of the formulas and pre-fabricated molds in the '70s and proven that you could sell more records if your country crossed over. Dolly Parton had followed up on Newton-John's lead, taking on Hollywood, building Dollywood, teaching by example that a hillbilly from the hollers could take the spirit of the Opry with her when she headlined in Vegas and acted in feature films like 9 To 5 and The Best Little Whorehouse In Texas. Dolly's Trio friends, Emmylou Harris and Linda Ronstadt, led by example with their country rock albums, exploring their own musical horizons because they had not undergone a Nashville make-over. With Shania there would be new lessons to be learned for the Music Row establishment, lessons she would pass on as she blew by everybody in the Music Row stables on her way to becoming the most successful female country record-ing artist of all time. Lessons that were at least as much about letting the music evolve and not merely recording according to proven but dated formulas as they had to do with emerging women's rights in the music business. Lessons that were more about making real music than they were about whether your music was rock, pop, or country.

By the time that Shania launched her world tour in 1998, a lot of the music being produced in Music Row studios sounded quite a bit like the recordings she had made for her 1995 breakthrough THE WOMAN IN ME. She had set fashion trends that had helped free country women from the cornpone stereotypes and rhinestone costumes of the past. She had championed the post-feminist stance with her saucy songwriting, demonstrating that a woman could stand up for her rights and not be confrontational or retributive while doing it. And she and Mutt Lange had changed country music forever with their forward-looking approach to production. A chick singer from the Canadian backwoods and a renegade rock producer from South Africa had refused to bow down to the powers that be on Music Row and make their music according to the worn-out countrypolitan ways accepted there. They had actually been encouraged to work together by Luke Lewis, one of a new breed of Nashville execs who succeeded to positions of influence in the '90s. Shania and Mutt also set new standards for dynamics on a country record and a new minimum requirement for crossover country. By the time that her tour had leap-frogged from North America to Asia and Australia, and come back to Canada and the U.S., before finally moving on to Europe, she had "rocked this country all over the world" and cast her detractors' allegations and contentions aside with the pure intent of making the best music she could. In the process of doing so, she had sold more than 25 million albums in less than seven years. Still, Shania Twain would begin her tour in Canada and return there for several shows before she was done. She had not forgotten where she had come from.

Billboard Music Awards 1995

Top of the Pops BBC1

Top of the Pops Special Edition

Grammy Awards, 1999: "Man! I Feel Like a Woman!"

CMA Entertainer of the Year, September 1999

The
Woman
in
Me

1
NASHVILLE RULES

OR SOMEONE WHO HAD CROSSED THE BORDER only once before in her
life, moving to Nashville in the summer of 1991 offered Eileen Twain
many challenges, including her surprise when she ordered a chicken-
fried steak at a Shoney's restaurant and discovered it was not ham, as it would
have been back home, but batter-coated, deep-fried beef. Her work for Mercury
was almost as perplexing. She had been signed on the basis of her songwriting
as much as her vocal abilities, but her songs were not crafted according to any
Music Row formula for collaborations. "I was pushed into this," she told the
producers of her VH1 Special *Behind The Music*, "three hour writing sessions —
'we need you to co-write' — and this kind of thing, and I didn't understand any
of it. This was very new to me. I was kind of intimidated by it . . . I didn't know
if I could fit into this. It was kind of weird."

Eileen had been writing songs since she was eight years old, but she was
used to being moved to do it, beginning with some emotion or vision, not writing songs from nine to five like another day-job. To her, songwriting is a highly personal process, a creative process fired by inspiration. She had yet to learn
the Nashville way of being a woman country singer, as Norro Wilson, who had
produced the successful demo session that convinced Buddy Cannon and
Harold Shedd to sign Eileen to the Mercury label, explains. "She was from
Canada . . . way the heck away . . . she didn't have a reference about this town.
And that's not fussing at her. It's the fact that the town does work in a certain
way. Whether it's formulas or not, it's just kinda how people do it. They get
together, and they go to the writin' room, and they write all day."

As her grooming by Mercury progressed, Eileen Twain found that she was
being pushed into other things she didn't fully comprehend, but she went along
with each dictate her label bosses issued. Shedd put Shania into the studio to
sing background vocals on both Jeff Chance's album WALK SOFTLY ON THE
BRIDGES and Sammy Kershaw's HAUNTED HEART, the corporate strategy seeming

to be to have her surrounded by hunks and hats. Changing her name, however, was one thing she wanted to have a say in. She knew that other Canadians had changed their names when they crossed the border. Wilf Carter had been renamed "Montana Slim" for American audiences, even though he had been born and raised in the Canadian Maritimes and lived in Alberta and Arizona for much of his adult life. When she was told that she would have to do it, she began to plot her own destiny. "They liked Eileen, which is my name," she told VH1, "but they didn't think it flowed well into Twain. So, they thought I needed to change my *last* name . . . It was something that I just couldn't let go of." She felt that giving up "Twain" would be a betrayal of her heritage and a denial of the beliefs Jerry Twain had labored to instil in her. So, she suggested something entirely different, an Ojibway name that meant "on my way" — *Shania*. "It's Indian," she explained, "and it flows so well with Twain." She had first heard the name at Deerhurst where she had befriended a young wardrobe assistant whose name was Shania.

Norro Wilson had produced her demo recording for Mercury in less than glamorous fashion, as he explains on the VH1 special. "We went in the studio and did three sides, in a little studio, low budget, basically, el cheapo." For Shania's debut, self-titled Mercury album, Wilson worked with Harold Shedd, the producer of such successful acts as Alabama and K.T. Oslin. The two men took charge of song selection. In the contract Mary Bailey had negotiated, no provision had been made for Shania to have any control of material to be recorded. *God Ain't Gonna Get You For That*, a co-write with Kent Robbins, was the only song with her artistic input, not an arrangement she had imagined when she moved to Nashville. As she would say in her VH1 special, "I could be a club act for the rest of my life. And make a decent living and do cover songs forever. Anybody could do that. I didn't want my recording career to be that — nine to five songwriting and being controlled by everybody else." She would have her day one album later when many of her songs Mercury producers had passed over became the core of THE WOMAN IN ME, the top-selling album of all time by a female country artist.

In an article billed as "Shania Twain's Lessons for Music Row" in the *Journal of Country Music*, Harold Shedd later told contributor Clark Parsons that "she'll probably say that the label wouldn't let her cut her songs. But she didn't have anything song-wise that would contribute to an album. . . . It was as much a search for a direction as it was a concept, because everything we did on it she could do so well, she was that unique. We had a variety of things on the first album, but nothing that was really her. *What Made You Say That* was probably the closest thing to Shania. We were just trying to find something to get her on the radio and get her exposure and give people a chance to hear her."

"My songs weren't really taken seriously then because I was a nobody and I was new in town," Shania told Parsons. To Denis Hunt at the *Los Angeles Times*, she added, "I had written some songs for the album . . . but Mercury Records didn't want to use them. My husband helped me reshape those same songs for THE WOMAN IN ME and arrange them in a way that is so much more listenable."

There were other factors that complicated the issue, which neither Twain nor Shedd chose to mention, factors that put country producers at a decided disadvantage when it comes to breaking new acts, as Clark Parsons observes. "Thanks to the power of country radio, country artists must first break through radio, sell tons of albums, and then develop a distinctive sound." Music Row had become hog-tied by a stuck-in-the-mud-country radio industry which had stifled creativity and innovation in country music for decades. Providing the artist with made-in-Nashville product so that the songwriting royalties and publishing royalties would be banked in Nashville banks was another Nashville 'rule' that guided the grooming process for new artists. As Norro Wilson admits, "I know that she felt that there was an area of dictatorship. And, you know something, there's usually a dictatorship with a start-up artist."

Fortunately for Shania and country music in general, this regime started to give way just as her debut album was released. As new Mercury executive Luke Lewis told Clark Parsons concerning the treatment Shania received from his predecessors, "I didn't have an appreciation of how good she was then. I don't think the producers of the record did either. I think she came out of the first album a bit frustrated that she didn't have enough input, but it was water under the bridge. I don't think anybody agonized over it. It was one of those things where creative talent has a way of hiding itself sometimes from those of us who are looking for it. I don't think she meant to be hiding it, but it wasn't as apparent as it became when she and Mutt got together and he encouraged her." Lewis subsequently changed the rules for recording artists at Mercury. "Our inclinations here, for A&R head Keith Stegall and myself," he told Parsons, "are to let artists have as much creative freedom as we can tolerate." This policy would serve the new regime well, making things easier for both Shania Twain and Terri Clark. With Garth Brooks redesigning the way deals were cut and several new country women adopting liberated views when it came to doing business, the old ways in Nashville were giving way to new practices. "Start-up" artists were no longer being viewed as chattel, as prize race horses in the stable built by the label. But as the disappointing months of 1993 slowly unfolded with only modest sales, there was less and less to be cheerful about, and it didn't make things easier to contemplate the reality that some start-up artists never got a second chance, not if the singles from their first album didn't get played on the radio.

There was little Lewis could do about Shania's debut after he inherited the project other than to promote the album so that Shania could put her best foot forward despite the song selection and the clichéd cover art. For her Nashville debut, Shania was presented as an Indian maiden from the Great White North. On the cover she is photographed wearing a fur-fringed buckskin parka with a wolf at her side, which simply reinforced the popular American belief that all Canadians must live in a frozen wilderness. This image wasn't entirely the brainchild of Nashville based record executives, for Shania and Mary had a hand in the proceedings. Shania researched the remote location for the photo shoot herself, reportedly slipping on grandmother Twain's snowshoes for her tramp across the frozen wastes of Ontario to find the ideal spot. A trained wolf, Cane, was flown in from the West Coast for the shoot.

To promote the album, Mercury sent Shania out on the road on what they called their "Triple Play Promotion" along with two other Mercury acts, Toby Keith and John Brannen. As Shania recalls, "this was quite a launch. Sometimes the three of us would joke around that we'll get together one day and have a platinum record reunion." When her career took a decided upswing in 1995, that platinum reunion was a distinct possibility. But in 1993, her debut album bombed nationally, selling only about 100,000 units at the time, although it did fairly well in regional markets (Seattle, Denver, and Salt Lake City) and very well in Canada. In *Country Music News*, Larry Delaney called it a "ten-song masterpiece" and expressed his Canadian pride in seeing Shania on TNN several times during the promotion of the package. The one bright spot on the horizon was that Mary Bailey received two phone messages as a result of people seeing the debut video. The first was from someone named Mutt Lange. She was unfamiliar with the name. The second caller was Sean Penn. Him, she knew about.

The video for *What Made You Say That* was a provocative performance by Shania filmed in Florida on a Miami beach. "I think it was ahead of its time," she commented during a CMT video retrospective. "What I wanted to do, and the way I wanted to express myself, was very overt for country television. Everybody was saying, 'Oh, I don't know — you ought to be a little more conservative . . .'"

Shania had been glamorously filmed and edited by director Steven Goldmann, a fellow Canuck who was beginning to establish himself in the music video world. With the successful videos Goldmann made for Michelle Wright and Patricia Conroy, his company, The Collective, soon found themselves fashioning videos for Kathy Mattea, Pam Tillis, Paul Brandt, and Faith Hill. Goldmann was named CMT Video Director of the Year in 1995 and 1996. For the *What Made You Say That* video, Goldmann simply continued the trend he'd set with Michelle Wright's *Take It Like A Man* video, filming glamorous closeups of Shania through five costume changes. She is depicted cavorting with a hunky stud on the deserted beach before splashing into the surf with this sex object. She is the predator — not the passive female. This successful imaging foreshadowed role-reversals to come in subsequent videos.

Sean Penn thought Shania Twain was gorgeous. Intrigued by the visual possibilities, he called Shania from Hollywood and volunteered his services. It was a good omen. Penn's earlier involvement with Madonna suggested that at the very least he knew a diva in the making when he saw one. Buoyed by the interest, Shania's team responded positively, and Penn brought some style to her second video, *Dance With The One That Brought You*. Veteran Hollywood actor Charles Durning played the mature male in a long-term relationship; Shania played the dual role of the young wife and the contemporary woman. "It was a great day for me," she remembers, "just to be around and watch real pros work. It was really cool to get to know Sean Penn. . . . He was really a terrific person. He's close to my age, and we really hit it off well. I was more involved in how I wanted to be, and we just kind of pieced it together."

While these videos drew fan interest to the new Mercury act, neither single cracked the Top 40, both stalling in the mid-50s on the charts. Touring along with Toby Keith and John Brannen had also failed to light any fires at radio, nor did the third single from the album, *You Lay A Whole Lot Of Love On Me*, a recycled publishing catalog item that had been a minor hit for a minor artist in 1980. The accompanying video was a romantic "French postcard" production set in Montreal. "Just being in Montreal," Shania remembered for "Shania's Video Vault" in *Country Music Today*, "really portrayed the video very well. It was the perfect place to go and do it. It was kind of like a little mini-movie. . . . It was a good experience for me. We were drinking cappucinos in this cafe and we were just playing with the froth." No doubt merely being in the old City, the Mount Royal environs, which had provided Canada with its most flamboyant Prime Minister, Pierre Trudeau, and its most eloquent poet,

Leonard Cohen, while walking along St Catherine Street, named for the first Native saint, provided sufficient ambience. Shania was enchanted by this old world ambience. "Montreal has lots of old buildings," she remembered for her video retrospective. "And when the French came over to Canada and built that part of Montreal, they built it very much in the same style they would have built in their own country. So, it really does have European structures." The romantic feel captured on the video clip was all for nought because few radio programmers chose to play the single. *You Lay A Whole Lotta Love On Me* really was a sappy record, no more and no less, no matter how cool the video may be.

2

ANY MAN OF MINE

TO A RECLUSIVE MILLIONAIRE PRODUCER AND SONGWRITER from the international rock music world, the songs and videos from the SHANIA TWAIN album were immensely intriguing, even if county music radio and fans largely passed them by. Although he was based in England, Robert John 'Mutt' Lange saw Shania's first video, for which she was soon named CMT Europe's Rising Video Star of the Year. He liked the video well-enough that he began playing the SHANIA TWAIN CD during his daily workouts. Wearing a tank top and exposing her midriff had been a natural thing to do on that beach in Florida for her first video. Little did Shania know at that time that she was exposing one of her most intriguing assets. Mutt Lange liked her country pop record, *What Made You Say That*, but he was attracted by all of her charms, including that flat tummy and that soon-to-be-famous navel. She was beautiful beyond words, and she could *sing*, too. Lange was usually attracted to tall, leggy blondes, pin-up models — like Bo Derek. He didn't know it then, but he and Bo Derek and her photographer-filmmaker husband John Derek would soon play a significant part in Shania Twain's future. The wheels were set in motion when he picked up his phone and dialed the 615 area code. He wanted to talk to Shania Twain. After making an inquiry, he learned the number of Twain's management company.

Mary Bailey had no idea who Mutt Lange was, and she and Shania merely sent him a signed autographed 8 x 10 promo shot in response to his call. Indeed, few people in Nashville knew Lange. "What is a Mutt Lange? Who is a Mutt Lange? And what has a Mutt Lange done?" Norro Wilson asked rhetorically in the VH1 Special. Mary and Shania's lack of familiarity with the name of the famed producer of multiple platinum albums for Michael Bolton, Def Leppard, the Cars, Foreigner, Bryan Adams, and AC/DC didn't matter because Lange persisted. Soon, Lange and Twain were chatting amiably on the telephone and he popped her the question. He asked her if she wrote songs herself. Then, he asked her why she hadn't recorded some of them on her album. Before the two hung up their receivers, Shania had pulled out her guitar and sung some of her material, including *Home Ain't Where His Heart Is (Anymore)*, to Mutt over the long distance phone line. It was the beginning of a promising relationship. These impromptu long distance songwriting sessions were a welcome diversion for Shania after her disappointing experience with nine-to-five sessions in a writing room on Music Row.

For the first time in a whole long while, Shania felt exhilaration, encouragement, and the stirring of deeper feelings she had almost totally forgotten — of a time when her spirit had not been fettered with worry and failure and compromise. Of a time when she had still had enough independence to at least oppose the idea that she had merely become a 'girl singer' on Music Row with little to distinguish her from the rest of the corporate label stable, all of whom were certainly talented, although most were as subdued as she had become.

"When Mutt said he was interested in my songwriting," she later told her VH1 audience, as a trembling quiver of excitement quickened the pace of her words, "I was *so* happy. I was thrilled. I was saved! I was gonna be creative, again." She told Clark Parsons, "I sang *a capella* a few songs over the phone to him and he said, 'Wow! Have you played these for other people? Am I the only one who's hearing this?' He was thrilled that I had so much to offer as a songwriter."

They continued to speak and share over the phone. Mutt was as successful a songwriter as he was a producer. He'd written hits for recording acts like Huey Lewis & The News (*Do You Believe In Love*), Def Leppard (*Pour Some Sugar On Me*), and Bryan Adams (*Everything I Do I Do It For You*) that had led to sales of millions of records, sales of more than 10 million of albums like Def Leppard's PYROMANIA and HYSTERIA. Co-writing was his strength. Canadian rocker Bryan Adams has said that Mutt could write with anyone, even Bryan's mom, and come up with a hit song. Bryan and Mutt's *Everything I Do I Do It For You* had sold three million singles and been at number one on nearly every chart in the world for several weeks in 1991, a record-setting 16 weeks at number one in the U.K., propelled to the top by being included on the sound track of Kevin Kostner's blockbuster film, *Robin Hood: Prince of Thieves*. The two songwriters had become close friends.

In June 1993, the 40-something Lange showed up at Fan Fair in Nashville along with Bryan Adams. They had been in Ocho Rios, Jamaica, snorkeling, writing, and recording 18 TIL I DIE together, and just dropped in to say hello. For world travelers like Lange and Adams, Nashville's Tennessee State Fair Grounds was not all that far from the island home of Reggae. With their label connections, it didn't matter that they were not among the 25,000 people who had gobbled up the limited number of Fan Fair tickets.

This was the first time Shania had laid her eyes on her mysterious long dis-tance songwriting friend. Their first meeting on the floor of the convention was an electrically charged hug. Shania was truly happy to meet her phone pal in person. Mutt was equally intrigued. He wanted to know if the warm, fuzzy feel-ings he got while he was sharing three-hour transatlantic phone conversations with Shania would be even more pleasant if they were in the same room. He also wanted to witness Shania's Fan Fair showcase later that week. The two hit it off big-time. Handsome and sophisticated and reclusively shy of crowds and reporters, Lange was able to offer more face-to-face with Shania than he was will-ing to divulge to most people. He was intrigued by her talent — *and* he was smit-ten. Shania has said that she had become hardened, had retreated within herself, into her music and her career in the years after Jerry and Sharon, her closest friends and beloved parents, were taken from her. She had almost come out of her shell when the deal with Mercury had gone through, but the Nashville makeover that followed immediately afterward had a brutalizing effect on her. She now felt herself being drawn back into the world of the living.

Mercury Nashville President Luke Lewis was the person who had tipped Mary and Shania off as to who Mutt Lange really was. When Luke learned that Shania and the famed producer were hitting it off on the phone really well, he wondered if there was any interest in Mutt producing her next album. There was. It was sufficient reason to believe there might actually be a second Shania Twain album. Without Mutt's appearance on the horizon, though, that second album had not been a sure thing.

Mutt was a busy guy, having jumped on a jet in the midst of working on Bryan Adams' album simply to be with her. He was a native of South Africa. His home was in England. He regularly roamed around Europe simply to attend soc-cer matches, his favorite sport. He wasn't about to move to Nashville. He had to get back to the project he was immersed in. As they mutually shared a disap-pointment over the small numbers of people attracted to her Fan Fair showcase, Mr Mysterious made a suggestion. He asked Shania to accompany him back to Europe. He was scheduled to mix Adams' album in France. Why not jump on the next Concorde flight and come on over? He was charmed by the fact that she didn't know what a Concorde was.

This was the beginning of a courtship that would be fueled by a kinetic yin-yang exchange of energy as they joyously created new songs, each bringing their own inspiration to each newfound lyric and melody, and, within the give-and-go of creating and debating — shaping the new material that was to change country music — they were falling in love.

While Mutt shared an affection for pop music with Shania, he was actually a closet country fan, perhaps even more fond of it than Shania herself. "Mutt's a huge country fan," she would later declare. "I may be the princess in his life, but Tammy Wynette is the Queen! The steel guitar is his favorite instrument." This could easily have been an overstatement, a burst of enthusiasm for her favorite producer and husband, because before Mutt began production on his first-ever country record, he took her to realms where country music was seldom heard at all: Ramatuelle, near St. Tropez in southern France, England, Spain, Italy . . .

Until this time, Shania had never made much mention of harboring intimate feelings for any man, except for her father, Jerry Twain, though an engagement that was short-lived has been mentioned by third parties and Paul Bolduc is mentioned among the thankyou's included on the liner notes of the SHANIA TWAIN album. If she had experienced true love, compelling, irresistible passionate love, we probably would have heard about it. Shania has not had much luck concealing anything; she's simply too outgoing to pull it off. However, there is no doubt that a real deal romance was beginning to happen for her in the summer and fall of 1993.

In the manner of characters from a romantic 19th-century novel, Shania and Mutt explored the "continent" together, and, by the time they came to Paris, Shania knew that Mutt was serious in his intentions because her sisters showed up, invited there by Lange. There had been precedents of couples doing the continent together before, famous couples who settled for a while on the shores of Lake Geneva like Elizabeth Barrett who married famed fellow-poet Robert Browning, and Mary Godwin who married the even more famous poet Percy Bysshe Shelley. Ironically, several of these women — who had been romanced in this same cradle of European culture where the architecture of classic Greek and Roman buildings has withstood the onslaught of time, where the paintings of the Renaissance masters still hang on the walls of museums and castles alongside Van Goghs, Picassos, and Klees, and the orchestral music of the baroque, classical, and romantic composers seems to echo from every cobblestone — had created masterpieces themselves. Elizabeth Barrett Browning's sonnet *How Do I Love Thee? Let Me Compare The Ways* has proved to be more memorable to most students than any lines Robert Browning composed. Mary Shelley's *Frankenstein* was the first science fiction novel and would become at least as influential as the famous poems that her husband had written. It would be the same with Mutt and Shania, once she got the support from her fiance that she had needed all along to put her over the top.

Mutt Lange believed that Shania possessed a remarkable potential and that all she needed now was an ally and a stronger sense of self-confidence. He understood what it would take to insure that confidence, and, when he finally got down on bended knee, 2.5 carat diamond ring in hand, he was not denied her hand in marriage. Before he proposed, however, he showed her his interest was genuine by including her sisters in their life so that she would understand that he did not intend to wrest her away from her beloved family members. The three sisters immediately went shopping and sight-seeing. They were in Paris, the fashion and romance capital of the world!

Carrie-Ann would later tell interviewers that it was as if Mutt were asking them, herself and Jill, in lieu of their departed father's presence, for the right to marry their sister. It was a cavalier and romantic approach and not unlike the respectful behavior that Mutt had extended to each and every artist he had worked with, only, this time, he wasn't thinking so much of merely producing this singer — he was also fixing his mind to marry her.

On December 28, 1993, Mutt Lange and Eileen Twain were married at the Deerhurst Resort in Huntsville, Ontario, a venue close to all of the bride's relatives and friends. He might be well-off, a rich and powerful influence in the mega record-selling pop music world, but Mutt was also sensitive to Shania's need to blossom and not intent on merely remaking her, as Nashville had done, to suit his own interests. After their visiting in Canada was done, the happy couple flew south to the Caribbean for a honeymoon in the sun. Since they had first spoken, their existence together had become a dreamy interlude. *This*, Shania knew, was every little girl's dream come true. She had waited until almost forever, long past the time that other dream — of Nashville — had been realized, but Nashville hadn't turned out all that well until she was rescued from Music Row by her Prince Charming.

3

SHIMMY, SHAKE,
MAKE THE EARTH QUAKE

W HEN SHANIA AND MUTT BEGAN TO RECORD TOGETHER, they laid down the bed tracks at Sound Stage Studio in Nashville. Most of the instrumental overdubs were also done there in Tennessee, too, at Battery Studios, Javelina Recording Studios, and Recording Arts. Drummer Paul Leim and bassist David Hundgate anchored an A-team lineup of specialists like Dann Huff, Brent Rowan, Larry Byrom and Brent Mason (guitars), Matt Rollings and Hargus "Pig" Robbins (piano), John Hughey and Paul Franklin (pedal steel), and fiddle players Rob Hajacos and Glen Duncan.

Shania's lead vocals and Mutt and Shania's background vocals were done at A.R.P. Productions in Sainte Anne de Lacs, Quebec. For mixing, they chose Le Studio in Morin Heights, Quebec, where Anne Murray had recorded. The setting was picturesque. The guest cabins were set on a lakeshore across the water from the studio itself. If you felt inclined, you could row yourself to the session in one of the row boats they had there. Amidst this rural tranquility, her life continued to be so nearly perfect that Shania could scarcely believe it kept on happening that way. She felt privileged to be working with someone who wasn't trying to make her over. Someone who wanted her music to come from her. That was so unbelievable, but she knew it was the approach that Mutt took with all of the successful acts he produced. There was no formula. As the music was created she found that it took on a life of its own. She would later proudly tell interviewers that this was her husband's true genius — he actually understood how to create, how to fashion music that had never been heard before. It was a miracle.

Mutt had encouraged her, sharing the songs he was writing with her over the phone, singing *I Said I Loved You But I Lied*, the song that he had written for Michael Bolton, to her during their first transatlantic conversation. And he had inspired her with his talent. "When we started working together," she told Robert K. Oermann, "I became such a fan of his voice. *No One Needs To Know* is kind of like a duet. . . . But he's always saying, 'Why don't you toot your own horn more? . . . Tell people.' He could have been a star himself. He's got rock & roll hair. . . . He's got such a great voice. But he's a producer at heart."

Of course, the intimacy of their relationship infused their music with a rare and special quality. Mutt's genius lay in bringing out the best in each act he worked with, and working together, he and Shania discovered the music that became THE WOMAN IN ME, the real Shania. "The advantage that we have together," she told me in 1995, "is that we love each other. . . . A lot of the success of this album has to do with the writing and what he has to do with the sound of it. Right from the beginning, he said, 'We need to go to your catalog. I need to know what you've been writing, then we'll go from there. You be the basis for the creativity of this album. Because it needs to be you, not me.'"

Despite this creative chemistry, Shania and Mutt had to address the harsh yet silly reality that country radio was at first reluctant to play the lead-off single from their album, *Whose Bed Have Your Boots Been Under*, an undeniably country record. Fortunately for Shania and Mutt, shortly after she had finished recording her debut album SHANIA TWAIN, Harold Shedd had been shuffled in a corporate restructuring to the newly created Polygram Nashville label and Luke Lewis had succeeded him at Mercury. The label had shown considerable innovation when it came to marketing Billy Ray Cyrus' breakout single *Achy Breaky Heart* and his multiple platinum selling SOME GAVE ALL, a year before her own more dismal debut. However, *she* had been treated like just another girl singer. Seated beside Cyrus at the 1993 Country Music Seminar, she had been ignored by all but a few of the 2,500 radio programmers that year. Mutt and Shania were heartened to believe that Luke Lewis would be more responsive to their creative input, to their vision of what Shania's music could be if she recorded her own songs — to what sales potentials might be if she were to take advantage of what set her apart from the rest of the girl singers rather than following formula approaches.

Lewis warmed to the Shania-Mutt combination right away. There would be no strings attached. She was free to record her own songs, no problem there, either. He has since called THE WOMAN IN ME "their honeymoon album." Lewis could see that things could work out very well for both Mercury Records and Shania Twain if Mutt Lange produced her album. There was only one stumbling block and that was the budget. Mutt Lange's productions cost a whole lot more than Music Row was used to spending. At least half a million dollars, sometimes more. When Mutt said that there was no problem, really, and that he'd absorb half the cost if he were given a shot at a better percentage of the profit, it was a done deal.

This compromise was similar to deals that Garth Brooks was hammering out with his label, although he had been compelled to change labels to make his point. The contractual arrangements Garth worked out, where he had a stake in the proceedings as an investor and was not merely an artist signed to a corporate entity, would include Garth in the marketing strategy and decision-making, helping him considerably to realize his goal of selling 100 million albums in one decade. Also similar was the fact that, as a producer and songwriter, Robert John "Mutt" Lange had also already fashioned records that were closing in on that impressive 100 million figure. His songwriting royalties alone amounted to millions of dollars per year.

In retrospect, the gambling producer, Lange, profited greatly. The cautious label execs would have reaped larger benefits if they had footed the entire bill, but when THE WOMAN IN ME began to sell in greater volumes than any country album by a woman had ever sold before, there were not very many unhappy campers on the artist-producer-label team. In fact, there were not too many sour faces anywhere in sight at all, not unless you count people who had not jumped on the Shania Twain bandwagon earlier when they had the chance, or others who seemed to resent her success simply because she was a woman, a person they had previously been able to refer to as a 'girl singer' but now had to acknowledge as the most successful female country recording artist, ever.

To promote the album, Shania embarked on a radio and media voyage but not a concert tour. That strategy worked very well at first. Her mall appearances attracted mobs of fans, sometimes tens of thousands of them, even though she was there to sign autographs, not to perform. Almost 20,000 people swarmed into the Mall of America in Minneapolis; 27,000 fans showed up for her fan appreciation day in Calgary. With her self-promotions, her fan appreciation days, her controversial videos and network television appearances, Shania was sowing the seeds for the Shaniamania that would follow the release of her third Mercury album. When asked why she wasn't touring in support of the release, Shania would say she didn't have enough original material to perform yet. She also soon learned that not touring would not likely hurt her record sales all that much. She would not upset the record label if she didn't hit the road because the label didn't make any revenue from an artist's tour. Luke Lewis warned Shania that she would be criticized for not touring, though, predicting that people would say "that you're Milli Vanilli and you can't perform." As Lewis explained to Clark Parsons, "and that puts an enormous burden on her when she goes out because it's going to have to be solid as a rock or she's gonna get creamed." What Lewis was saying without actually voicing it was that, although he and Keith Stegall had adopted a more forward looking agenda at Mercury, there were plenty of people in the country music business who still played by the old rules.

Meanwhile, Mutt and Shania were getting used to married life, busily creating music, too, and love flowed all around them. Life was sweet and simple there in up-state New York. During their long walks and horseback rides, they were already propelled forward into new and more wondrous creations, already writing songs for a sequel to THE WOMAN IN ME. They were not deterred from their single-minded purpose by anything written or said by nay-sayers.

The only cloud on the immediate horizon was something they hadn't anticipated. It began right there on their own property, which they had reportedly purchased for $1.2 million. The land surrounding Dexter Lake and the nearby town of Waverly was located within Adirondack Park and was designated for resource management. Mutt and Shania had plans for a dream home, not a mere summer cottage, with a state-of-the-art recording studio, complete with apartments to house the visiting recording artists and musicians. The Adirondack Park Agency was not sure these ambitious plans fell within the area of "resource management."

An article published in *The Buffalo News* on Sunday, November 26, 1995, bore the title: "Controversy Over Country Music Studio." Acting Park Agency Executive Director, Daniel T. Fitts, was quoted as saying, "the first thing we're going to do is to sit down with the landowner and discuss the facts of the case."

Shania and Mutt thought they had edited the bureaucratic red tape out of their lives, along with the other problems of urban living, when they had left the city life behind them and moved "back to the country where we all belong," as Neil Young had suggested in his 1985 song *Back To The Country*. Was it their fame that had betrayed them? Was it because they were well-off successful people who made hit records that sold millions of copies? Had their association with the music industry triggered fears of some monstrous '90s Woodstock rearing its contentious head right in the midst of this environmentally sensitive parkland? Right there in St. Regis Falls?

Of course newspaper stories, which reported that they lived in a 12-bedroom, 24,000 square-foot mansion on 20 square miles of private land with their own private lake, sometimes exaggerated the situation. These stories seemed to indicate that they were flaunting their wealth and fame. Again these reports were a result of Shania's enthusiasm for life. In 1993, she had been openly expressive about her days as a teenaged tree-planter, and now she raved about her wilderness home. She was so happy to go on long walks in the woods. She was thrilled to be riding her horses in this inspiring setting. Some journalists fixed upon this as an example of opulence and chose to build up the details as evidence of her wealth rather than her peace of mind. Their acreage was located in an unsullied wilderness area, and they had gol' darn gone and built their studio and residence on their land despite bothersome flak from park officials. But by sharing her happiness with the press, Shania had exposed this parkland preserve to unwanted publicity.

The privacy Shania and Mutt had coveted now seemed to be slipping away as they found themselves under increasing scrutiny. Even when she donned bulky clothes and a baseball cap as a disguise, she was recognized at local supermarkets. This loss of privacy led to Mutt and Shania moving to Switzerland, as Shania explained to Jennifer Gerlock at *Country Song Roundup*. "We didn't have to move at all. It was just a decision we had to make for the studio. It all boils down to where we want to spend the rest of our lives making music and where we can. You know, it's kind of hard to record when you've got helicopters flying over and private planes and everybody wants to know what you're doing all the time. . . . So, we are going to go somewhere in Switzerland where they have a lot of music stuff going on anyway. Making music there is going to fit in as opposed to sticking out. . . . I'm not leaving the States, but we're moving the studio. . . . I also have a home in Florida, and that's where I'll be spending my time off."

Shania simply was not conforming to Nashville expectations, becoming even more of an outsider by moving to Europe. Commentators like Robert K. Oermann would observe that she "wasn't working the room like everybody else." More rabid voices declared that Shania was a studio Barbie and Mutt was a rock & roll Svengali. Together, they were ruining everything that country music stood for. Their mere presence in the country music world was a black eye on the Opry and everything previously held sacred.

Some women-bashing journalists like Charles Earle, who writes for the Nashville publication *In Review*, would declare Shania Twain was involved in a "conspiracy to change country music into a big, awful fashion show." Of course, Nashville writers were not the only ones to bash Shania, not by a longshot, nor did the attack come only from the male flank. In the *Birmingham News*, under the title "Shania's Star Zooms As Mutt's Trophy Wife," Mary Colurso wrote, "Shania was just another big-hair chick with a self-titled album, trying to get noticed among all the hoopla. Excuse me if this sounds crass, but I can't imagine she took one peek at Mutt from under those fabulous eyelashes and said, "Whoa! That's the guy for me! Lange might be dynamite behind a stereo console, but he looks like a roadie reject from some grungy, unwashed, let's-all-wear-black-t-shirts AC/DC tour." For Colurso, Shania's achievement thus far in her career was "not bad for a lightweight vocalist who has never been on tour, has rarely performed live, and whose greatest asset is clearly her luscious, come-hither appearance." While comparing Mutt and Shania with Mariah Carey and Tommy Mottola, she concluded, "Babes glom onto star makers because these men can boost their careers. That principle has long been etched in stone in the music business. . . . If it sounds like I begrudge these women their success, it's only because so much of their popularity rests on sexy feminine appeal."

At five-foot-four, with auburn tresses, soft green eyes, and classic high cheekbones, Shania was a slender wisp of a woman whose curvaceous form had emerged from the full-length red gown worn on the *Whose Bed Have Your Boots Been Under* video to reveal more skin than any female country artist had ever exposed, certainly more than had previously been seen by any good ole person in the South during the performance of a country song. When backlash set in, it was not a cleavage issue — the sort of thing that had worked so well for Bardot, Monroe and Madonna — but rather Shania's innocent little navel, all above her belt, so to speak, that set the South on fire. If Shania Twain and Mary Bailey had decided to create some controversy to spark interest in her records, they could have wracked their brains till they had migraines and not come up with a game plan that worked as well as the publicity that was being made for them at no charge at all by the Shania-bashers who could not have been anticipated or fabricated. Everyone, it seemed, had an opinion about Shania's navel.

When the first rumblings of controversy began to swell, Shania was off on her media tour promoting her lead single, *Whose Bed Have Your Boots Been Under*. The companion video of a barefoot Shania strumming her guitar on a rural veranda, inter-cut with her in a red dress table-dancing for the patrons of a roadside diner, was hurried over to CMT, where reactions were lukewarm. *Whose Bed Have Your Boots Been Under* (known as 'Boots' among fans) was scrutinized by a committee of CMT employees, which commentators have alleged was comprised of more women than men. Regardless of the gender politics, these committee members were not ready for the fun-loving sensuality being offered up. So, again, the morality issue, not the music, kept CMT from playing the video in heavy rotation. "They thought it was redundant and too sexy," Luke Lewis told Clark Parsons. "I'm not sure if they ever told me what their objections were, but they didn't play it much. I was calling them out there every week. 'We've got a hit record, would you guys play this thing?' And they just were not happy about it. The truth is they never played it like it was a hit." The video for the next single, *Any Man Of Mine*, was so heavily requested that CMT caved in. It didn't seem to matter that this track was a whole lot more experimental than 'Boots', with complex tempo changes, dance track breaks, and a driving country rock intensity. There was a fiddle in the band, wasn't there? A pedal steel, as well. The harmonies were traditional as all get out. Radio programmers who had been reluctant to playlist the first single now chose to ignore the fact that Shania seems to be rapping on the spoken extro, a line-dance call that hips and hops. Rap or not, the final verse *was* a call to the dance. "You gotta shimmy, shake, make the earth quake," she instructs. "Kick, stomp, stomp, then you jump. Heel to toe. Do si do . . ." She sure was a sexy dancer. Everyone agreed on that point.

Seldom mentioned at all by critics were some truly spectacular moments in this video, where, for example, Shania is dancing in her red dress in a field near a fence and a tight flight-pattern of starlings whirs into frame and out again. Their flight becomes the illustrated swirl of a pedal steel swell. Her video was bursting with an exuberance for life that appealed to both hardcore CMT addicts and casual viewers. All of her videos have been so well made that they don't immediately wear out their welcome. The videos were the visual equivalents of the exciting music that Shania and Mutt had made on THE WOMAN IN ME and simply showed her to be irrepressible.

'Boots' and *Any Man Of Mine* had been filmed on and around Bo Derek's ranch in Santa Ynez, California. These videos would become crucial to the eventual success of THE WOMAN IN ME, with *Any Man Of Mine* streaking all the way to the top of the charts to become Shania's first number one. John Derek was first called in to shoot the cover photography for the album. There would be no more pursuit of the "Indian maiden" imagery from the debut album. It was hoped that he could reveal Shania to the world as the "10" she really was. He did.

Shania credits Mary Bailey with coming up with the idea of calling Derek. Both John and Bo worked with Shania in New York City during this image making process. John Derek's photos of Shania were stunning. Bo's back cover shots of Shania with her horse showed the other side of Shania. The video project, begun in England where the initial version of the video for *Whose Bed Have Your Boots Been Under* had been made by an animator, was at first a disappointment. Animated boots just did not cut the mustard. Although he was reluctant to do so, John Derek was called in to rescue the project. Bo and Shania were hitting it off as friends, so John couldn't say no to their request. "John Derek was the director and Bo Derek was the producer, and her sister Carrie was her assistant," Shania told *Country Music Today*. "It was a whole family affair. Bo's mother, Norma, is actually a professional hair and makeup artist and does movies and everything. So, she was my hair and makeup. . . . Bo convinced John to do it and in the end we all became great friends."

For the video of *Any Man Of Mine*, John Derek was once again put in charge, but after the label rejected Derek's initial cut, Charlie Randazzo was called in to shoot additional footage — the belly-dancing sequences near the barn and the wagon in which no less than 50 glimpses of Shania's belly-button have been counted by avid Shaniamaniacs. *Any Man Of Mine* became Shania's first number one CMT video. The next four video releases would follow suit.

Derek stuck with the usual rural images used for country videos but his direction, his camera work, and Randazzo's eventual video editing, which combined footage from Derek's shoot and Randazzo's dance sequence, showed Shania to be a "10" even though she was fully clothed. Well, almost fully clothed. Shania rode horses, herded cows, and danced her butt off for the cameras. The form fitting levis, denim vest, and cotton tank top (with midriff bared) she wore in the *Any Man Of Mine* video were working girl's clothes, but Shania's navel was quickly becoming the most famous ever exposed to public viewing since the days when Cleopatra won Julius Caesar's favors with a bellydance designed to save her country from Roman conquest. These outdoor scenes were interspersed with vignettes of Shania in a bubble bath, a horse playfully sticking its head in the barn window to fetch her towel; Shania dressing for the evening in a black formal; and Shania checking herself out before her full-length bedroom mirror. She had traded her boots for heels, her working girl image tossed into the laundry hamper. These contrasting outdoor and indoor sequences portrayed both sides of Shania: the raw cowgirl *and* the sophisticated pop diva. Country girl — bare midriff, jean jacket, and jeans. City woman — full-length bedroom mirror, heels, and a glamorous designer gown. Women related, men stared, and the patriarchs and matriarchs of the old South whispered behind their hands. They were shocked.

Shania would claim to be surprised at this reaction. "So many other people bare their midriffs," she declared during the taping of her VH1 Special. "I don't know why mine is such an issue. I don't understand that." She also seemed mystified that people said she was making any kind of fashion statement at all. "I didn't know America all that well," she confessed to Bruce Feiller. "I'm from Canada. I didn't know things were all that different . . . I don't like to offend people. I'm not out to make a statement." Feiller noted that Shania actually chose her wardrobe to appeal to the women in the audience, not the men. "Women are the people who read *Vogue*," she told him. "They're into the Calvin Klein ads. They're into the Guess? ads. If it wasn't for the music, I would be the sort of person who would wear the same thing the rest of my life. I'd be terribly boring."

Professing her innocence of the impact she had made was an endearing quality, but surely frustrated anyone who tried to pin her down during an interview. Her behavior and her fashion sense jolted the country music world out of the moral conservatism that had been established during the '50s. Country label execs, publicists, and even the artists themselves had been restrained for so long by the fear of violating so-called good ole values that country music had very nearly died.

Country music had been set in its ways for nearly half a century — ever since the music had become the slave of radio formats in the late '40s. The music had become as prim and proper as the twin-bed Hollywood films of the 1950s that featured the likes of Doris Day and Rock Hudson. Become as stereotyped as the early black & white Hollywood "westerns" where good guys wore white hats and bad guys wore black. And as dated as the dialog of the Vistavision color-by-deluxe "dusters" that Hollywood had stopped making 30 years ago. Country music lyrics, especially those deemed acceptable for women, simply had not changed since they were set in place by this mid-century puritanism. When censors demanded that all men and women depicted sleeping in bedrooms together were to be in twin beds, Hollywood toed the line. When radio stations began replacing many of their live shows with disc jockeys and playlists of popular records, the record industry fell in line, too. In the rock & roll world, the, the Doors, the Stones, the Mothers of Invention, and many others may have rebelled, but the Nashville equivalent of John & Yoko's Peace demonstration sit-ins was the elopement of George Jones and Tammy Wynette. In Nashville, the cultural upheaval that took place elsewhere in America in the

1960s was scarcely noticed. On Music Row it was business as usual behind closed doors. While Merle Haggard never intended *Okie From Musgokee* to be a redneck anthem, the song was the 1970 CMA Single of the Year. Women's rights organizations found their efforts met considerable opposition in the South, more so than anywhere else in North America. By the early 1970s, country music had become a reactionary backwater, isolated from the mainstream by its ever narrowing views, increasingly watered-down content, and syrupy Nashville sound.

How had country music become so reactionary? Country artists who had recorded songs that had contained sexually explicit lyrics in the 1920s and '30s simply quit doing it by the late '40s. There was no airplay to be had for songs where the vocalist blatantly sang of "banging Lulu," as Roy Acuff had done on his 1936 recording *When Lulu's Gone*. Or Gene Autry had done on cuts like *Do Right Daddy Blues*, where he sang about the wild side of life with unabashed frankness before radio censorship shut down lyrics like, "Now you can feel my legs / And you can feel my thighs / But if you feel my legs / You gotta ride me high."

By the 1970s, country radio had accepted drinkin' back into the equation along with the usual cheatin' and hurtin', lovin' and leavin', but some topics were untouchable, unless you were Loretta Lynn and prepared to go against the grain. And there was a strict dress code. While the outlaw movement may have changed the music, it didn't change the way country artists dressed all that much. Some now wore blue jeans and denim jackets, but most still wore rhinestone studded suits, and with few exceptions the men all wore hats and the women all had big hair. Johnny Paycheck sang *Take This Job And Shove It*, Barbara Mandrell sang *I Was Country When Country Wasn't Cool*, but you could see a country star coming a mile away. They were always duded up. And once they had lived in Nashville for a spell, whether they were from Halifax, Bakersfield, Oklahoma City, Austin, or Boston — they all spoke with southern drawls like characters from the *Dukes of Hazzard* or *The Real McCoys*.

MTV provided viewers with the sex from the old 'sex, drugs, and rock & roll' phrase, but early CMT was as hokey as country radio. Country women could flaunt their beauty and they could dance in their videos, but not sexually. In the late 1980s, rockin' new country artists like Steve Earle, Tanya Tucker, and K.T. Oslin bravely broke new ground. Pam Tillis and Michelle Wright tore down barriers with their sensual performances in their sultry music videos for *Cleopatra Queen of Denial* and *Take It Like A Man*. Shania's performance in the *Whose Bed Have Your Boots Been Under* video went even further. Her dancing was overtly sexual. Shania was going against the grain — and she knew it. "Even though I was kind of going against the grain at the time," she told *Country Music Today*, "in the end it was the best thing I ever did — not being intimidated by the fact that it might be a little risqué." Luke Lewis had taken a walk on the wild side, not only in backing these videos but also when he took out an advertisement in the Swimsuit issue of *Sports Illustrated* and issued a Shania calendar featuring John Derek's photographs from the photo shoot for THE WOMAN IN ME. But he had come to believe in Shania, wholeheartedly. "I remember the day she told me, she wanted to be as 'big a Garth,'" Lewis told *Cosmopolitan*. "I looked into her eyes, and knew she could do it."

In the *Any Man Of Mine* video Shania plays directly to the camera as if she *is* a private dancer and the camera is the guy she is intent upon turning on. Doing this fulfilled every cowboy's dream. Steve Earle was moved to quip that Shania Twain was the "highest paid lap dancer in Nashville." Shania's image and attitude began a revolution among country 'girl singers'. Following suit, Mindy McCready would upstage Shania for a while by displaying a gold ring in *her* exposed belly-button, and Dixie Chicks arrived on the scene as liberated as Shania with their politically incorrect post-feminist attitude. Other singers would also willingly abandon the cumbersome Nudie costumes and rhinestone-studded jackets for tank tops, harem costumes, and all manner of fetching and alluring fashion before the decade had run its course.

As time went by, Shania found herself answering many of the same questions over and over again. She had challenged country norms and changed country music, but interviewers still asked the same old questions about her navel. Shania would respond to interviewers questions about her sexy videos by quipping that she thought George Strait was sexy. Was it alright for country guys to be sexy but not country women? Was there some unwritten rule she was breaking? If there was, surely it was a double standard and unfair. Was she less of an artist because she was sensual? After fielding these questions repeatedly, she came up with answers that were designed to put them to rest for once and for all. "If I had an office job," she told *Los Angeles Times'* New York correspondent Elysa Gardner, "I wouldn't show up for work baring my midriff. But this is entertainment . . . I'm aware there's this mentality that you're not allowed to be intelligent and good-looking, or that you're not credible if you wear your hair like this or your shirt like that. But I will not accept that. It's not right."

The choice of a ballad, *The Woman In Me*, as the third single released from the album, was Mercury's attempt to widen Shania's audience, to draw in some older record buyers who might have been put-off by the bold sensuality of the first two videos and the brash, up-tempo country rock approach. "We had our international people at Polygram saying they thought they might be able to break her with a ballad," Luke Lewis told Clark Parsons. "And it turned out that didn't pan out either. But it seemed to work real well for us here." The Mercury execs were still thinking in traditional marketing terms, although the Markus Blunder video, shot in a historic mosque in Cairo and a location near the Egyptian Pyramids, was anything but traditional. Again, horses played a central role. This was the lengthiest video shoot Shania had done, four long days in the sweltering desert heat during which she sustained a welt from the Arabian-style metal stirrups, a scar that has stayed with her to this day.

"Of course, I had never been to Egypt," Shania would reminisce in *Country Music Today*, "so I was kind of going as an observer of the culture and the country and the whole thing. So that was kind of interesting. . . . The surroundings were very inspirational for me. I was enamored and absorbed by the whole mystique of the place. . . . We were in the oldest mosque in Cairo, so it was really special, and we felt that it was really special. This was sacred."

Shania couldn't understand a word the people she was working with said, and they couldn't understand her, either, but communication wasn't really a problem because her producers, George Everage and Nabil Shalzi, bridged the language gap. The heat was a far more difficult obstacle to overcome. It took ages for video director Marcus Blunder and his camera crew to climb to the top of the pyramid at Giza simply to film one of the sequences. "I don't know how he didn't just have sunstroke or something," Shania told interviewers. She was respectful of the privilege of filming in these holy locations and would not forget Cairo's most distinguishing feature, telling journalists, "it's a city of a thousand mosques." Respecting tradition in a Moslem country meant that no matter how hot she felt, she had to remain fully clothed for the mosque scenes. She had to remember to remove her shoes. The sailboat scenes on the Nile River were more fun and a whole lot cooler. There was now a sense of mystery added to the Shania Twain mix. The diaphanous garment she wore and the exotic location appealed to a growing number of fans. Shaniamaniacs were able to count six belly-button glimpses. No one seemed to care that the video itself made no sense at all.

The 'pyramid' video (as people came to call it) was released in August, and, while *The Woman In Me* fell short of the Top 10, the album was selling at the rate of 50,000 units per week.

In late November 1995, Mercury released *(If You're Not In It For Love) I'm Outta Here*. As the single began its climb toward the top of the chart, the world learned about the troubles that Mutt and Shania were experiencing down on the farm, a.k.a. their wilderness paradise in the Adirondacks. The Associated Press bulletin, emanating from St. Regis Falls, went out over the newswire, and the readers of *The Buffalo News* were not the only people who puzzled over the news item and compared the person mentioned in the story to the fun-loving Shania they saw in the music video for *(If You're Not In It For Love) I'm Outta Here*. Public opinion seemed divided. Country fans sympathized with Shania, but again some of them had a bit of trouble digesting the video. Shania had not returned from the sands of the Sahara desert to the familiar setting of Bo Derek's ranch. Shania had left the barnyard behind, altogether, trading in her levis for New York street clothes to perform against the marble backdrop of a New York City courthouse. The people dancing and drumming in the *(If You're Not In It For Love) I'm Outta Here* video weren't two-stepping or even line-dancing, they were boogeying on down. Directed by Steven Goldmann, this video vaulted Shania to the next level in the music video game.

While the video appeared to be extensively choreographed, the dance act was much more spontaneous in the making. Taking their cue from the line, "You could be a beauty queen in a magazine," Shania and Goldmann assembled a cast of students from La Guardia School of Performing Arts and several other Big Apple schools. When the cameras were ready to roll, Shania knew instinctively what to do to get things started. "I just said, 'I want everybody to have fun, we're going to dance, we're going to move, just film us.'" Mutt's hook-laden groove proved to be irresistible. Shania fed off the energy as the dancers and drummers revealed to her just how effective her record would be when it was released as a single. "I'd never had such a large group of people in a video," she explained later in *Country Music Today*. "It really was fun seeing other people performing the song . . . that I had written . . . and giving it attitude! They were just into it. So that really inspired me and gave me extra energy. . . . It was like a party all day."

Shania just seemed to want to have fun, a spirit clearly felt in the scenes from *(If You're Not In It For Love) I'm Outta Here* where she and the assembled troupe of dancers jockey for position at the microphone stand. The multi-racial dancers revealed that all sorts of people were getting into Shania's music, even children. In one of the more effective scenes, a student with the miniature kiddie guitar is cut into the mix each time the studio musician's stinging guitar riff rings out on the track. Shania's respect for her youthful enthusiasts anticipated the 'Show Me Your Shania' contests once she went on tour, with the guest appearances by the winners. Shania was willing to share the spotlight with members of her audience. She was not aloof. She knew that without an audience there just ain't no show. The singer, the band, and the audience were all there in the same room, and, if they worked together on it, they could all have one heck of a good time.

Shania next appeared in a skin-tight black leather racing outfit as she donned her crash helmet and squeezed herself into a racing cart for the action-packed sequences of the *You Win My Love* video. Now, viewers saw cleavage, Bardot-style. Her crop-top became famous overnight, and there were — count them — 53 belly-button glimpses. Everyone loved the sequence with the bumper cars. "I liked the image change in this one," Shania told *Country Music Today*. "It was a fun direction for me to go for a while. Different hair. Different makeup. I was really putting on a different character for this one, a little more spunk." This was Mutt's solo songwriting effort on the album. Shania had requisitioned it the first time Mutt played it for her, before he might be tempted to pitch it to someone else. "I said, 'Ah, I think we should do that one!" she told interviewers. "It's got more of a rock edge to it . . . and that's how I wanted it visually." Some of the stunts were physically challenging. The flips were the most difficult. "Here I am," she remembers, "in those big heels, heavy platforms. Good thing the pants were stretchy. It was three in the morning, and we were doing these gymnastics on the stage." Shaniamaniacs noted the first glimpse of a beauty mark on her face.

There were two versions of the video for *No One Needs To Know*: one features film footage of a real tornado, the other was tied in with footage from the feature film *Twister*. Both begin with a totally funky front porch rehearsal while Shania counts in the song and strums along on her guitar with a small group of musicians. Shania had already appeared on a porch singing in the video for *Whose Bed Have Your Boots Been Under*. The barefoot country girl who smiles into the camera lens in that video exudes an innocence and warmth that is both traditional and personal, but here on the front porch of this two-story wood-frame house, which seems set out on the prairie horizon outside Nashville like a target for the Hollywood special effect tornado, Shania portrays a take-charge musician rehearsing her acoustic band. *No One Needs To Know* is such a light-weight vehicle, a simple country song, really, with an almost rockabilly feel to the band track, yet somehow — once they've taken their instruments into the living room and shut the door — the strength of the verse and chorus lyric, combined with the straightforward melody, stand up to the hurricane force assault of the twister. All hell is breaking loose in the outside world, but Shania continues to sing and strum. There's nothing in this world more powerful than a simple country song. "I really wanted it to be more organic," Shania told *Country Music Today*. "They're all real musicians. They aren't in my band or anything like that . . . it was a real jamming kind of thing. And I'm singing live there, and we edited that live. It was very understated. I think the way the song relates to the movie *Twister* is directly to the love story. Because, you know, the song really is about being in love but not wanting anybody to know."

Many journalists have written that all three up-tempo, country-flavored singles, *Whose Bed Have Your Boots Been Under, Any Man Of Mine,* and *No One Needs To Know,* are not the usual country fare, but listening again to these tracks on the album, you may be struck by just how country all three productions really are. At the end of *Whose Bed Have Your Boots Been Under,* you will hear Mutt and Shania's backing vocals — very traditional harmonies here — and beneath the lead vocal and running contrapuntally to the harmonies you will also detect a deep baritone vocal, which is enriching the track and creating a group harmony, in the same way that renowned acts like the Statler Brothers and the Oakridge Boys harmonize in the vocal arrangements on their records and in their live shows. The music is quite traditional, a country two-step.

What is not traditional is the subject matter where the roles are reversed. It's not the woman who has a cheating heart and wayward shoeware; it's the man who does. And he is put in his place here. Shania is not wracked with grief because this person has strayed. She knows he's been "sneakin' around with Jill;" she's aware of his "weekend with Beverly Hill." Instead of tearfully accepting him back and setting herself up for more of the same treatment (as country boys all want her to), Shania is hip to his sweet-talking ways. She realizes he tells all the girls the same line and proceeds to shoot down his come-on by casually asking, "This time did it feel like thunder, baby? And who did you run to?" The woman she portrays in her lyrics is wise enough not to be heartbroken, but she is not bitter, either. She takes her dignity back by giving this suave stud the brush off with a flippancy that lets him know he will not have his way with her, no matter what lines he peddles: "So, next time you're lonely, don't call on me. Try the operator. Maybe she'll be free."

This assertion of such a detached woman's point of view into such traditional cheatin' lyrics and melody is the element that some radio programmers resisted. This was not a weeper. Shania was singing about a cheating philanderer whose approach would no longer work, empowering all of the women who sang along with the same resolve. The message she was ultimately sending was that the time was up for cheatin' and hurtin' songs. They had worked for several decades, but they were no longer believable in the '90s. Coincidentally, this perception led to the theme of the next release where Shania lays out the ground rules in Any Man of Mine. "This is what a woman wants . . ." she declares at the beginning of the track. Singing directly to the men in the audience, she offers several helpful suggestions: "Any man of mine better be proud of me. Even when I'm ugly he still better love me." The bottom line is, "Any man of mine better walk the line."

In the lyrics for The Woman In Me (Needs The Man In You), Shania tells her audience what a man must provide in a relationship in order for it to work from the woman's point of view in the '90s. Despite the force of her opinion, she admits, "I'm not always strong. And sometimes I'm even wrong." Shania was saying that she did seek comfort in her man's embrace, that she welcomed his strength, but the underlying message in all of these songs was that love between a man and a woman brings fulfilment only if it is felt sincerely by both partners in the union. This theme was re-enforced with the message contained in the title and hook of the fourth single, (If You're Not In It For Love) I'm Outta Here. The gospel according to Shania was a far cry from the cheatin' and hurtin' songs where alcohol and spousal abuse were condoned, leading to infidelity, misery, divorce, and alienated children who often suffered the most from broken marriages. But she was not merely issuing bible-thumping 'Thou Shalt Not' sermons from a Sunday pulpit — she was suggesting in a playful way positive solutions that could lead to happy relations between women and men.

For Shania's portrayal of a single-mother in Home Ain't Where His Heart Is (Anymore), Steven Goldmann employs black and white footage of the marriage breakdown cut with color footage from happier days. Although glamor isn't part of the scene here, Shania sympathetically portrays an attractive single-mother in dire straits. It really is raining on her parade. "It was so cold," she later remembered in Country Music Today. "Again, we were in Montreal, and Steven Goldmann directed it. It was very cold outside, and the doors all had to be open in this studio. Rain coming down on me, I was so cold I could hardly take it. . . . But I wanted the drama of the rain and being wet and just so lost in sorrow."

The final release from THE WOMAN IN ME was God Bless The Child, a gospel song released during the Christmas season. The re-recorded track for the video took the original a capella song fragment and dressed it up for Shania's tour-de-force gospel vocal. She is accompanied by a full choir. Larry Jordan directed the video, the eighth from the album. When they were packaged up together for home viewers, all eight became the full-length video THE COMPLETE WOMAN, which was listed as a best-seller by *Billboard*. Shania and her video-making associates were systematically putting together, piece by piece, video by video, a 'full' image of her character, sensual and sensitive, bold and daring, intelligent and reverent, though her detractors chose to fix on slogans like, "sex sells." Shania, herself, was more articulate. "The success started with the music," she told *Ottawa Citizen* reporter Betsy Powell. "And it will continue with the music. No one's going to care what Shania Twain looks like in '97 if the next album isn't great."

And the music *was* good. Ever since I first listened to THE WOMAN IN ME before my first interview with her, I had a deep appreciation for her music. I had been won over that first morning I met her by her sincerity and her spontaneity when she had learned that my favorite song on the album was *No One Needs To Know* and had sung me a verse and chorus to a finger-popping rhythm right there in that hotel restaurant. That February morning in 1995, Shania was eagerly interested to learn my opinion of her new music. Off the record, I told her that I'd written a very positive record review. "This splendid CD is infused with the deep love and affection felt between husband and wife team Lange and Twain who co-wrote all of the 12 tunes. From the opening strains of the tour-de-force ballad *Home Ain't Where His Heart Is (Anymore)* to the closing strains of the a cappella lullaby *God Bless This Child*, we are treated to songs which inspire rather than the usual cheatin', hurtin', drinkin', tragi-comic formula stuff. There are plenty of twisted cliché Nashvillisms, waves of twangy guitars and spicy cajun fiddles, and even a number that has line dance mania served up with hand-claps and drum programs (*Any Man Of Mine*). But the bottom line here is country music through and through. Sometimes it is 'new country' as in the runaway chart hit *Whose Bed Have Your Boots Been Under*. Sometimes it is straight up traditional like the tear-jerker *Leaving Is The Only Way Out*. Always, you hear the expressive rich vocal from Shania. Continually, you get a changing, adapting production-mode from Lange that chooses to highlight the natural vocal, rather than force it into conceptual radio niches. . . ."

As I continued to paraphrase my review, I could see that Shania was pleased to hear that someone had accepted her husband's production of her record at face value. I commented that Mutt had not come up with basically a pop album. . . . It is very country!

Shania's, "Yes!" confirmed my speculation that there had been some people, perhaps at the record label itself, or at radio, who may have been hesitant, because it *was*, after all, a country album like none of us had ever heard before. In the days to come, I would learn just how much controversy would swirl around the release, and in the final analysis, see this new music find widespread acceptance among both country and pop music fans.

After Shania went on to say that a lot of people were pleasantly surprised, we began to talk about the music in more detail. I mentioned the cajun fiddles. Shania confided, "We wanted fiddle that really *dug in* and was really aggressive, not just fiddle as a background instrument." From reactions such as these from Shania Twain, I immediately felt a confirmation that she was far more than a pretty voice and face who obediently fronted the male genius efforts of her producer and the calculated marketing efforts of her male record label executives. She had been thoroughly involved in the recording and production of this breakthrough album. In fact, Mutt Lange's real genius came in his recognition of Shania's vision as an artist — and her ability to deliver that vision — if he steered her raw talent rather than slotting her into any sort of formula at all as the team at Mercury had done in 1993 for her debut album.

Tom Roland was another reviewer who had immediately recognized what a great album THE WOMAN IN ME really was. His February 13, 1995 record review in *The Tennessean* declared that Shania Twain's mix of rock and country could be a "recipe for success. This is an absolutely stunning album. A lot of country artists have melded the idiom with rock & roll in a way that's become entirely predictable, but not Twain. Working with husband/producer Robert John 'Mutt' Lange, they wrote the entire project and created an album that blends elements from the two styles without watering down either one." Roland would remain a Twain supporter throughout the Shania-bashing era when some male journalists filled their columns with surprisingly hateful accusations. For a while it seemed as if the battle lines were drawn and the gender wars had begun in earnest.

Typically, Shania took an optimistic view. "I'm very thankful," she told James Muretich, "for any of the hardships that I've gone through because I think it's easy to become an egomaniac in this industry. Everybody's always telling you how great you are." It was an interesting way to regard the opposition she was encountering. Luke Lewis in his usual easygoing manner put this antagonism down to the fact that Shania wasn't doing business with the locals. She didn't have a Music Row publishing deal. She didn't have a Music Row manager or press agent. And, until she began to make plans to tour, she didn't have a Nashville-based representation at all. Others saw the initial antagonism to be deeply rooted in the gender issue. This was the Nashville good ole boys' last stand. So much seemed to hinge on the success of this release. The fate of country women appeared to have been put on the line as if their bid for independence and control of their music and their careers had been piled up like a stack of casino chips to be wagered at the most strategic moment. The next roll of the dice could decide everything. It was now or never. Ultimately, it would be up to the fans to decide. Without their wholehearted endorsement at the cash register no ground could be gained.

There was no doubt that country fans loved what Shania was doing. They were buying THE WOMAN IN ME at a furious pace. As they continued to do so, they put Shania over the top. Her phenomenal record sales were proof that there was a market waiting to be exploited if women were allowed to record country music that expressed a woman's point of view. But would Shania and Mutt live to see the day that the country music industry itself would acknowledge their accomplishments. Or would Shania find herself shut out of the awards, punished for her trespasses. Fortunately, some of the jousting for position took place in Ontario and California, far from the staid environs of the Row itself.

4
FAN APPRECIATION

WITH EIGHT MUSIC VIDEOS RELEASED from the WOMAN IN ME album in less than 24 months and a host of cover features in music magazines, Shania seemed to be everywhere you turned. Five of the videos were number one hits on the CMT chart; four of her singles went to the top of the *Billboard* Hot Country chart. Many country traditionalists who had resisted listening to Shania when THE WOMAN IN ME was first released now went out and bought the CD. George Jones, perhaps the most traditional of all Nashville artists, told Twain biographer Scott Gray, "I love this girl's singing. And I'd love to do an album with her. She caught my ear above all the rest of them." Soon, the music video networks learned that Shania's videos were also attracting new viewers who didn't change the channel after they had watched her doing her thing on CMT or TNN. Shania might not be a politically correct country artist, but she was definitely turning a lot of new fans onto country music, especially women.

THE WOMAN IN ME was the perfect title for the album. Shania credits Sandy Neese, Vice-President of Media Relations for Mercury Nashville, as the person responsible for choosing the name. As music critic James Dickerson explains, "unknown to Twain, Neese was a member of a loosely organized 'good ole girl' network in Nashville that years ago had pledged its membership to give breaks to female artists who were deserving of a helping hand. In time, she would have a profound influence on Twain's career, although the singer would never quite understand why." Shania told Dickerson, "Mutt and I went through everything possible for the title. Then Sandy came out one day and said, '*The Woman In Me* should be the one.' Just the way she said it, I said, 'Yep, that's it.' "

Sandy's influence went further than simply giving the album a name. "We really had a struggle with that first single," Neese told Dickerson. "Radio didn't want to play it. It was too pop. It was too this, too that. Luke went back and pounded week after week on the promotions department. 'I know this is a hit.

I know we've got something phenomenal going here.' He wouldn't let go." Through canvassing listeners at the few stations willing to playlist the song, Lewis and Neese learned a single fact that helped the Mercury team to understand their dilemma. Nearly all of the phone callers who responded positively to Shania's single were women. "Unknown to Twain," Dickerson asserts, "the 'good ole girl' network fell in behind THE WOMAN IN ME. Behind the scenes, women worked hard to make the album a success. Their hopes were riding high with Twain's hopes."

Once Luke Lewis and Sandy Neese had identified their market, they had their work cut out for them. Women buying records by women was something new. Although women had always been known to buy more records than men, they had bought music by men, and record labels had accordingly recorded hunks who would attract sales from women. This strategy had led to male artists dominating both radio airplay and record sales. Now, for the first time since Elvis had appeared on the scene, women were buying records by women in significant numbers. This revelation would lead to Shania's 'Fan Appreciation Days' where she took to the malls to meet her fans.

Shania's extensive "Fan Appreciation Tour" had evolved from this recognition of her audience being primarily women. While men might be found watching sports, women went shopping. So, Shania hit the malls in February 1996. As CMT's February Showcase Artist, she was featured on the 30-minute CMT Showcase program that aired at various times throughout the month. Her fan appreciation day at the Mall of America in Minneapolis prompted Newsweek magazine's Karen Schoemer to title her full-page story, "The Malling of Shania." In Newsweek all of America could read that "more than 10,000 people are here to see her, and they fill the floor all the way back to the Stampede Steakhouse, the Great Train Store and the Screaming Yellow Eagle ride in the mall's centerpiece amusement park. Fans line the three chrome-plated balconies and the whirring escalators that connect them. You'd think they were here to see a heck of a show. But today, Shania's not singing. She's just, well, appearing. She's here to celebrate a marvel of marketing genius known as Fan Appreciation Day, a four-hour autograph-signing session, photo-op, and smile-athon."

This celebrated mall appearance was one of many successful promotions Shania Twain and her record company staged during 1996 and 1997. A story filed by Tennessean writer Robert K. Oermann claimed there had been 20,000 present at the Mall of the America, twice as many as mentioned in Newsweek. Oermann also noted yet another broken rule: "She defied another country rule of thumb, the one that says you can't sell records to other women if you are *too* beautiful." Another way of phrasing this would be to say that Shania's music appealed to women in a way that no country female had before she arrived on the scene. No one except for Patsy Cline. Shania was no longer singing made-on-Music Row formula songs. She was singing songs written from a woman's point of view. She was celebrating her womanhood. She was doing things her way and her fans loved her every time she appeared. Shania always had time to step down from the podium and visit with disabled or physically challenged fans during the event, and she signed every bit of memorabilia the worshippers thrust into her hands. "It's been a wonderful year. I have no one else to thank but you, the fans," she told them. "You're fantastic!" Repeating this simple truth mall after mall, day after day, she took North America by storm, with no army, not even a country band, to help her in her conquest. Suddenly, getting your picture taken with Shania had become a national pastime.

Shania's 'feel' for her audience was nothing new. She had shown such respect during her 1995 media tour when Shania and Mary Bailey arrived at a Toronto TV studio to perform a short set of her songs for the syndicated radio show *Today's Country* with hosts Greg Shannon and Sharon Edwards. Just before the show, they discovered that the DAT tape, which was supposed to be tracks of four songs complete with back-up vocals, was the wrong tape. "There were no back up vocals on the DAT tape," Jan Cody, the producer of the radio show, remembers. "All the instrumental tracks were there, but no back up vocal tracks. These were songs from her new album THE WOMAN IN ME, and the way they were mixed the harmony vocals were very important to her performance." When this was discovered, Bailey and Twain huddled in the control room for many anxious moments discussing the situation before they agreed to Shania performing *Whose Bed Have Your Boots Been Under*, acoustically, with show band guitarist Mike "Pepe" Francis before doing the interview with Greg Shannon. This rare impromptu performance ran live to air on syndicated stations from coast to coast.

"People are buying my record because of the music," Shania told Robert K. Oermann. To her, this was the bottom line, but for the *Tennessean* journalist the impact of her "rewriting the rule book on country stardom" held significance because by doing so she was confronting Music Row's biblical commandments, the Thou Shalt Nots of country music. For girl singers there were many "nots." As a longtime Nashville resident and journalist, Oermann was most impressed by this feat. "Shania Twain," *Dallas Morning News* writer

Mario Tarradell declared, "is writing her own rules for country music success." But Shania preferred to speak about her music rather than to get into any kind of discussion about Nashville rules because she simply no longer acknowledged that she was bound by any of them. She took her music directly to her fans. "It's the fans who have kept all this momentum going," she told Oermann. "And the industry is refreshed by this. . . . There may be some people who don't get it. But that's okay. They don't have to 'get it,' as long as the fans do."

During this period, a number of women's magazines began to see Shania Twain as a desirable cover story. The May 1996 edition of *Chatelaine* featured her as "The Unstoppable Shania Twain." While in the entertainment sections of dailies, fanzines, trade magazines, and even in *Newsweek*, Shania was portrayed as a glamorous, sexy, elusive country star, in women's publications, she was "Runaway Twain," shown in comfortable, loose-fitting, sensible clothing. She was carefree, hardworking, and successful, the practical girl next door who would back-comb *Chatelaine* reporter Johanna Schneller's hair, gently chiding the journalist all the while because she didn't know how to do it, teaching her how.

Schneller would respond with distinctive descriptions of a sort not being found elsewhere in 1995 and early 1996. "I'm sitting down, even with flat hair, next to the petite-yet curvey Twain, I feel as big as a Santa Claus Parade float . . . 'You don't know how to do this?' Twain asks. Her voice is friendly and full of energy, it turns up at the ends of sentences like a verbal smiley face. (She also possesses a jawline like a speedboat and melted-chocolate eyes.) 'It's very easy. You just hold a handful like this . . .'"

Schneller would also discover a fascination for wardrobe, which led to dozens of similar articles by other journalists in the months to come after this story ran. The two women were putting in time prior to the filming of Shania's *(If You're Not In It For Love) I'm Outta Here* video in Manhattan. "She's waiting for her wardrobe woman to arrive with the pair of black velvet, lace-front, bell-bottom hip-huggers made to Twain's specifications during a five-hour fitting," Schneller informed *Chatelaine* readers. "The pants were cut too low, emergency procedures were performed with spandex. The reconfigured pants fit like the skin of a sleek seal."

In responding so directly to Shania as a woman, Johanna presented what readers of the magazine felt was the *real* Shania. Schneller may not have known it, but she was helping Sandy Neese and the woman's network out, for prior to this feature, Shania was viewed from afar — or from a position below a pedestal upon which she was placed. Or she was roughed up by one of the distraught male journalists, her fame and success denigrated with every dripping, vindictive adjective and adverb. Of course, many journalists of both sexes had merely been blinded by her radiant beauty.

"In the caramel-colored marble lobby of a Manhattan courthouse," Schneller continued, setting the scene, "Twain winks at a large camera that zooms around on a U-shaped track above her like an oversize model train. She's wearing The Pants, plus a red chenille cropped turtle-neck (Twain loves to wear black, red or white) and an expanse of flat stomach. 'This is mid-riff year,' she says, laughing. 'Who knows what it will be next year?'"

In keeping with her mandate, Schneller also divulged a diet tip. How did Shania keep so trim? Easy, she was a vegetarian. While the rest of the cast and crew were woofing down take-out Chinese, Shania had snuck away to her trailer with a bowl of rice. Just rice. Plus, her poverty years have taught her not to waste food. "When I make dinner," she confided, "I'm perfect at just making enough. My husband says, 'What — are you trying to starve me?' But it's the mind-set of my childhood, the grooves that end up in your brain.'"

While Shania had become glamorous, she still had not realized she had made it. She was still Cinderella waiting for the limo to turn back into a pumpkin. She had told me that her story was "rags to something" but she wasn't rich, yet. Here it was — a full year of record-breaking album sales, several number one hits, a sweep of the CCMAs, two Juno Awards, and two ACMs later — and when Johanna Schneller asked, "So have you had a moment when you realized that you have everything you've worked for and dreamed about?" Shania said, "No. I don't know why that is. I'm just so focused when I'm doing things. I've just got so much to do . . ."

As the months fled past, the world soon came to learn just how much more there would be to do before Shania Twain would finally take an extended vacation. There were times, of course, when she was down on the farm, so to speak, wood-shedding her new songs with Mutt. Times they would spend on long walks. And times spent with her horses and dogs. Times spent shoveling out the horse stables, even. But every time you turned around, there she was in the headlines, again. There she was on the cover of a magazine in the racks at supermarket checkouts. Again. The tabloids had begun to feature her, too. Which to someone in showbiz means that you've made it, even though the silly stories are seldom more credible than the sort of stories that declare to the world in banner headlines: "Woman Gives Birth To UFO!"

When she finally addressed the subject, Shania told *Country Song Roundup* reporter Nancy Brooks, "Nothing (in the tabloids) is true at all. I'm not getting divorced; I'm happily married. I'm not going back with my old boyfriend, and I've never had an affair with a married man." She had, however, given birth to an unidentified flying soap opera, which had a momentum all its own.

The first industry test of popularity Shania faced came in September 1995 at the Canadian Country Music Awards in Hamilton, Ontario. She arrived in a flurry of media hype in time to attend an early Sunday afternoon press conference that was held in a medium-sized room at the conference center where the Canadian Country Music Week celebrations had been underway since Friday. I hurried over from the Anglican Cathedral where producer Randall Prescott had assembled most of the other Canadian female country vocalists for his production of Dick Damron's video, *Jesus It's Me Again*, though Shania was not part of the video shoot because Damron had been unsuccessful in his solicitation of Twain's manager, Mary Bailey. A few months later, Bailey was officially relieved of her position.

Before Shania's press conference got underway, Doug Chappell, President of Mercury Polydor Canada, presented her with a triple-platinum award, which acknowledged her Canadian sales of THE WOMAN IN ME. Questions at the press conference centered around how many awards Shania Twain imagined she would win. If some of these journalists had thought they could bait her with such queries, trick her into presumption that she was going to win, then later use her statements as evidence of her alleged arrogance, they were wrong. No doubt, most writers were merely interested in scribbling down a colorful quote or two. Whatever the expectations were, they did not find a wigged-out superstar that afternoon. Instead, Shania Twain offered a series of elusive answers that could be summed up in very few words: "I'm not in the business of winning awards, I'm in the business of making music. The music comes first." She *was* going to sing on the show — that was why she was here.

Again, I was impressed by her intelligence. I slipped out of the back of the interview room and returned to the church where a good deal of fun-loving camaraderie was to be had with jolly old Dick Damron and the women who had come to pay tribute to him. Lisa Brokop, Patricia Conroy, Tracey Brown, Stephanie Beaumont, and Jennifer Johnson were fitting themselves around the grizzled veteran like a bouquet of pretty faces and even prettier voices; Sylvia Tyson, Colleen Peterson, Cindy Church, Caitlin Hanford, Kelita, Lyndia Scott, and Laura Vinson had been filmed singing with him earlier in the day. In a basement dressing room beneath pulpit and pews, Michelle Wright had just arrived and was exchanging greetings with the other women. They were all friends and the others were excited that Michelle would host the Monday night awards show.

The following night, I filed a feature story on the awards show with *Country Music News*. Shania Twain was spectacular during her show-opening performance of *Any Man Of Mine* and *The Woman In Me*. The 1800 people who filled the auditorium to the rafters showered their enthusiasm on Patricia Conroy for her *Keep Me Rockin'*, on Lisa Brokop for her duet with Steve Wariner, and on Susan Aglukark and her Native dancers. Cassandra Vasik won an award for her vocal collaboration with Jim Witter, and Farmer's Daughter were named best new artists. Host Michelle Wright, winner of the fan favorite award as Entertainer of the Year, declared that the show had been a "Girl's night out!"

Shania did not disappoint anyone as she came up to accept award after award, five of them in total. Now that she was receiving recognition from her peers, she *did* break down. Tears flowed as she clutched the CCMA trophy for Song of the Year, awarded to her and Mutt for *Whose Bed Have Your Boots Been Under*. By the time that she got around to accepting her third award, the CCMA Single of the Year for *Any Man Of Mine*, she had the thanking-folks-routine down pretty good. Sagely, she saved some of the lengthier lists for her fourth and fifth awards, Album of the Year and Female Vocalist of the Year. By then, she was spreading out the mentions like a pro.

In the press room, during the post-awards interviews, writers poked their tape machines at Shania Twain with a newfound zeal. Now, they wanted to know, did she expect to repeat this feat at the CMA Awards later in the month? Would she sweep the Juno Awards? Would she win a Grammy? I hid my smile behind my hand as the new reigning Queen of Canadian Country patiently instructed her people, "Yes, this was a good beginning . . . it was encouraging," but no, she didn't expect anything. She wasn't in the business of winning awards — she was in the business of making music.

I personally didn't hold my breath in anticipation of the CMA handing Shania Twain any awards in Nashville. My pessimism was fueled by *Tennessean* columnist Brad Schmidt on September 20th, two days after the Canadian Country Music Awards show. "Those crazy puck-slappin', ice-fishin', moose-lovin', Dudley Do Right worshippin', Molson-swillin', pasty-skinned Canadians," Schmidt wrote, "they actually have their own country music awards, which just cracks me up. The competition among the THREE Canadian country stars must be something fierce . . . the CCMAs are kinda like the Mexican ice-hockey awards . . . or, the Citadel's annual women's achievement awards." If Schmidt's attitude towards Canadian country stars was a typical Nashville response, then Shania would be shut out at the CMAs until hell froze over. It wasn't going to happen. Not while good ole guys like Brad Schmidt were calling the shots. A gossip-columnist by trade, Schmidt could have been the original inspiration for the line, "So, you're Brad Pitt . . . that don't impress me much," but that is pure speculation. Schmidt does rhyme with Pitt, though, and if you feel rankled by his diatribe, you, too, can insert his name at the appropriate place in the song when you're singing along in your car.

More respectful was *Tennessean* writer Robert K. Oermann who filed a far more positive story on the CCMA Awards show on the day it was shown on TNN. "Twain kicked off the show with a medley of *Any Man Of Mine* and *The Woman In Me*," Oermann reported. "Among the standout performances during the show, which was taped earlier, were a country rock tune by Patricia Conroy, native American Susan Aglukark's number with dancers and multi-ethnic chorus, and a sterling ballad from Lisa Brokop that featured harmony and guitar from Nashville star Steve Wariner." Oermann noted that Shania had swept the awards, winning five times. She had "rocked Canada's Country Awards."

A few weeks later, Shania performed on the 1995 CMA show in Nashville, provocatively mussing Johnny Cash's pompadour during her romp through the audience to the stage while singing *Any Man Of Mine*, but she did not win an award. In November, Shania entertained Hillary and Bill Clinton. On the deck of a float during the Macey's Thanksgiving Day Parade in New York City, she danced with a gigantic turkey. On January 20, 1996, she performed the Canadian national anthem, *Oh Canada*, at the NHL All-Star game in Boston. On the 29th, she was named best new country vocalist at the American Music Awards in Los Angeles. Shania was a star worthy of winning awards everywhere but Nashville, it seemed.

As the awards shows came 'round again, Shania continued to be featured in performance, picking up some new hardware, too, though, with no new album, her wins were less spectacular. One of her more unusual 1996 prizes had been the "Great British Country Music Awards" where she had been honored as the International Rising Star. For a cover story printed in the British magazine, *Country Music People*, Shania discussed her British connection, David Rose, who had been credited on the liner notes to THE WOMAN IN ME. "David is a British guy," she explained, "who had been hooked on my video clips and had persuaded Mutt to look at them, so, he (Mutt) was aware of me though we had never met. I certainly was not aware of who he was." She also told a humorous anecdote from the "Triple Play Tour" in 1993. "Toby Keith said, 'Don't you starch your jeans?' I said, 'Pardon me? Is *that* how you get your clothes like that?' I didn't want to ask him, you know, '*Why* do you do that to your clothes.' So, I was the outcast! I don't know too many people who iron their jeans to a crease and then starch them at the same time! I've been told a few times I wear the wrong jeans." The British audience could appreciate this culture shock vignette from Shania's early days in Tennessee. Nobody in jolly old England ironed their jeans, let alone starched them. "It just wasn't done, old chap."

As she headed out on her Fan Appreciation Tour in February 1996, Shania did so carrying nominations for Grammy Awards, Juno Awards, and People's Choice Awards. In L.A., she won her first Grammy for THE WOMAN IN ME, Album of the Year. She won Canadian Academy of Recording Artists Juno awards, too. But nothing was forthcoming from Nashville, the price she and Mutt seemed to be paying for recording there, using top notch Music Row pickers like Dann Huff, Brent Rowan, Paul Franklin, and Rob Hajacos, but then stealing away to mix things in a whole new way in Quebec.

Two years after that mixing session, Shania 'crossed over' into the francophone market in Quebec. Quebec is a unique North American radio market. Because a provincial French dialect is the language most frequently spoken there, this quaint area has remained both the most isolated area in Canada and the most European of the ten provinces. Euro-pop dance mixes were immensely popular in urban areas like Montreal when THE WOMAN IN ME was released. Country music was not the music of choice for very many Quebec residents. This Francophone audience had given birth to Celine Dion who became an international star long before she learned to converse fluently in the English language. Dion did so primarily in order that she could make appearances on network TV shows in the United States and chat amiably with the likes of David Letterman.

"Shania Twain has been the hottest thing in North American country music for more than a year now," Lucinda Chodan reported in a story syndicated by the Southam Newspaper chain during the second week of May. "But it wasn't until a dance-mix version of Twain's *(If You're Not In It For Love) I'm Outta Here!* hit Quebec turntables that la belle province tuned into la belle country." The video was number one on MusiquePlus. The single was at the top of the chart on Montreal's "highly rated francophone station CKMF. . . .

More than 100,000 units of THE WOMAN IN ME have been sold in Quebec since January," Chodan noted, "when Mix 96 began playing the percussion and atti-tude heavy *I'm Outta Here!*"

In June, Shania performed at Fan Fair in Nashville along with a growing Canuck contingent of artists, including Michelle Wright, Terri Clark, Paul Brandt, Lisa Brokop, and the Moffatts. No longer ignored, she sat at a table in her Fan Fair booth pen in hand ready to sign autographs. She was a popular player when she suited up for the annual celebrities softball game. Garth Brooks hit a yardstick home run when he signed autographs for 27 consecutive hours, but the real news of Fan Fair 96 was the coming-out of 13-year-old debutante and newest Curb Records recording artist LeAnn Rimes, the real-deal voice behind a recycled, written-for-Patsy tune, called *Blue*. She was already being hailed as the "next Patsy." LeAnn would make an immediate splash and sell millions of records before settling back into the pack running far behind the leaders at the clubhouse turn as Garth and Shania headed for the finish line that would mark the end of the first century of country music.

By August 1996, THE WOMAN IN ME had sold eight million records. Shania went home that month to Ontario. On August 16th, the town of Timmins was scheduled to pay homage to their most celebrated former resident. They were prepared to do it in style. Nothing, not even the inclement weather, could dampen the enthusiasm the locals felt that day.

Despite the black smudge the publishers of the local daily newspaper had earlier attempted to put on Shania's image by questioning her Native heritage, her fans were as undaunted as ever. And well they should be. Shania Twain had never forgotten them. She'd frequently acknowledged their support from awards show podiums in both Canada and the United States.

On 'Shania Twain Day', her fans waited, several hundred strong, in a massed assembly outside the Timmins City Hall for a first glimpse, some beneath umbrel-las, others braving the cold, driving rain, shivering, soaked to the skin in their Shania t-shirts and windbreakers. Some had come from as far away as British Columbia to be here. All of them were more than ready to erupt into a rowdy sea of enthusiastic cheers, applause, and catcalls once the moment they awaited arrived. Joelle Kovach, a Timmins native herself and a journalism student, had come home, too, from Concordia University in Montreal to witness the event for *Country Music News*. " 'We're tough, we're not made of sugar,' said Twain, as she stepped outside City Hall," Kovach reported. "A dazzling genuine smile spread across Twain's face. A few wisps of brown hair falling from her elegantly upswept coif, a smooth tummy peeked out from beneath a green striped midriff shirt. 'We're Northern Ontarians . . . we can deal with the weather!' she pronounced."

This mix of student journalism and fan adulation is the sort of regional report that makes Canada's national country newspaper more immediate than glossier rags. Kovach interviewed several fans, including Suzanne Vachon. " 'She sure got famous fast, eh?' chuckled Suzanne Vachon, 61, of Timmins. Like many fans, Vachon, a friend of Twain's family, owns all of Shania's posters, CDs, and videos. But Vachon especially covets a snapshot of a two-year-old Twain holding a guitar because, 'She has a cowboy hat on in the picture.' "

In Timmins "on a typical evening," Kovach wrote, "the local Tim Horton's donut shop is crowded with bored teenagers making plans to move to the bustling cities as soon as they finish high school." But as Twain confided when the budding journalist got a moment alone with the superstar. "I was too busy to be bored. I had two jobs. I worked at the MacDonalds, and I played in a band." Riding in the rear of a silver limo where she sat beside her German Shepherd guard dog, Tim, Shania was whisked back and forth across town for various functions. Her former boss at the burger chain outlet was one of many to fashion his personal tribute, an employee of the month plaque, something that the star had not won as one of his teenaged employees. "My sister won, but I didn't!" the star exclaimed in a video-taped moment later included in the footage shown on her VH1 Special.

Shania was presented with ceremonial keys to the city, the main street of Timmins was renamed "Shania Twain Way," and a delegation representing the Mattagami First Nations People made her an honorary member, making official her earlier adoption into the Temagami tribe by her father Jerry Twain. An Associated Press story that ran in newspapers from coast to coast displayed a photo of Shania, her medical-gloved hands plunged into cement, above the caption: "Thumbs up. Shania Twain makes her mark in cement during celebrations held in her honor in Timmins yesterday." Before moving on, Shania planted a tree in honor of her late grandfather, was toasted at a gala dinner, and serenaded by the Timmins Symphony.

The very next day, Shania was at the scene of another tribute, this time before thousands of fans during "Fan Appreciation Day" at the Canadian National Exposition in Toronto. Recording artist and songwriter Eddie Schwartz (author of Pat Benatar's 1980 Top 10 release *Hit Me With Your Best Shot*) presented Shania with four SOCAN Number One plaques in recognition of her chart-topping singles, *Any Man Of Mine, The Woman In Me, (If You're Not In*

It For Love) I'm Outta Here, and *No One Needs To Know*.

In September, Shania received two CCMA awards in Calgary, the Canadian Country Music Association's Entertainer of the Year and Female Vocalist of the Year honors. Newcomer Terri Clark picked up best single and best album honors, while Paul Brandt won for his song *My Heart Has A History*. In Nashville at the CMA awards, George Strait had a big time, as did Brooks & Dunn, the 1996 CMA Entertainers of the Year. But Patty Loveless was named Female Vocalist of the Year, not Shania. No CMA awards were waiting for Shania, though her influence on Music Row had become evident.

Whether or not Shania and Mutt had broken the rules (for which they may or may not have been punished by the establishment), they had renewed Nashville. Tim McGraw's producer, Byron Gallimore, seemed to have torn a page out of Mutt Lange's studio production manual and posted it on the double glass partition between the control room and the studio. And a new wave of young women led by LeAnn Rimes, Jo Dee Messina, and Chely Wright had begun to create a new brand of country called "contemporary" which often made Shania Twain's THE WOMAN IN ME sound totally traditional in comparison. Lila McCann's approach to country owed allegiance to the roots of cheerleading, not to any knowledge she had of the history of country music, but she was a cheerful new component of the contemporary country era. Mindy McCready followed Shania's footsteps, eager to explore the corridors beyond the doors Shania's fresh approach to country lyrics and fashions had opened. While 'contemporary' country may have breathed fresh air into Nashville, Music Row went a little overboard, exiling the genre's traditional older artists from radio. The whole industry was committed to a youth movement.

Faith Hill's fresh approach was not an imitation. Her history was not that different from Shania Twain's. As a child, Faith did not know either of her biological parents. She was adopted by Ted and Edna Perry and raised in Star Mississippi, a town of no more than 1,500. "I'm 32 years old," she told Josh Rottenberg for a *US Weekly* cover story, "and I started singing when I was just a kid. I've developed my own thing. I don't know what you'd call it, but it's kind of a quilt of all the music I grew up listening to." In searching for a new formula for success, the town that had for so long done things one way simply found it difficult to accept Faith and Shania's declarations at face value that they didn't use any kind of formula at all.

Despite the clear impact Shania had on country women's music for the good, tabloid-style journalists still tried to stir up some mud to sling. Because

Shania had not toured yet, some claimed she was merely a studio singer who could not actually entertain live audiences. The silliest rumor mill sewage of all was the suggestion that she could not really sing — that Mutt had digitally connived to deceive everyone — even though Shania made several network TV appearances during 1995 and continued to do so in 1996, performing her songs to millions of viewers. As such slanders increased, so did her record sales. Her fans paid little attention to these negative barbs, as little attention as the artist herself. But no one could deny that Shania, more than any other single performer, had changed both the look and the sound of country music. Shania and Mutt would accomplish even more with their second collaboration when it was finally released in late 1997.

Shania Twain's *Come on Over* - Best Selling Country Album Ever! Certified by the RIAA

CMT

JUNE/JULY
$3.95
Issue 3 Vol. 1

Country Music Today

The Country Music Magazine with an Attitude

VIDEO VIXEN
Shania TWAIN'S REEL LIFE STORY

SPECIAL FEATURE
Oh Say, Can You Sing

Trace Adkins has 'Lunch with Lisa'

Checking In with Juice Newton

In Focus with Collin Raye

Edgar Winter's Salute to Yankee Grey

US $3.95/CAN $4.95

From Video Vixen: Shania Twain's Reel Life Story

COUNTRY Weekly
YOUR Country Music And Entertainment Magazine
June 22, 1999 $1.99 Canada $2.49

Shania Twain: I'm still country ...and I love it!

SALUTE TO COUNTRY FATHERS

Summer Country Travel Guide
- Where the stars eat
- #1 vacation spots
- 75 fun things you can do, and much more!

e Ann Womack, Tracy Byrd & many more

COUNTRY WEEK
The World's #1 Selling Country
April 4, 2000

Randy Travis

Chely Wright

AT SEA WITH
Mindy McCready,
Tracy Byrd,
Mark Wills &
The Wilkinsons

George Strait's new CD

$2.49/$3.49 Canada

COUNTRY VS POP

The battle's on! And stars like Alan Jackson and Shania Twain find themselves on opposing sides

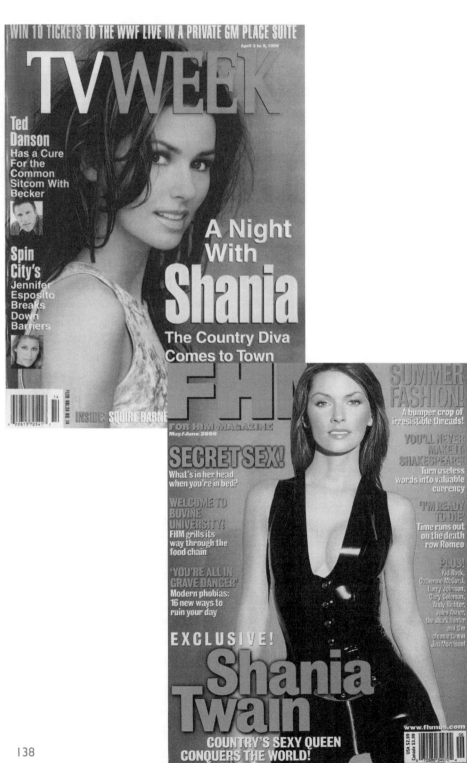

IV

Come
on
Over

1

A WOMAN'S PREROGATIVE

OR A WHILE DURING 1997, SHANIA TWAIN AND MUTT LANGE were out
of the public spotlight busily creating their second album together. As
the label and Shania's management geared up for the impending release,
a flurry of preview stories hit the news stands. By this time, writing a story on
Shania Twain had solidified into a standard approach. Inevitably, when a
reporter prepared a story for a magazine, first to be mentioned was a description
of Shania and what she was wearing. "As she enters a stage complex in
Brooklyn to shoot a video for *Don't Be Stupid (You Know I Love You)*," Elysa
Gardner wrote in November 1997, "she's decked out in form-fitting black velvet pants and a matching sleeveless top. Her brunette locks teased just slightly
to affect a sensuous look. Twain makes playful gestures into the cameras while
lip-synching the lyrics and sways her hips with an athletic but distinctly feminine grace. . . . This sweet-and-spicy style served the Canadian-born singer well
on her 1995 breakthrough album THE WOMAN IN ME, which is fast approaching
the 10 million mark in sales." Titles for Shania stories had a style of their own,
too, and Gardiner called her *Los Angeles Times* entertainment section feature
"Throwing Nashville a Curve." The author asked the provocative question:
"Shania's debut album hit sales marks beyond anything country music had ever
seen. Will her follow-up keep pace?"

As Gardiner continued, "The songs on THE WOMAN IN ME . . . mix lithe
country textures and a feisty female perspective with glistening pop savvy and
Twain promoted them with television appearances that presented her as a lat-
ter-day Raquel Welch for country fans." And as Shania explained, "There are
people who thought that there were hints of male-bashing on my last album.
The odd person would say, 'Don't you think you're being a little hard on the
guys?' But for the most part, both men and women enjoyed it and related to it.
So, that gave me the license on this new album to do what was truest to me.'"

Times record reviewer Randy Lewis was not willing to credit Shania as a songwriter who was saying much in her lyrics. "What made Twain's THE WOMAN IN ME the best-selling album ever by a country female? A lot of sex appeal, a little vocal sass and a sound that made it equally inviting to pop and country listeners. In short, style, not substance. The follow-up continues, while mostly embellishing that recipe. These 16 songs, all written by Twain and her husband . . . are outfitted with the same edgy pop-rock textures. (Lange again makes her voice so viscerally prominent you worry she'll leave lipstick prints on your speakers.) Where the record improves over its light weight predecessor is in *Black Eyes, Blue Tears*, the confession of a woman opting out of an abusive relationship, and *When*, an inner dialogue that tackles romantic self-deception with humor and honesty."

"A lot of fans who approached me about the WOMAN IN ME," Shania told James Muretich "were mothers and daughters or uncles and nephews and it was like the generation gap was bridged by my album. They were saying that, in the car, my album was the only thing they could all agree to listen to. That was the biggest compliment. So, I realized that I wanted to do that again."

People eager to buy the record and form their own opinions had two more days to wait until it appeared in retail outlets. COME ON OVER, Shania Twain's third Mercury Nashville album, was released on November 4, 1997. Record stores were busier than usual that day throughout North America.

The 16 tracks on Shania's new album took quite a few people by surprise. THE WOMAN IN ME had been longer than the usual 10-song country album that Nashville regularly issued. Twelve songs, maybe, but *this* was heresy. Of course, the rock or pop fan was used to finding at least 45 minutes on an album. Less than that, well, it was a rip-off. Much more, and you couldn't fit it all on a 12-inch vinyl LP, not without moving the grooves so close together that quality was severely compromised. With the arrival of the CD, rock and pop acts stretched their sets out even further than the usual 45 minutes. Nashville albums were seldom longer than 32 minutes, and this did not change significantly with the arrival of the CD.

Ten songs, most of them cut short, approximately two-and-a-half minutes in length, usually not more than three minutes at the outside, was the usual country album. Nashville cut records so that they would have ten potential singles. After these were mixed, the label would select the best of these for their radio singles. Country music was, as they say, a radio-driven medium. In the 1970s, Willie Nelson had begun to lead the way out of this commercial single mentality with albums like RED HEADED STRANGER, where a concept drove the audience to listen to the album as a set rather than as a collection of singles. Others had followed Willie's example. Emmylou had made her own concept album, THE BALLAD OF SALLY ROSE. And when new country rolled up and the CD replaced the LP, artists like Garth Brooks and Mary Chapin Carpenter had extended the length of their singles. When Emmylou broke away from Top 40 country and collaborated with Canadian-born Daniel Lanois in 1995 to record the alt-country gem WRECKING BALL, the music program was longer than Shania's THE WOMAN IN ME.

COME ON OVER was created to erase the radio-format and record-bin mentality that a record had to be country *or* pop, country *or* rock. This was new music that defied categorization. THE WOMAN IN ME had broken new ground: traditional country was blended with rock on dynamic tracks like *Whose Bed Have Your Boots Been Under* and *Any Man Of Mine*; ballads like the title track and *Home Ain't Where His Heart Is (Anymore)* explored the possibilities of melding a country vocal with pop production. On COME ON OVER most of the tracks rock, taking the earlier explorations on *(If You're Not In It For Love) I'm Outta Here* to their logical extension. Country rock moments include the infectious *Love Gets Me Every Time*, *That Don't Impress Me Much*, and *Honey, I'm Home*. Even the pop productions *You're Still The One*, *When*, *If You Want To Touch Her Ask*, and *Black Eyes, Blue Tears* romp right along. *Man! I Feel Like A Woman!* defies categorization altogether. The one thing you can say with certainty about this number is it cooks! But is it pop? Is it country? Is it rock? Perhaps the designation country dance track fits best. One thing you learn while listening to the album is that Shania *is* rocking her country, really rock & rolling, which meant she was also treading on hallowed ground, Elvis territory, a domain dominated almost exclusively by men during the rock & roll era.

Shania's fans didn't care what critics called it. With COME ON OVER Shania seemed to be inviting us all over to her place, but we had already learned that she and Mutt cherished their privacy on their 3,000 acres of wilderness near Lake Placid. Surely, she wasn't going to announce that she and her husband would host a country Woodstock in their back-forty. It didn't seem likely. These were the speculations that went through my mind when I read advance release notices and heard the lead single *Love Gets Me Everytime* on the radio. When I peeled the shrink-wrap off the CD jewel case and sat back to enjoy Shania's new music for the first time, I liked what I heard. Right away, I believed that I knew the answer to all of the questions. This was material that would tour very well. Many of the tracks were tailor-made for live performance. COME ON OVER was clearly a blueprint for Shania's long-anticipated tour. Tracks like *Don't Be Stupid (You Know I Love You)*, *Honey I'm Home*, and *That Don't Impress Me Much* were country dance tracks. *Rock This Country* was a performance manifesto that I could already envision being released as a single and video near the end of a tour that just might prove Twain's detractors to have been very, very wrong. It was material that would translate into live shows as dynamic as Bruce Springsteen and Garth Brooks had been able to deliver. "Get ready, we're comin'. . ." her amplified whisper on the CD announced to her fans. "It was on my mind the whole time," she told Jay Orr for a November 1997 cover story in the *Nashville Banner*. "This is going to be my 'live' album. I'm taking this album on the road. I was definitely thinking 'live' and how exciting the live arrangements would be."

A closer look at the tracks reveals that her assertion was not a frivolous one at all. The opening track, *Man! I Feel Like A Woman!*, begins with the call to action, "Let's go girls!" Shania is rallying her troops. On the road, this would easily adapt to further and further modifications becoming, "Let's go Cincinnati! Let's go Miami!" etc. The song is also a post-feminist statement where Shania declares her woman's prerogative "to have a little fun" while bopping to Mutt's ZZ Top-meets-Canned Heat guitar-driven groove. "That song started with the title, then it kind of wrote itself," Shania told *Billboard* magazine's Chet Flippo. "The whole expression is a celebration of being a woman these days. I think we're kind of spoiled in a lot of ways, with the advantages we have. Feminists may not feel that way, but I do. It's pretty darn fun to be a woman."

In video format, role reversal depictions abound. A hunky male band performs behind Shania's torchy strip-show action. These guys are glued on merely for their pretty bods and pretty faces — they've never strummed or picked an electric guitar in their lives — the gratuitous equivalent of a bevy of showgirls prancing around a hat act. If the hats can have their Vegas showgirls and their cheesecake posing, Shania can employ a little beef, eh? She begins in formal attire, top hat with a hint of a black veil, a white shirt, black tie, and a long-rider coat tailored up to suggest a tuxedo jacket with tails, and she provocatively sheds this garment and the man's shirt she is wearing to reveal the black bustier, mini skirt, and thigh-length boots that provoked so much interest and controversy during her Grammy show appearance where she wore a fetish fashion dog collar and abandoned the coat and shirt, altogether.

The mini that fashion designer Marc Bouwer had sewn onto the bustier was shorter than Twiggy's miniskirts, which had outraged British Royalty in the '60s;

the boots appeared to be a mail order item selected from an S&M catalog. Bouwer, who includes Pamela Anderson, Toni Braxton, and Sigourney Weaver on his list of clients, was indignant at this licentious interpretation of his artistic creation. Music Row Dominatrix? Hell, no! Had no one noticed that she had also appeared on the Grammy show in a gorgeous white gown? This was about contrast, not morality. It was not about dog collars and S&M. "It was a silk satin collar with little jets of crystal beads hanging off," he patiently explained to Vancouver *Province* reporter John P. McLaughlin. "So, it was anything but S&M. It was more Victorian. The corset's actually based on a Victorian shape. What I like about it is, you have a very clean line across her bust and you have the clean line of the gloves breaking at the same spot as the bust." Most Shaniamaniacs hadn't even noticed the gloves. Bouwer continued, "And she has a tiny little waist and I said to her, Shania, I'm going to corset you like you've never been corseted before. And really, I didn't need to make it that tight because she has an incredibly tiny waist. She's a vegetarian, she eats very healthy."

In recent years, these Grammy performances have become a forum for the rich and infamous where a fashion statement can often create even more buzz than winning a trophy. Madonna had often walked away from the Grammies having created the most buzz of all, but in 1999 it was country dominatrix Shania Twain who got most of the press. Few people could even remember Madonna's kimona-clad geisha girl appearance. No one thought of Shania as a Victorian.

Shania's relationship with Bouwer was also a two-way street. "She recognizes good ideas," the New York Fashion designer said. "For Twain's *That Don't Impress Me Much* video," McLaughlin reported, "Bouwer was given only a sketchy concept of Twain in the desert trying to hitch a ride while a lot of guys are coming on to her. He immediately and appropriately enough thought of Little Red Riding Hood and the wolf." "And I liked the idea of the hood," Bouwer told Mclaughlin. "But I didn't want her dressed in red because that would be too weird in the desert. Then I thought of *The French Lieutenant's Woman*. I loved that hood on Meryl Streep, that silhouette. So, we'll do that but we need a much more natural looking fabric. I toyed with the idea of snake first but I found the leopard and showed it to Shania and she's like, 'Oh, yeah, it's great.' Then she had the much lighter hair and the beautiful red mouth. That would be my only reference to Little Red Riding Hood."

The second track, *I'm Holding On To Love (To Save My Life)*, is a soaring pop confection that seemed to have little to do with country music at all. Nice fluff. An exquisite guitar solo paid tribute to Mark Knopfler's *Sultans Of Swing*.

With the third track, *Love Gets Me Everytime*, we hear the first prominent country elements, other than Shania's vocal twang, which seldom gets so pop that you forget she's just a country girl. Here, ganged fiddles played by Rob Hajacos, Joe Spivey, Glen Duncan, and Aubrey Haney ride the twangy guitar groove like a country breeze rippling the leaves of a grove of poplars. Mutt Lange's favorite instrument might be the pedal steel, but from experience he knew that fiddle and pedal steel had also become the clichés most people iden-tified with traditional, singin'-through-your-nose, country, which everyone except diehard country fans hated. For most of the cuts, Mutt mixes Paul Franklin, Bruce Bouton, and John Hughey's pedal steel guitar licks into the wash of guitar and piano sounds. Mandolin, accordion, organ, and synthesizer are also used sparingly. The fiddle is the instrument he chooses to feature more prominently. On track three, the ganged fiddles and twangy guitars are liberally spiced with tasty but minimalist pedal steel riffs. Lange's mixes are so skillfully executed that this detail work, along with the background vocals and rhythm track, works in such a subtle way that the overall effect is a bouquet which sur-rounds Shania's lead vocal. Still, Mutt kept the country tradition of the vocal being the most prominent element in the mix. People liked Shania's country rock because they could hear what she was saying in the lyrics, which is not always the case in rock mixes. Once again, it was an astounding album.

Canadian Musician magazine reporter Karen Bliss thoroughly researched the "Tracking of COME ON OVER." Karen spoke with tracking engineer Jeff Balding, the closest anyone was likely to be able get to learning how the intensely private Lange put the music together. She backgrounded her story with care paid to detail. "The tracking for COME ON OVER was done at Masterfonics in Nashville, with Mutt Lange producing and engineer Jeff Balding, a 14-year veteran who has worked with everyone from Trisha Yearwood to Megadeth. All beds were laid down in three weeks with core play-ers Paul Leim (drums), Joe Chemay (electric & fretless bass), and Biff Watson (acoustic and nylon string guitars), and Twain singing scratch vocals. Later, Lange and Twain returned to Masterfonics for some overdubs."

"She was spot-on on her vocal tracks," Balding told Bliss. "The vibe and everything was there. What's great about that, is that she really gave the musi-cians something to play off of. They can really grab on to the tune that way. And since she's such a great singer, just in case there was something that she did that we want to keep, we made sure that we got a sound that was usable. We tried two or three different mics."

Finding just the right location for the drum kit for each track proved to be an adventure. Several locations were tried out including one of the hallways. For most of the cuts, the stone room with its highly reflective rock-face walls and stone-slab floor turned out to be the most effective. For ballads, Lange and Balding moved Paul Leim into one of the small 'dead' booths where there was no bounce-back at all.

"Mutt's great to work with," Balding told Karen Bliss. "I've worked with him on a few other things before that, some Michael Bolton and an artist called Stevie Vann. Mutt has a lot of ideas in his head that he comes into the session with. . . . Both of them (Shania and Mutt) really put a lot of thought into the direction. They wanted a real fun Motown feel. I probably had three or four conversations with Mutt before he came down, where he'd play me stuff over the phone and he'd tell me about what he was thinking, the concept, so a lot of thought went into it before we came into the studio to do the tracks."

Once the bed tracks were done, Lange and Twain headed off to specialty studios in Nashville and elsewhere. Slide guitar tracks were done at GBT Studio. Backing vocals were done in Toronto at Glenn Gould Studio, programming at Sven Studios in Mamaronek, New York by Olle Romo. Then it was back to the Masterfonics Tracking Room and Jeff Balding.

"They came back down," Balding explained to Karen Bliss, "in the middle of the record. We did the fiddles. . . . We had a fiddle player that we used during the tracking, and he came back in and brought four fiddle players. On some of the tunes, we'd mic the fiddle very up close, maybe six inches, eight inches off the fiddle, just in front of the bridge. . . . And on the gang fiddles that we did with all four fiddle players playing at once out in the room, we set them up in a semi-circle and used two Neumann KM 582s."

The making of COME ON OVER was in every way a labor of love. We have come to accept the lushness of the layered background vocals as Shania's trademark sound. It's helpful to remember when you're listening to her records that she and Mutt stacked those BGs together. He sometimes squirted a miniscule frosting of synthesizer on the high register harmony phrases. It was the icing on the cake, so to speak, and contributed to the "crispness" that some reviewers mentioned. Mutt sang many of the harmonies himself. The backing vocal bouquet and the guitar textures are re-colored each time a song moves from verse to chorus, bridge to chorus, or chorus to verse. Sometimes, this floral arrangement of vocal harmonies, keyboards, and guitars is varied within sections, shifting beneath Shania's more constant lead vocal. Such painstaking attention to detail demands talent, innovation, and many hours of labor in the mixing process. The luxury that pervades their music at every bend in the road comes from the heartfelt love they feel toward each other. It was not the usual method employed on Music Row or, for that matter, in the rock world, either. Mutt Lange's approach to making records was original. He kept it that way. He might repeat some of the clichés in his hooks, now and then, but each record he has turned out is like an original oil painting by one of the masters. There is no formula, no assembly line, to be discovered.

Shania seemed vibrantly alive in both her delivery and the lyrics she was singing. She was holding on to love to save her life; she had no time for the Doctor Ruths, horoscopes, psychics, or internet chats, which she told interviewers were "superficial crutches" that distracted people from real life. She had "gol' darn gone and done it!" She was in love and wanted the whole world to know just how fine it felt.

Because he and Shania worked so closely together, and because they also co-wrote their songs, their collaboration became topic for much discussion. "There are still those who make snide remarks about Lange making her the star she is today," Karen Bliss noted, "or assume she's not bright because she's attractive, but regardless of her Covergirl image, Twain is very much a songwriter. Elton John and Bryan Adams both have songwriting partners; it doesn't lessen their credibility. But for some reason, Twain is taken less seriously as an artist by some."

Shania wrote the songs initially, and Mutt added the big picture. "He writes more from the producer's mind and can see the end result musically," she told Chet Flippo, "whereas I think more conceptually, like, 'What is this song going to be about? . . . Do I want the song to be serious or light?' A lot of these songs have a cheerful or comic surface to them, but they have a deeper thought behind them. I write better lyrics now, because of Mutt, he's always pushing me to come up with something better . . . I influence him with the music because I pretty much dictate where I want to go melodically. He's really a master at arranging things. You can hear where the rhythm will change from a verse to a chorus or have a completely different feel in a bridge."

Shania had told Susan Pocharski for a March 1998 story in *Cosmopolitan* magazine, "we collaborate when we feel it's time to do that. If anything, writing is a wonderful chance to get together, period." As she told Larry Delaney for a December 1997 cover story in *Country Music News*, "we don't have any kind of formula for writing hit songs. For most songs, I am composing the lyrics and

Mutt is working the arrangements. He's really into how a song is put together and builds around my ideas and my song lyrics. Sometimes I have to trim the lyrics, and sometimes I have to put more into what the song is saying. Mutt can really zero in on those kinds of things, and he's able to turn something sluggish into something that has much more definition to it. It's really remarkable how we think alike on these songs . . . seldom do we even disagree about the way a song should go, and Mutt has never interfered with what my songs say. He's always encouraging me to say exactly what I feel in a song, and I've always prided myself on being assertive and progressive and unique. So, I hope the messages I am dealing with in my songs are being accepted that way."

"Acceptance," Delaney pointed out, "especially in Nashville itself, has often been reported to be strained and even non-existent." Twain downplayed that, saying, "It would be naive of me to expect a wholesale acceptance of my music . . . there'll always be detractors, I guess, but the negative reaction has been very minimal. . . . I am personally always well received by the industry people in Nashville. The fans have been unbelievable." She put the impression that she and her husband were "outsiders" down to the fact that they didn't live in Nashville. But she wasn't planning to move there. "I really think if I spent all my time in Nashville," she told Delaney, "I would begin to 'fit in' to the point that it would defeat my ability to be original and unique." As embarrassing as their loud bellyaching has been for her, Shania's detractors have remained a small minority of dogged journalists and disgruntled good ole persons. They make a lot of noise but their dissenting views come from far fewer individuals than you might imagine. The impression they create is like that age-old expression: 'heap big smoke, no fire'. Their motives are difficult to comprehend.

Being taken less seriously because she is also attractive and flamboyant is something Shania has learned to live with. "It goes with the territory," she told Karen Bliss. "There's a lot of people out there that will always jump to that conclusion. So, yeah, my talents . . . get under appreciated or get overlooked. But it's my choice to be entertaining visually. I know that it's going to be misunderstood at times, but I don't care. If I wanted to downplay my looks, I could. I could shave my head and not wear makeup. I could not be feminine if I wanted to. We can *all* be unattractive and we can all be attractive. I choose to be as attractive as I can be, because that's the way I feel best." It was this very wholeness of feeling that attracted so many people from so many divergent lifestyles to Shania Twain and her music.

While some journalists still attacked Shania, Music Row had paid attention to the sales results she had been getting. Faith Hill, Pam Tillis, Martina McBride, and Trisha Yearwood had all broken new ground before Shania hit big in 1995, but now they were meeting less opposition when they said they wanted to become more involved in the production of their own records. Before Shania's breakout success, McBride had faced stiff opposition to her desire to become involved in her recording sessions. "I wanted to give a little feedback to the production," she told *Country Song Roundup* reporter Bob Paxman, "and it was kind of like, 'Oh, now don't you worry your pretty little head about all that . . .'" After the release of THE WOMAN IN ME artists like a McBride, Deana Carter, and Sarah Evans found they no longer faced the 'girl singer' mentality.

Mutt Lange was also seeing some of his songs accepted by Nashville acts like Lonestar and Blackhawk. The initial walls of resistance were slowly crumbling. Credit was being paid where credit was due. Mutt and Shania had enlisted the services of some of the best players in the business. Paul Franklin had recorded and toured with Dire Straits. Brent Mason was the most in-demand session guitarist in Nashville. Dann Huff was the guitarist credited with playing "Electric Riff & Rhythm Guitar, all guitar textures, Talk Box, Electric 12-String, Wa-Wa, and 6-String bass electric guitar on the sessions." Dann Huff was a guitar monster, a creative player who had already tried his hand at producing and was eager to do more. When Shania learned that Faith Hill was looking for a new producer, she mentioned Dann.

Over time, Faith and Shania had become friends, and during one visit, Shania made her suggestion. "I didn't even know Dann Huff was producing," Faith told Janette Williams for a feature story published in *Country Song Roundup*. "We were talking about what I was gonna do as far as producers. Shania said, 'Did you know that Dann Huff produces?' She said that Mutt Lange said that he had incredible talent and was a diamond in the rough. So, I took her advice and called up Dann."

The resulting production team of Byron Gallimore (who produces Faith's husband Tim McGraw), Dann Huff, and Hill herself explored new ground. Shania and Mutt, Faith and Tim were not only happily married couples, they were also partners in the creative process. Faith and Tim's duets and their marriage, when compared to George Jones and Tammy Wynette, were everything that Mr & Mrs Country Music had yearned to be but had not been able to harmonize and sustain in their personal lives 25 years earlier. "It was a very creative process for me," Hill told Williams. "It was a real team effort." That team effort eventually led to the recording of *This Kiss*, Faith's biggest radio success which powered the sales of her album FAITH into multiple-platinum figures. The song was written by Beth Nielsen Chapman, Robin Lerner, and Annie Reboff, while other cuts were written by Matraca Berg, Diane Warren, Gretchen Peters, Sheryl Crow, and Bekka Bramlett, a representation of the new pantheon of Nashville songwriters finding a common ground. While it was convenient for some journalists to say that Shania and her fashion designer Marc Bouwer or her video director Steven Goldmann had changed the face of country now that Faith had become another of their clients, in reality the changes were taking place within the music and lyrics.

Gretchen Peters is one of the best of the new breed. Gretchen nearly always writes from the woman's point of view. And she is articulate when it comes to speaking about the songs she crafts. "Writing *The Secret Of Life*," she says, "was really a matter of wrapping music around a simple philosophy; don't listen to the TV gurus, don't buy the self-help books, don't waste your time searching for happiness. It's not a big Cecil B. DeMille moment anyway. It's usually waiting for you when you're not expecting it — in a cup of coffee, at a baseball game, or while you're driving and your favorite song comes on the radio. The secret of life is just recognizing it when it happens." While *This Kiss* was fueled by pop crossover potential, Gretchen Peter's *The Secret Of Life* was fashioned from material that was more familiar to traditionalists than the pop-tinged *This Kiss*: two people drinking in a bar. The song is contemporary as well because the protagonists grapple not with each other — they wrestle philosophically trying to find the answer to life's dilemma. This was a whole new style of barroom philosophy, full of insights suited more to the progressive attitudes now accepted by post-feminist women and liberated men.

This Kiss and *The Secret Of Life* are but two examples of a wealth of post-feminist expression that flowed into the mainstream in the span of time between the release of Shania Twain's THE WOMAN IN ME and COME ON OVER. For years, Tammy Wynette had been topic for discussion between hard-line women's rights organizations who criticized her for recording *Stand By Your Man*, which became her signature tune, and those who praised her for recording *Womanhood* and *Woman To Woman*, citing her as a leader of the feminist cause. But Country Queens were still hokey as all get out, especially Tammy and Dolly.

Following the British-Australian-Nashville country rock stylings of Olivia Newton-John who graduated into pop superstardom, Dolly became a superstar, too, but no matter how pop she got, how glitzy she became, she often played a caricature of herself, a Daisy Mae. She seemed to drag the Opry along with her wherever she went. It stuck to her. She paid the price heavily for pushing the envelope as much as she did. And she seemed so much more at ease with herself singing bluegrass than she did when she rocked.

There are intriguing similarities between Linda Ronstadt, who belted out *You're No Good, When Will I Be Loved,* and *Poor Poor Pitiful Me* while selling more than 10 million albums during the 1970s by fitting herself onto both the pop and country charts, and Shania Twain, who accomplished the same feat and sold more than 30 million in the '90s. Linda's recordings evolved from folk rock (with the Stone Poneys) into country rock (on HEART LIKE A WHEEL), through to covers of New Wave songwriters like Elvis Costello and Reggae artists like Jimmy Cliff by the early '80s. Linda also tackled some of Patsy Cline's records, most notably the Willie Nelson penned classic *Crazy,* and reminded country fans of just how well Patsy had sung while she was alive. Although not a songwriter herself, Linda endorsed women songwriters like Karla Bonoff, Dolly Parton, Wendy Waldman, and Maria Muldaur, all of whose songs she introduced to the pop audience for the first time.

When Reba McEntire took hold of her career, she told Mark Bego, "I'm just as good and as capable as anybody (in show business), male or female. I don't think there's anything I can't do." When Reba rocked her country, she did it R&B style, like Gladys Knight and Aretha Franklin, and she rocked Music Row by constructing her own office tower, a building taller than most of the corporate label headquarters, in the downtown core. Reba is feisty and, like Dolly, she has proved to be a smart businesswoman, forming her own management and publishing companies. She understood how the men manipulated things to their advantage and quickly began to rake in a fair percentage of the money her career was generating, revenue she had not always seen before she had taken control of her affairs. In the '90s, kd lang, perhaps the best country female vocalist next to Patsy Cline, chose to record an evolving pop style music, and cuts like *Ingenue,* when contrasted with Reba McEntire's pop productions like *Sunday Kind Of Love, Cathy's Clown,* and *You Lie,* serve to point out just how country Reba is, no matter how much production is piled up around her vocals.

Tanya Tucker had always rocked up her country and she kept doing it in the New Country era when Carlene Carter, Pam Tillis, Mary Chapin Carpenter, Martina McBride, Wynonna, and Trisha Yearwood began celebrating their womanhood on rocking new country records. When Shania Twain got into full gear, she began to celebrate her womanhood, too. All of these artists aimed to break free from half a century of serfdom for women in Top 40 country. Having any fun at all while singing a country song was not the usual approach for girl singers before K.T. Oslin's 80's Ladies. Carlene Carter's single and video I Fell In Love developed the theme. While traditionalists have decried the move to contemporize country music in the '90s, you only have to look to women like Ruyter Suys and Corey Parks of the heavy metal group Nashville Pussy to realize that "new country" is tame compared to the rocking women can get into. And while some people found it a stretch to find anything at all redeeming about the Spice Girls, the Spicers seemed to have become a rallying point for something called "girl culture."

Hardcore '90s Girl Culture fans lived in a Spice Girl world where attitude and rock were cemented into a bubblegum philosophy that was difficult for people over the age of 14 to comprehend. Their hero-bands bore brazen bandnames like the Slits, Bratmobile, and Pottymouth. And for readers of magazines like Spin the term "Women in Rock" was no longer gender-specific; it was now a political term. "Being female wasn't enough," Karen Schoemer informed Newsweek readers, "you have to be correctly female. Do you pledge allegiance to the Spice Girls? Do you accept Sabrina the teenage witch in all her multidimensional personae? Do you promise to wear torn slip dresses, smeared makeup and a constant expression of Fiona Apple-style fetishistic victimhood?" These bratty types were claiming W.I.R. as their exclusive domain. "Raising your voice with a thousand other earth mothers to a Holly Near ballad," Schoemer explained, "just doesn't cut it but spitting out the sexy defiant words to an Ani DiFranco song sure does. Under these guidelines, no one is likely to mistake Shania and Celine for Women In Rock. Their politics are all wrong. They do womanhood the old-fashioned, un-ironic, hyperfeminine way . . . They comb their hair and flaunt their bellybuttons," Schoemer argued in Newsweek, "and it's *not a statement*. Their music is unabashedly domestic, without complicated subtexts; rock critics don't often write about them because there isn't a lot to explain. But out there in the real bedrooms of America, Twain and Dion have had real impact."

Despite the attitude and politics of both traditional feminists and girl power extremists, an emerging post-feminist attitude sees women liberated from confrontational attitudes and elitist stances adopted as appropriate behavior during the early decades of the struggle to establish women's rights. Shania's "message is female empowerment without male bashing," Chet Flippo correctly observed in USA Today. Country women have been less angry and far less iconoclastic than their rock and pop contemporaries. For the most part, country women prefer to celebrate their womanhood.

Women's rights were not established without some casualties, however, and hard-line feminists sometimes found it difficult to function in the world they had fought so diligently to create. Despite all the progress that had been made by 1998, some women still told reporters that life was tough in a male-dominated world. Some feminists were unhappy that a new generation of women no longer felt it necessary to deny their sexuality and no longer felt antagonism toward men. Some were outraged that women like Shania were using their sexuality to sell records. But Shania was not alone. Women who made reference to post-feminism were no longer viewing life in terms of sexual politics at all. These young women wanted to put all of that behind themselves and have a little fun. In days past, it would have been unheard of for someone like Faith Hill to say, "I think FAITH is a mirror reflection of where I am in my life. Musically, for sure, there's no question about it. I could not have gone deeper to find what this record is. As far as the personal side, there are a lot of positive songs." Faith's happy family life and fulfilling pregnancy during this same time was also a huge contributing factor. "I found it hard to sing about something sad," she said at the time of the album's release, "and then go home where I was exuding happiness all the time."

By the late 1990s, people of all gender orientations openly sought a vocabulary for more effective communication, and the expressions "appropriate and inappropriate behavior" were regularly in use. They were being applied to behavior by women as well as by men. Liberated males found this a welcome relief from the accusatory language used in recent years during the all-out conflict of the gender wars. There were still some guys, of course, who just didn't get it. And it was to these men that Shania directed her comments in the lyrics to several of the songs from COME ON OVER.

"Let me let you in on a secret / how to treat a woman right," Shania suggests in *If You Wanna Touch Her, Ask!* "If you're lookin' for a place in her heart / It ain't gonna happen overnight." This stop, look, and listen approach spoke of inappropriate touching, but it also suggested for the sincere male that a woman wanted to be sure they could become friends before she could open up. Here, she was going a little deeper than some of the TV Doctor Ruths. The fact that both men and women continued wholeheartedly to endorse Shania's new music suggested that some progress was being made in what a few years earlier had been referred to as the 'war between the sexes'.

Still, there was far too much violent behavior going on in the form of spousal abuse, and Shania's *Black Eyes, Blue Tears* addressed the need for women to make the decision to walk away, but focused more fully on what happened next. This was a song that, like a support group, urged the battered woman to regain her self-esteem, not to blame her ex-partner's abuse on some flaw in herself, as was frequently the case in reported incidents. "I'm very passionate about that song," Shania said at the time of the album's release. "I definitely can relate to this subject. I wasn't at all sure that I wanted to talk about this in a song, but I guess I needed to. It's a very important issue, especially since the O.J.(Simpson) case. I wanted to write about it in a more optimistic way. I put it more in the light of a *Thelma & Louise* who don't drive over the edge. See, the freedom that they experienced in liberating themselves is the spirit of the song, but the ending (of the song) is about using your freedom. Driving over the edge is not the answer."

On FLY, their second album, Dixie Chicks Natalie, Emily, and Martie would make their own modest proposal with *Goodbye Earl*, where a wife beating repeat abuser, who walks right through a restraining order and puts his estranged wife in the intensive care ward, is murdered and dumped in a lake by the victim and a friend. The Chicks, like guardian angels, look on during the video, starring *NYPD's* Dennis Franz as Earl, but are invisible to the protagonists. This song proved to be so controversial that nearly 20 percent of country stations refused to playlist the song. Feminists wrote angry letters to the editors of the dailies. Post-feminists answered them. The Chicks were not telling women it was okay to murder their abusive husbands. They were making a satiric statement. This was, after all, a lot like *Gulliver's Travels* author Jonathan Swift's satiric *Modest Proposal*, a tongue-in-cheek essay suggesting that to remedy the starvation in Catholic Ireland, eating babies was a meat-and-potatoes solution, especially so since Ireland's only other surplus other than too many children was spuds. *Goodbye Earl* was satire, not an instruction manual. The hope was that the men in the audience would take the hint. No one really wanted to be Earl, did they?

Franz pointed out that, as Andy Sipowicz, he was used to arresting the Earls of the world in his role on the cop show. He thought the video to be funny, especially the finale, a musical romp in which he comes back from the dead to dance with the cast just to show it's fiction and not fact. "I used blue jeans, boots, muscle t-shirts, sleeveless jean jacket, cheesy sunglasses and a big hairpiece that looks like a bad Elvis wig to become Earl," Franz told *Country Weekly* feature writer Larry Holden. Of the Broadway musical style finale, Franz said, "I'm decomposing during that scene. I look like I've been in the ground for a while. Worms are coming out of me, my face is all white, my hair is rotting away and my clothes are ripped."

Oddly enough, Shania was cited by some reviewers for not spending enough time on the blood and bruises in *Black Eyes, Blue Tears* and criticized for focusing on what came afterward. She did not treat her subject seriously enough, other reviewers claimed. Both of these songs, Shania's and the Dixie Chicks', provoked debate that could only be helpful in the educational process. While the debate between feminists and post-feminists raged in the media, many of the alarming statistics and facts about spousal abuse, which did not usually receive as much attention, became public knowledge in a way that could not be easily be swept under the carpet. The times they were changing, once again, and this time a Nashville outsider from Canada and a trio of politically incorrect country singers from Texas were the ones who were "blowin' in the wind." Women making statements in folk, rock, and pop had long been accepted, but in country . . .

When *Saint Paul Pioneer Press* pop music critic Jim Walsh asked Shania what being a woman in the late 1990s meant, she said, "There's so many different perspectives. There's so many different types of women now, that it's hard to speak for women in general. But for myself I see a new sense of freedom that I never felt as a younger woman, as a teenager. As a girl, I felt so much more inhibited, socially. And I'm shedding that now, somehow. And I'm writing about it. I was a little angry as a teenage girl, as far as understanding boundaries for boys. You know, why do they think they can just grab your butt when you're walking by?" Referring to the midriff issue, she said, "I got such a reaction from country from that. They thought I was being overly sexy or something. They were a little bit shocked. And I was, like, 'Don't you watch television? Don't you see that half the women on the streets walk around with bare midriffs and are very conservative decent women?'"

"Historically," Walsh said to Twain, "in pop music and in music videos women who have appeared the way you do have been viewed as bimbos or play things. That's not what you get from your stuff — it's sexy, but part of why it's sexy is the vibe that you're in control." Shania agreed. "That's the difference. I think there are women out there who have a problem with other women being comfortable with their sexuality. And I'm not one of those women. I'm not an angry feminist in any way, shape or form. I don't want to be a man . . ."

"You say you're not an angry feminist," Walsh said. "Do you consider yourself a feminist?"

Shania's answer was revealing. "No, I don't," she said. "I think I'm too old-fashioned to think that way. I think more than anything, I just like to express that it's okay to be proud to be a woman, as opposed to feeling inhibited about it."

Where women's issues had not been considered as subject for discussion among country music critics, they were now regularly discussed in interviews with country women artists. These issues were now the subject of country songs, and women were meeting less opposition when they sought creative input during the recording of their music. In his book *Women On Top: The Quiet Revolution That's Rocking The American Music Industry*, James Dickerson writes, "Today, women are doing more than topping the charts; they're transmuting popular music. They're taking it to a new level, just as Presley transmuted country and blues in the 1950s. This is as much a creative struggle as it is one of equality between the sexes." A case in point was Shania's lyric, "Okay, so what do you think you're Elvis or something? / Whatever / That don't impress me . . ." Elvis was there in the lyric, referred to as the King to whom insincere men pretended, and, creatively, the track soared beyond gender politics to pop splendor, yet dropped back into a twangy guitar groove that could still be identified as country rock. *That Don't Impress Me Much* was especially popular with kids, who choose their favorites without a thought in their heads about whether the song is pop, rock, country, or hip hop. Or, whether a lyric is politically correct or not.

Also difficult to categorize was the rollicking *Don't Be Stupid*. The video was to be filmed on a beach in Los Angeles, but the weather didn't cooperate. A storm blew in from the Pacific, driving the video crew indoors. "We did a lot of it in a beach house," Shania told *Country Music Today*, "right on the beach with waves crashing up, rain blowing sideways. . . . It was really quite a storm." Despite the difficult working conditions, the result was Shania's own Riverdance with the cloggers and fiddlers dancing in the rain. The lilting Celtic freedom unleashed by the fiddle-playing recorded on the album track contributed to the decision to have Leahy, a Canadian Celtic band from Lakeland, Ontario, join Shania on her tour.

Shania had written *From This Moment On* with the idea that it was better suited for someone else to record. "I wasn't writing it for myself at all," she said of the song, "I didn't have it on my final list and Mutt said, 'What about that one?' He convinced me to do it." On the North American release, the track was cut as a duet with Bryan White, which pulled it into the country mainstream for country fans. On the international release, the song became a tour-de-force solo ballad. Duets with singers from other countries were also released during the tour.

Several critics cited Mungo Jerry's *In The Summertime* as the inspiration for the lite-country-pop of the title track *Come On Over*, but this was only one of several sources accessed in Mutt Lange's production. The groove was not stolen from the British skiffle group Mungo Jerry or anyone else, as reviewers bent on slamming the album alleged. All popular music depends, at times, on refurbishing clichés. Country music lyric writers do it all the time. And within the aural tapestry of COME ON OVER, you continually hear tributes to records from the past as Mutt Lange invokes pleasant memories in order to color the music. Beatles' guitar stuff. Stones' guitar stuff. Dire Straits' guitar stuff . . . Few producers are able to locate the sweet spot in their track, which guarantees the song will be a radio hit, as well as Mutt does.

With *You're Still The One*, Shania came up with a heartfelt love song, her tribute to her loving relationship with Mutt. "I think a lot of the people in the industry think (our relationship) is based entirely on career," Shania said when the album was released, "which is so ridiculous. They say, 'Well, he married a young, good-looking girl, and she married a successful producer.' So, people thought it was based on that and certainly couldn't last. But it isn't based on that, and this song is about us . . . I'm glad we're making it. So, this song is a celebration of that." The production on *You're Still The One* soars. Shania nails her feelings into her vocal with confidence. Her vocal is the sole country element in sight, yet country and pop radio programmers both found enthusiastic endorsement for the track from phone-in listeners as their request lines clogged with callers wanting to hear the song. The music video filmed in black and white was another seaside experience for Shania and her video crew. Director David Hogan features his subject in closeup shots that border on the extraordinary. The contrast between the outdoor beach-side scenes and the interiors is spectacular, reminiscent of the romance captured in b&w '40s films featuring box office stars like Cary Grant and Ingrid Bergman.

Shania's initial vision was to have the lighting create the mystique. She explained this to Hogan, and he sent her some books with examples of lighting imagery and effects so that she could choose what she wanted. "I was able to pick out some things and he duplicated it perfectly," she told *Country Music Today*. "And just the whole kind of dappled lighting . . . It's very dramatic in black and white . . . Artistically, it's one of my top five." The song is now her signature tune, still the one most people attach to her name, a pop and a country classic.

2

ROCK THIS COUNTRY

FACED WITH MARKETING COME ON OVER in the fall of 1997, Mercury Nashville President Luke Lewis told *Billboard* magazine's Chet Flippo, "Thankfully, there doesn't have to be a big marketing spin on it. Reaction to the first single *Love Gets Me Every Time* has been better than I expected." Flippo noted that some 33,000 singles had already sold before the album's release; adding in the pop sales, the figure was more like 45,000 singles. There had been some pleasant surprises at country radio, too.

"I knew I was getting singles from two women superstars the same week," KKBQ Houston programmer Dene Hallam told Flippo, "from Wynonna and Shania Twain, and I was frightened by the prospect of getting two rock singles. Now, I think it's ironic that the new Shania single is much more country than Wynonna's. I'm flabbergasted by that. Shania's song is fabulous; it's very exciting, and it's great for the format."

"*Love Gets Me Everytime* is really about the woman playing the fool or the sucker," Shania explains. "I mean, guys usually sing about these things where, you know, they just fall apart when they see a beautiful woman. . . . Of course we, as women, go through the same thing, but we seem to keep more cool. . . . We lose control, too, as much as we are control freaks." The video for *Love Gets Me Everytime* showed Shania choosing a wardrobe in a high fashion setting. Plenty of closeups and glamor is the focus all the way. It was a video about making a video. Because there was no storyboarding and no plot, vignettes such as perfectionist, control-freak Shania fixing her own hair — which has become dislodged, just as a production assistant rushes to her aid — became significant moments. "The director, Timothy White," Shania explains, "really saw the whole thing as, 'Let's just capture some candid moments and see what we come up with . . .' and that's what we did. I mean how easy can that be? They're filming me picking out the things I want to wear, and just having fun, basically, eating and all the stuff that happens during a photo shoot." The video was wholesome, humorous, and glamorous. Exactly what the video channels wanted.

Mercury Nashville's senior VP of sales, John Grady, told Flippo his marketing plan would not be anything unusual. "Marketing didn't sell her last album," Grady said. "When you get a record this good and you've sold 10 million the last time, it's just about getting back to your core. Mainly, you just need to let them know that it exists. Retail is very excited about it, and they need big records as much as we do. We'll be up against Celine Dion and everybody else, and this can compete as a pop album." With artists like Garth, Wynonna, and Shania, Mercury VP of promotion Larry Hughes was aware that there was a "great deal of leeway with country radio. You can be a little more left of center. When the public takes hold of an artist like this, it behooves radio to follow the public's demand."

Inevitably, Chet Flippo found himself discussing the upcoming tour and the controversy surrounding it. "In my opinion," Shania told the veteran reporter, "I've paid my dues as far as touring is concerned. I was able to prove that you can sell records through radio and television just on the basis of the music. You don't have to have all the hoopla. Sometimes the industry underestimates the fans. There are only two women who have sold what I have in North America. [Whitney Houston's WHITNEY HOUSTON and Alanis Morissette's JAGGED LITTLE PILL also sold more than 12 million.] And the only one who achieved those sales without touring was me . . . But now I can add the touring element."

As the expectation built, people stretched their imaginations in efforts to envision what a Shania tour might be like. Would it be like Reba with theatrical stage settings and elaborate costume changes? Would Shania be as pumped as Garth? Would her show be more of a Vegas show as Anne Murray's shows always were? Or would her stage presentation be more like Bruce Springsteen and the E-street Band, laden with dramatic moments and over-the-top extended versions of her hit material? She *was* a singer-songwriter like Springsteen. And . . . Jon Landau *had* stepped in to manage both artists' careers at a critical juncture when initial management fell short of realizing their artist's vision of themselves.

Landau, a rock critic and *Rolling Stone* magazine's record review section editor before he became involved in producing and managing Springsteen, had helped springboard the Jersey rocker into the limelight when he wrote, "I saw the future of rock & roll and it is Bruce Springsteen" in a review published in the *Real Paper*. His comment was then used successfully as a marketing slogan by

Columbia Records. As soon as an exploitive contract with the singer's previous management was out of the way, Landau had stepped into the breach acting as both producer and manager. Springsteen began to write and record the working man's music that had been bursting to get out of him all along. Armed with that music he had toured his buns off and become a rock legend. When it came to touring, Bruce was the Boss.

When Landau first met Shania, he must surely have seen the future of country music. "I think her approach to her life experiences is to strive for a kind of positiveness that animates most of what she writes," he told *Rolling Stone*, "that's her philosophy. She works her butt off. She's very results oriented, no-nonsense. And, to me, she is utterly real." With Shania and Mutt there was no need for Landau or his partner Barbara Carr to tinker with the music at all. And marketing was being handled very well by Mercury Nashville. What was needed was a strategy for the long anticipated tour. Such a strategy was not in place after the release of THE WOMAN IN ME. Although Shania had done very well on her own with a promotional tour during which she spoke to radio and media . . . and very well making mall appearances at dramatic and strategic moments . . . she *had* born the brunt of criticism for not touring. Because of the controversy, Shania could not afford to embark on a half-hearted tour. There was no one better equipped to mastermind a successful touring strategy than Jon Landau.

Going on tour solo as a woman country artist was potentially disastrous. Reba was the only female country artist who had successfully headlined her own stadium shows before this time, but Brooks and Dunn had opened for Reba, bringing their own legion of fans with them. As a solo artist, Wynonna had not sold out the big arenas. For independent-minded women, Emmylou Harris's approach to touring her WRECKING BALL album, playing medium-sized venues and festivals, worked better than tackling stadiums and arenas.

Sarah McLachlan's Lilith Fair approach worked for a wide variety of singer-songwriters and pop acts, but, although Shania certainly generated the necessary girl power, she had sold considerably more albums than all of the women involved in a Lilith Fair show put together. So, that made no sense, banding together with so many women from so many diverse musical styles. Putting together her own country women show didn't seem like the answer either. That had worked for the CBS Special *The Women of Country*, but it was not likely to sell sufficient tickets night after night in all 51 states and all 10 Canadian provinces.

What had become apparent by late 1997 was that Shania could scarcely afford to tour with a male act. In the end, the choice of Leahy, a showy instrumental family group of cloggers and fiddlers from Shania's home province, turned out to be an excellent choice as an opening act for Shania. While Leahy likely sold few tickets themselves, they put on a spectacular display as an opener. They also helped build the audience expectation to a fever pitch for Shania's dramatic appearance. Which, in a perfect world, is what you want an opening act to do. No more and no less.

And what was seldom mentioned was that Leahy also fit the bill because they had no single front person or personality at all who might conflict with the superstar's identity and thus skew the show in any undesired direction. In a way, they were merely an extension of Shania's band, and the fact that Leahy fiddled their butts off for her before she went on also helped establish a fiddle *feel* that, although it was more Celtic than country, had a cutting edge aggressiveness that was similar to the playing style of the three fiddle players in Shania's own band.

In 1994, when Mutt had begun to produce Shania's tracks, he had dropped the pedal steel down in the mix. He simply didn't use it as a lead instrument as often as was customary on traditional country records. But he had kept the fiddle prominently up in the mix, especially an aggressive cajun-style fiddle, which often was the defining country element in an otherwise pop production. Having any act that was more country than Shania as an opener would merely serve to point out to people how pop Shania was. Because Leahy wasn't really country at all, they served a more functional purpose of actually making Shania sound *more* country by comparison. The fact that Leahy was not a pop or rock act, either, proved to be ideal. And it added a flourish of *Riverdance* excitement, just as the cloggers and fiddlers in the video for *Don't Be Stupid (You Know I Love You)* had.

The overall effect of the prominent fiddles throughout the show discouraged critics and fans alike from thinking they were at a heavy metal country performance, although, for much of the evening, they were. People had come to accept Garth's heavy metal shows. They didn't seem to mind Tim McGraw's approach, either. However, there was no telling in advance what attitude they might take toward a woman doing the same thing. Look what had happened when Shania had worn a tank top and a denim vest in her first two videos from THE WOMAN IN ME.

During the weeks in which she rehearsed her show with her new band, Shania rose early and roamed the grounds of her secluded estate near St. Regis

Falls in the Adirondacks. Within the grounds, which were surrounded by a high fence and an electronic security gate, she was safe enough, but at least one of her dogs would be with her whenever she went further afield. From the cozy interior of the studio and apartment complex, she could look out over a small lake to where a rustic unpaved road wound its way into the inviting stands of thick forest. Outside, she savored the natural soundscape, the nearly noiseless early morning air disturbed only now and then by the cry of a bird, a bark from one of the dogs, or a hissing snort of one of the horses. It was something you could breathe in and let out again. She would spend some time with her horses even if she did not intend to ride that morning. Here, she felt at peace with the world, at home, or almost at home, because this wilderness was not all that far from the hustle of big city life, not nearly as remote as her northern wilderness, the wilderness she had carried in her heart ever since she had moved south to take her music to the world. There was wildness here but it was contained and vulnerable to intrusion. There was mist rising from the lake, though. The fragrant aroma of woodstove smoke. The trees breathed and sighed when they were caressed by the wind. She could feel her spiritual connection to the earth here.

If she rose early enough, she would just be coming back from the stables when the 'Twain Zone' personnel would begin to wonder where she was. Each morning, her new bus stood ready to carry her into Lake Placid for the rehearsal. Rehearsals were going well, but there were new hurts to absorb as well as triumphs to be felt when the music felt right. Two weeks earlier, John Derek had passed away. Bo Derek had called with the sad news and she had shared her friend's grief over the telephone, carried it with her in her heart, although she had braved it out during that day's full rehearsal.

On days when Shania wasn't rehearsing, she could canoe or swim or go hiking. She has an adventurous spirit and she loves to be outdoors. "I do very daring things with my horse," she told Susan Poharski. "We jump trees; I've seen bears on our trails. It's pretty scary, because I go by myself a lot of the time, but it's exciting not to know what's around the corner."

In addition to excitement, Shania found the Adirondacks with their densely forested slopes and cold mountain lakes to be a strangely spiritual retreat where she could step outside her door without a care in the world. Here, her horses, dogs and friends did not expect her to be 'Shania, the Covergirl Superstar'. Here, she was merely Eileen, the denim-clad person who roamed around the acreage with the assurance of an old hand and the wide-eyed wonder of a greenhorn. Here she could shovel horse manure and clean out her horses' stalls because someone had to do it. And she could smile when she remembered that few of the journalists believed that she really did do it. She had made discoveries here, however, that were as much to do with smelling manure as they were to do with keeping her ears wide open and her spirit as free as was humanly possible. Here, she could manage all of that and continue to discover new songs, even if her efforts to tell people from the outside world about her revelations fell far short of the immediate experience.

"There's a certain mystique about these mountains," she confided to Michael Bane, a journalist who showed up one day while she was rehearsing in Lake Placid. "The fog in the morning; the clarity that you have during the day. The lakes are kind of mysterious — not as panoramic as what you have up in the Rockies. But mysterious, with a haunting calm about it. And the loon adds to the whole thing . . . They sound like a flute. When a loon cries out — and it has several different cries — it echoes throughout the foothills. It's a cry, too — not like a regular bird. And it sounds like someone has an echo-effect on these things, a very throaty, very full-bodied sounding . . . flute." She was not always successful at convincing the journalists to hang around long enough to hear a loon. She had come to accept that. And she had learned to cherish her early morning moments before anyone else was stirring. Soon enough, once she began to tour, there would be too many mornings when she would awaken to unfamiliar horizons with no chores to do at all. No fog rising from any lake.

One morning, a little later than usual, when she poked her head into the bus, a reporter from *Rolling Stone* magazine, Erik Hedegaard, was there. His presence was no more of an intrusion than any of the people who were invited there to her home, but it meant that the world was now listening in to every little thing she said. Every gesture she made could be reported. Erik would need to report the details. It was what good journalists did. The ones who said, "Just the facts, m'am," like Joe Fridays intent on carrying out an interrogation, often missed the details altogether. But the good ones noticed everything. Looking out the window of the bus, as the greenness of the forest flashed by, she gathered her thoughts.

"Pleasantly, she settled in," Hedegaard later reported, "and began to give an accounting of herself as, among other things, a simple Canadian girl from a rugged gold-mining city called Timmins, in the frozen reaches of Ontario, 500 miles beyond Toronto. She was a shy teenager, a little at odds with her sexuality, even angry at times over the unwanted attention of boys. She said she preferred not to think of herself as a country artist or a pop artist but, simply, as an artist who had done 'whatever it took to get work.' She said that for as long as she could remember, she had but one dream. 'My goal has always been to be international,' she said. 'It's what I've always wanted right from the start.' To that end, she wrote songs that were clever and decidedly commercial and used her looks to give them visual punch, and she made no apologies for either."

Rolling Stone is noted for excellent journalism, and Erik Hedegaard did not let the editors of the magazine down. His story is among the clearest portraits painted of Shania since she had first become known to the world at large. Readers of the magazine appreciated this accurate reporting of her situation, although in other quarters the very fact that she was "on the cover of *Rolling Stone*" was bandied about for entirely spurious reasons. Nevertheless, it was a landmark for a country artist to be featured on the cover of the respected rock magazine, the first time since Dolly Parton had been featured on the cover nearly 20 years ago that a country woman had made the cut. Of course, it also acknowledged, as Shania was now doing in her interviews, that she had crossed over to becoming not merely a pop-country crossover artist but an international star. It was what she had always wanted to be.

Then in April 1998, Shania appeared in the VH1 Special "Divas Live" with Aretha Franklin, Celine Dion, Mariah Carey, and Carole King. Journalists began to refer to her as a 'Country Diva'. The designation suited her. She was not merely the next Queen of Country Music. She was more. She was something new.

On May 29, 1998, Shania Twain launched her long-awaited world tour from northern Ontario in the city of Sudbury, near Timmins, where as a child she had sung in rural dance halls, hotel beer parlors, and senior citizens homes. Kicking off her tour in Toronto's Skydome might have been more lucrative, but her decision was made for well-thought out reasons. The head offices of the Canadian subsidiary of Shania's Mercury Nashville label were located in Toronto, but she had not done business with a Canadian label. She had "made it" in Nashville. Although as a teenager Shania had appeared on national radio and television shows broadcast from Toronto and had even lived there for while in the 1980s, her heart was with the hard-core fans found in the mining and logging communities that dot the Canadian Shield who had followed her career since the 1970s, long before she ever entered a recording studio. For these fans, she was willing to forego the obvious prestige of beginning her tour in the big smoke. In fact, she did not play Toronto until several months down the road.

Shania would have taken her maiden arena performance right back to her home town, to Timmins itself, but the local arena was simply too small. Nearby

Sudbury would have to do, with two shows scheduled in a hockey arena seating 6,000. Despite the $42.50 price tag for a ticket, some 5,000 Timmins residents made plans to head south down Highway 144 for the overnight excursion.

After the wall of controversy that had built up during Shania's supersonic ascent to the top of the country music sales charts, the sonic boom that announced her arrival on the touring circuit was far louder than the thunderous applause in Sudbury itself. As Shania traveled west across Canada, playing Edmonton, Saskatoon, Calgary, and Vancouver, before heading into Washington State, reviewers' reports were awaited with the same intense anticipation that speculators await the opening of trading on the New York Stock Exchange. The world wanted to see if Shania would stumble and fall as her detractors had predicted, or if she would prove to be as exceptional at entertaining as she already was at selling records. As show after show drew the highest accolades and journalists thumbed through their pocket Thesaurus pages in search of fresh superlatives, there seemed to be no doubt about it. Shania could deliver the goods on stage. In fact, her shows might even be better than her records. By the time that she arrived in Calgary, the word was out — Shania Twain was nothing short of spectacular in concert.

Critics who had panned Twain's 1995 release THE WOMAN IN ME had watched that album go on to become the biggest ever by a woman. She had proven detractors wrong in the past. So, some writers were cautious in their reports, especially those who wrote for Nashville publications where reaction to her collaborations with Mutt had fueled most of the controversy. *Tennessean* staff writer Tom Roland was in Sudbury, where he filed a review titled "Twain Concert: 'The Singer in Me.'" His report began, "O.K., her detractors can now stop questioning Shania's singing ability. . . . It is not perfect. Nor was the show. But both were good enough to solidify her as a talent to be envied. . . . Throughout most of the show, Twain held her own vocally, particularly admirable since her more than three years off the road have no doubt left her a bit rusty in front of an audience. As a result, she was subpar on three different numbers." Roland complained that Twain's "pitch was simply shaky" on *Come On Over*. Keeping pitch and staying in tune is tough during a stadium show. During her four-song showcase at the Venom club in London, England, in the summer of 1995, Shania had stopped her band for a moment following the intro of *The Woman In Me* because one of the guitars was seriously out of tune. She knew that she and her band would be held accountable if they soured any of the notes that night — they were playing to an audience of critics and industry people in a small venue. During her arena shows, she did not stop when problems arose, and pitch corrections were an ongoing process. Any musician who has sweated it out under the sweltering glare of stage lighting will tell you that changing temperatures and stage gymnastics play havoc with the tuning of their string instruments, though online guitar tuners have made the process more graceful because the instrument is tuned to a strobing pattern of lights, and, with the volume control turned down, the audience is unaware that these pitch corrections are going on. Guitar techs are ready to hand you a freshly tuned guitar whenever you break or shred a string, and prepare for each instrument switch, from acoustic to electric, from mandolin to fiddle (as Shania's bandmembers were doing).

Creative Artists Agency's Ron Baird had told Tom Roland that skeptics would not be a factor once the tour got started. "Most of that cynicism," said Baird, "has come from non-fans and industry types. I don't think the fans have any doubt or worry about her ability to sing. They'll be very pleased when they see the show." Baird's words were prophetic. Several reviewers of the early tour shows glimpsed the direction Shania was headed. *Ottawa Citizen* staff-writer Norman Provencher, in his May 29th preview, "Shaniamania," was likely the first journalist to apply the Beatle-like slogan to the tour, taking his cue from the local karaoke contest held in both Timmins and Sudbury to select two winners to sing with Shania on stage and a rehearsal he attended where a hastily assembled choir of nine young women struggled to perfect both the slow, shorter version of *God Bless The Child*, and the quicker-paced video version, because no one had been able to tell them which one they would sing with Shania on the show. "I really thought this was a huge joke when they first called me," choir-member MacKenzie Hill told Provencher. "I mean, this is the opportunity of a lifetime — and I'm getting it?"

"I haven't stopped smiling since Monday night," Margaret Manchester told Provencher. Winner of the Timmins' karoake-style competition, she didn't know Twain when the singer lived in Timmins but became a fan "as soon as I first heard her first song." Provencher's description of the 25-year-old tanning salon operator's instant celebrity pointed out a key ingredient in the phenomenon. Unable to purchase a ticket, Manchester had entered the contest — and won. She'd won singing before an audience of 150 in the Maple Leaf Hotel in Timmins. How did she feel about singing in front of an audience of 6,000 in Sudbury? "I think I'll be nervous," she told Provencher. "I think I'll be *really* nervous — but I'll do it." "This is completely excellent," 24-year-old Suzanne Nault told Provencher after winning the Sudbury contest. "I've lived here all my life and I really love it here, but you can't really say a lot of things happen here. I couldn't even get tickets. So, winning the contest is beautiful, although I don't know if I'll have the guts to actually sing. I might just faint." This was indeed the opportunity of a lifetime for north Ontarians. "A large part of the attraction," said Jim Hamm, program director for CIGM, the local Sudbury radio station staging the competition, "was that this is Shania Twain country, both because she grew up in Timmins and spent a lot of time in Sudbury, and, because a lot of us like her music."

The next day *Calgary Sun* critic Anika Van Wyk began her report, "Shania-mania has hit this city, but no one is more excited than Shania Twain herself." A rare photo of Robert John "Mutt" Lange and Twain manager Jon Landau accompanied her full-page *Sun* story. Recently converted hockey fan Lange was shown studying the Sudbury Wolves trophy case. Longtime Shania fan Kathy Leger, one of the first to join her fan club, could remember the time Shania had come to Sudbury and performed during an in-store promotion at the Records On Wheels outlet. "There were only 12 of us there," Leger told Anika Van Wyk, "and she sang about half-a-dozen songs acoustically. It was so cool. It was like we were all family." The 45-years-young Leger had stood in line for 16 hours in the rain to get her tickets to the arena show.

Calgary Herald music critic James Muretich was in Sudbury for the opening show, too. "Before a devoted crowd from Sudbury and her nearby home of Timmins," he reported, "every little move Twain made was magic. And if there were any jitters, the well-rehearsed superstar didn't display them during her slick show. She waved at a woman she knew in the audience, had a local woman join her for a duet, and another one draw ticket stubs so that two winners could move from their back row seats to the front row of the arena. For any doubting Thomases, Twain proved she's got great vocal chops." Muretich had correctly gauged the situation in Sudbury when he wrote, "Twain says that opening her tour in Sudbury, so close to her home of Timmins and with more than 50 family members in town (not to mention her dog and her horse) has given her a strong sense of security." As Shania also told Muretich, "I feel the greatest support here. I feel that I'm among friends." Shania was anxious "put to rest the ignorance that I'm not a live performer. I'll be relieved when people finally understand that it's the studio, television and videos that are new to me — not this." Muretich concluded with a prediction that paraphrases Chuck Berry's song *Roll Over Beethoven*, the Beatles' record that had introduced Beatlemania to the world in 1963. "If anything, she seemed to be genuinely enjoying herself performing in front of a 'home' audience and, at long last, removing doubts that she was just a video recording star and not a concert contender. She is. Move over Garth Brooks and tell Nashville the news."

Anika Van Wyk was equally enthusiastic. "When the applause reached a fever pitch," Van Wyk reported, "Twain skipped to the front of the stage and screamed, 'Let's Go, Sudbury!' and went right into *Man! I Feel Like A Woman!* Despite the cold steel-gray stage and overhangs that looked like snow and ice dripping from a roof, Twain heated up the stage with her smile, hip swings, and, of course, that world-famous belly-button. Wearing track pants, platform sneakers and a short metallic top, she looked like a sexier, more sophisticated version of Sporty Spice." The way Anika saw it, "Shania Twain made history last night. . . . And judging from that debut show, now that this Twain is rolling, there'll be no stopping her." This prediction became fact before the tour left Canada for the first U.S. show in Spokane, Washington.

Tom Roland was not the only Nashville critic to make the trek to Sudbury. Robert K. Oermann was in town, coincidentally promoting the reissue of his book, *Finding Her Voice: The Illustrated History of Women in Country Music*, a ground-breaking publication co-written with his wife, Mary Bufwack, a cultural anthropologist, the first book about country music women to not use the "country gals," "rhinestone cowgirls," and "Opry queens" euphemisms so familiar in country journalism. Without intending to, most writers, myself included, who had commented on country up until the 1993 publication of this book, had fallen in line with that girl singer attitude.

"Historically," Nashville author and journalist, Robert K. Oermann, explained to a reporter from the Canadian Press on the day after Shania Twain's first Sudbury concert, "Canadian country music and pop performers for that matter have been perceived as imitative of (their) United States counterparts. For the first time you have a performer who is not following, not imitating but leading the genre." And for Oermann, "one of the most significant things about Shania Twain is the fact that she is breaking rules. . . . Her polished, intimate show may have put to rest allegations, fostered mainly in Nashville's heartland, about her ability to perform live. But Twain's triumph is also a shot fired across the bow of the country establishment." During his time in Canada, he also told *Edmonton Journal* writer Alan Kellogg, "If nothing else country has always reflected the times. Shania has taken these elements of new country, added dance-club savvy and an unprecedented technological edge, so crisp, to the recordings. She's got little kids up on stage with her doing the shows, the middle-aged housewives, the whole thing. I don't find it off-putting. I find her just presenting another option. I get irritated at the rock critics who sneer at all this for not being hip. This stuff is not about hip, it's about inclusionary, making country music for an audience that ranges from six to 60. To attack it because it's commercial is absurd. Of course it's commercial, that's just the point." Like Calgary journalist Anika Van Wyk, Oermann saw Shania's Sudbury performances as a "vindication" when he concluded, "Everything she's done has turned a page and made something new."

Shania was praised for reaching out to touch her audience, for nimbly high-stepping on a treadmill with her three fiddlers, and for winning everyone over with her warmth. The sound was said to be excellent because Mr Mysterious himself, Mutt Lange, was on hand supervising the mixing board in the wings, and because the speaker cabinets were suspended in strategic locations located by the latest laser technology. Leahy drew rave reviews of their own for their step-dancing and fiddling. They were not the usual record label rookies out to prove themselves — they were Celtic maniacs.

The Canadian shows were sold out, a scalper's paradise. Everyone wanted to experience country's enigmatic superstar sensation in action. When Janet E. Williams of *Country Song Roundup* magazine reported on the Canadian stretch of the tour, she sounded as if she was testifying. "It finally happened: Shania Twain has gone on tour! It's a much awaited, highly anticipated occurrence that many country fans feared would never come. But they can relax — or, more likely, rush to the closest ticket outlet once they know Shania's on her way to their town, for a seat at a Shania Twain concert is likely to be the most coveted seat of the year."

An entourage of Canadian and American journalists followed Shania west. In Edmonton, Saskatoon, Calgary, and Vancouver the cast and crew continued refining the Shania show nightly, improving the pacing, staging, and special effects each time Shania went on. The audiences were close to 20,000 screaming fans per night now, and the show was drawing rave reviews from everyone in the press gallery. In Edmonton, where the Shaniamania continued to build, Shania was presented with an Edmonton Oilers' jersey. The number 98 on the back referred to her 1998 tour, but it was also the ultimate Alberta-style tribute: she was now playing in the same league as number 99, the Great One — Wayne Gretsky. At the Edmonton concert, the *Calgary Sun*'s Lisa Hepfner became an early tour fashion commentator: "Shania came out in a purple top that might well have come from a scuba shop. Her midriff was bare. Her black pants flared out at the bottom with two purple stripes down each leg. Her sneakers were big-soled and gray. Later, she changed into a tight, white, half-shirt and gold lamé vest with tight vinyl pants. Her long, reddish-brown locks were pinned on top with two long tendrils flanking her face." The Twain was comin' down the track and it was gathering steam at each whistle stop along the way. Back in Calgary to file a preview for the two Saddledome shows in the *Calgary Herald*, James Muritech wrote that even though Calgary Mayor Al Duerr had not proclaimed an official "Shania Twain Day," as the mayor of Sudbury had, "every day is Shania Twain Day whenever she's in town, whatever town she's in." Anika Van Wyk's Saddledome preview in the *Calgary Sun* bore the title: "Vindication!" The *Sun* ran a color poster of Twain. "Heck, even veteran music promoter Ron Sakamoto, president of Gold & Gold and five-time winner of the Canadian Country Music Award for promoter of the year, has caught Shania Fever," Van Dyck wrote. "'This is a part of history. It is a privilege to be a part of it,' said Sakamoto, who is presenting the shows across the country. 'She bares her soul out there and it's all her. It's an awesome show! For your entertainment value, this is just as much as Garth.'"

As the Shania Twain Experience headed south into the bigger U.S. market, which had for so long eluded Canadian women who sang country and yearned to become a headliner in the stadiums and arenas across of the border, a buzz of excitement preceded her. Shania's shows were frequently compared to Garth Brooks' concerts, and fans eagerly snapped up tickets with an appetite that before this time had only been inspired by pop divas like Whitney Houston, Janet Jackson, Celine Dion, and Madonna. Sales of both of Twain's critically acclaimed albums, THE WOMAN IN ME and COME ON OVER, continued their unprecedented record-setting pace. Six months after its release, COME ON OVER eased its way back into the number one spot on the *Billboard* country albums chart, a position it would occupy off and on during the next two years.

As the tour headed down the West Coast, a few critics sniped at Shania, now and then, but all commentators were compelled to admit that the Canadian country rocker's fans embraced her performances 100 percent. Neva Chomin's *San Francisco Chronicle* review of Shania's show at the Shoreline Amphitheater bore the title, "Twain Makes Mark on Adoring Fans." "The crowd," Chomin wrote, "a mix of burly truckers, suburban cowboys and their bottle blonde babes, and families of gum-chewing kids — was up and dancing through most of the set. . . . Twain quieted the crowd by sitting on a stool to deliver a medley of syrupy ballads, including *You're Still The One*. For all their treacle, such moments spotlighted the singer's connection to her audience. . . . Near the close of the two-hour show, a young girl presented Twain with a pink rose. The singer responded by bringing the eight-year-old onstage for a duet of *I'm Holding On To Love*." San José reporter Michael D. Clark reviewed the same show for the *San Jose Mercury News*. He found the acoustic set even more enjoyable. "Sitting on a bar stool, guitar in hand," he wrote, "Twain sang and strummed a note-perfect rendition of her latest hit *You're Still The One* demonstrating how effortlessly she shifts to lite-rock."

Three days later, *Orange County Register* reporter Gene Harbrecht wrote, "The Grand Ole Opry never sounded like this. O.K., so Shania Twain never pretended to be a traditional country act, but she makes pop country queen Reba McEntire sound like Loretta Lynn. However, that didn't seem to matter to a capacity audience at Arrowhead Pond on Sunday as Twain delivered two hours of mostly driving rock & roll in a performance that was more Patti Smith than Patty Loveless. Even the crowd was classic crossover, with young and middle-age country clad folks peering somewhat askance at boppers and headbangers." *L.A. Times* critic Robert Hilburn reviewed the same show. "She disproved those conspiracy theories with such ease Sunday at the Arrowhead Pond that it was only fitting that she was carried around the arena like a triumphant gladiator near the end of the two-hour set. Appearing confident and comfortable during this early stop on her first North American tour . . . Twain showed she could handle all the notes with ease and that the beauty in the videos wasn't just built around careful camera angles."

By late June, the Shania Show was in Milwaukee. Each success along the tour continued to build expectations higher and higher. Journalists noted that her Detroit show had sold out in record time: 15,000 tickets in less than half an hour. *Milwaukee Journal Sentinel* pop music critic Dave Tianen gave his full-page spread the title, "Twain Sets a New Tone," while his subtitle exclaimed, "There's nothing submissive about this independent country babe!" For his Garth-Shania comparison, Tianen quoted an explanation that *Dreaming Out Loud* author Bruce Feiller had told him: "Garth paved the way for the hunky movement in Nashville. Garth also brought rock & roll theatrics to Nashville and savvy marketing. He got the baby boomers. I think the women were probably there, but Shania gave them a role model. These women weren't responding to Wynonna and Trisha Yearwood and Pam Tillis. She brought in a new, young audience. The way it's spoken of in Nashville is, she brought in the babysitting money." When it came time to refute the naysayers, Tianen quoted WMIL-FM program director

Kerry Wolfe: "The formula has been that you get a record contract, move to Nashville, write with all the same people and end up sounding like everybody else. Shania is different . . . She didn't go out there and pay her dues doing 20 minutes before Reba as an opening act. Why should she have? She was selling 20 million albums anyway." Tianen continued, "Feiler's description of Twain's sound as country dance music is apt, but incomplete. There are elements, such as the weeper *Home Ain't Where His Heart Is (Anymore)*, which could have fit easily in a Tammy Wynette album. There are occasional fiddles and pedal steel guitars but country is but one of a myriad of influences on her. The encore of *Any Man Of Mine* roars with a guitar riff that is light years closer to Jimmy Page than Chet Atkins. *Rock This Country* is just what the title implies. *No One Needs To Know* is cheery country pop. During *Don't Be Stupid*, she was joined by her opening act the traditional family band Leahy. As much as anything, the notion that Twain would pick a largely unknown Celtic band to open her tour says volumes about her disdain for musical categories. Production-wise the show is very much an extension of the arena rock theatrics that Garth Brooks introduced to country in the '90s; big projection screens, fireworks, multiple costume changes, head mikes to allow the star to roam all over the stage. At one point she disappears in a cloud of smoke and on another she plunges into the crowd carried aloft by security men to press the flesh. Of course, none of the high tech production would particularly matter if Twain was the wooden diva at the center. Fortunately, she's a vibrant, flirtatious, open-hearted, high energy, immensely likeable entertainer. Twain's music isn't devoid of interest, but to truly appreciate her gifts, you need to see her in concert."

While reviewing the show for the *Denver Post*, Eric L. Reiner was caught up in the audience's enthusiasm. "Twain — her to-die-for physique displayed in tight pants and a silvery cropped top — boarded a small platform that security guards hoisted above their heads and carried into the crowd. How did the folks handle seeing the stunning singer up close? The guys were, well, guys. When Twain removed a jeans jacket and flung it into the throng, men fought each other for a piece of her clothing. Women also embraced Twain, as if saluting her at leveraging her beauty. As Twain paraded by, a Littleton woman remarked, 'If you've got it, flaunt it. I would, too.'" As Reiner commented, "Adoration from all quarters of society — not a bad end to a hungry child's story."

By September, Shania's tour bus was rolling through Texas on the way to her Friday, September 25th show at the Gaylord Entertainment Center in Nashville, the home arena for the Nashville Predators hockey team, when she took a call on her cellular phone from Tom Roland. Roland had already blocked out some of the text for his preview story, "Shimmy, Shake, Hear the Earth Quake," which would run in *The Tennessean*, with the subtitle, "Any audience of Shania's will walk the line, pulled in by her energetic delivery."

During their conversation, Tom and Shania debated the issues raised by her flamboyant photo on the cover of the September 3rd, 1998 issue of *Rolling Stone* magazine, a shot of the singer standing in a field in Ohio with a wispy scarf draped across her bosom, her navel proudly displayed several inches above the low-cut waistline of her form-fitting stretch-velour pants. "There's absolutely nothing revealing about that photograph," Shania told Tom. "It isn't revealing at all. It's even less revealing than if I was in a bathing suit top. There's zero cleavage. There's absolutely nothing showing."

This friendly banter between the two led Roland to write, "Twain admits she's walking a very fine line. But she feels strongly that she's remained on the side of acceptability. The difference, she says, is the difference between sensuality and sexuality, between suggesting and revealing. 'There's nothing wrong with a suggestion,' she defends. 'I almost find that sexier. If you look at all the old movies (it's) almost more exciting to watch people almost kiss than it is now to watch movies where they're just naked all over the place. That's what I'm drawn to. I think that's more sensual, and it's more decent.'"

This same wholesome attitude had endeared Julia Roberts — who had become famous playing a street prostitute with a heart of gold in the feature film *Pretty Woman* — and Shania Twain — who had become famous for displaying her belly-button while dancing to the beat of her music in her videos — to a demographically diverse group of fans during the 1990s. Both stars walked the line between sensuality and sexuality, managing to do so with an admirable sense of self-dignity. They were hot properties because they acknowledged their femininity and celebrated their womanhood yet had a sense of decency that had all but disappeared from the entertainment realm before they came along.

Looking back at the May shows in Sudbury, Roland was now openly enthusiastic. "Twain does play up her physique in concert. At that Sudbury gig, she wore three different shrink-wrapped outfits. But it didn't overshadow the music. Neither did the production elements: a few gadgets, loads of audience interaction and plenty of movement. Toward the end of that tour-opening show, she admitted to the crowd that the evening taxed her physically. 'I thought I was in shape for this, but, whew, you guys are giving off a lot of energy.' Four months later, Twain still isn't comfortable doing the entire show. Now, however, it's on purpose. 'It's almost like I have to be slightly out of breath and really hot and worked up to enjoy it. It just wouldn't feel exciting otherwise.'" When Roland asked her to assess her performance on stage, she replied, "If I wanted to get a perfect vocal — not miss a beat, not miss a word, not miss a note — I wouldn't be able to be as energetic as I am onstage. It's a bit of a compromise, but there's no way I could get up there night after night and not give an energetic performance."

Two days before her arena show in Nashville, Shania was scheduled to make an appearance on the Country Music Association's 32nd Annual Awards show. Since 1995, she had used this opportunity to make an indelible impression on the television audience; there was no chance, it seemed, that she would make any impression at all on the voting members of the association. This year she had been shut out of the nominations in all but one category, album of the year. In 1995, she had swung down the aisle of the Opryland Theater and saucily delivered her signature tune *Any Man Of Mine*. In 1996, she had performed the full-length version of *God Bless The Child* with a team of male dancers and the renowned gospel group Take Six. In 1997, she had debuted the lead single from the soon to be released COME ON OVER, performing *Love Gets Me Everytime* for CBS network viewers, which propelled the single to the top of the chart. For the 1998 CMA show, Shania had something entirely different in mind. She was merely drawing upon her past experience with the "Viva Las Vegas" show in Deerhurst and creating mini-Vegas events for the Nashville awards show appearances, which were choreographed and staged to stand out in people's memories from the usual stand-by-your microphone and sing-through-your-nose performances.

Shania's performance of *Honey, I'm Home* on the 1998 CMA Awards show was designed to let the world (and Nashville) know that she was alive and well on the tour circuit. As Shania took the CMA Awards show stage that night, a river of Nashville high-school students streamed up there to join her. Having gathered these youthful participants to her bosom, so to speak, as if she were a female incarnation of the fabled Pied Piper, Shania and her troupe proceeded to blow everyone's mind with her good, clean, fun approach to rocking the country world. The fact that Shania was clothed in a costume that more resembled someone working out to one of Jane Fonda's exercise tapes than a rhinestone cowgirl opened a lot of eyes. This loud and enthusiastic display of rowdy behavior ended with pyrotechnic eruptions that were obviously stadium show style fireworks precisely cued for maximum drama. The effect was so dazzling, so different from the usual CMA show fare, that awards show host Vince Gill was moved to quip, "That was Shania Twain with *Honey, I'm Deaf . . .*"

Backstage, Shania told a reporter from *Country Weekly* magazine, "I wanted to take some of my live performance and show it here tonight. I wanted to have that same live energy. In every city that I perform in, I bring up a high-school chorus and drum corps. I also bring up a guest singer — usually a teenager, but sometimes as young as eight years old. Being on the road touring is easier than anything I could do. It's funny because I'm sure everybody was waiting for me to drop dead after the first month, but it's a lot easier than promotional stuff where you're on a plane twice a day — long, long, long, long days. Instead, I go onstage for two hours and have a great time. How hard can that be?"

Earlier that same month, Shania had made a similarly spectacular appearance when she had performed this same song on the Canadian Country Music Awards show in Calgary and walked away with six CCMA awards. Her performance had been broadcast throughout North America, live by CTV, and a week later on TNN, and, in Europe, Japan, and Australia by CMT. When viewers tuned in to her performance video of *Honey, I'm Home* on CMT, they saw her dressed in the *same* outfit, form-fitting athletic wear — short sleeveless top and full-length pants — that she wore for both Awards shows. And they saw the Shaniamania that was breaking out everywhere she performed. Everyone in the audience was singing along, high-fiving Shania — they had spontaneously become her backup singers, and they were all in her video.

3
COUNTRY DIVA

THIS REITERATION OF SHANIA'S IMAGE, re-enforced everywhere fans turned, was especially effective and served her very well when it came to selling tickets and records and perhaps even winning awards. After a break for Christmas, some time spent in Miami filming the CBS Special *Shania Twain's Winter Break* with Elton John and the Backstreet Boys, and a detour through Australia, Shania began the second leg of her North American tour. Flanked by Whitney Houston, Mariah Carey, Jewel, Madonna, and Celine Dion, Shania appeared on the cover of *People* magazine in January 1999 under the title, "The New Pop Divas: They Have Chefs, Masseuses, and Private Shoppers. Here's How Today's Singing Superstars Play, Work — and Spend!" At the Grammys in February 1999, Shania led a contingent of Canadian stars who were nominated for an unprecedented 27 awards. She won two Grammys, the first for best country single, the second for best country vocal performance for *You're Still The One*. She would also accept trophies at the *Billboard* Awards, the American Music Awards, and from VH1 whose viewers voted *You're Still The One* the sexiest VH1 video of the year. In April, at the Academy Of Country Music Awards in L.A., she accepted two Diamond Records from special presenter Dick Clark, which acknowledged that both THE WOMAN IN ME *and* COME ON OVER had surpassed the 10 million mark in sales.

By this time, it had become obvious to everyone that Garth Brooks was not the only country artist on the planet who was maximizing his record sales via skillfully executed marketing strategies. A few weeks before Shania Twain had begun her triumphant march across the continent in May 1998, Canadian magazine publisher Larry Delaney had predicted in *Country Music News* that Shania was about to launch the "concert tour of the century." At that time in early 1998, few people were prepared to believe Delaney was serious in making such a statement. Garthzilla was still the King. Whitney Houston was the boss diva. Madonna was the fearless female leader, a dominatrix diva who had revolutionized herself several times over — as the material girl, as Eva Peron (the world's first female dictator) on the silver screen, and now as a proud mom. Madonna had negotiated herself into the smartest artist-label-management deal of all time. She had taken womens' rights issues where they had never gone before, all the way into the decision-making corporate boardrooms of the rock world, and she had won a huge victory without compromising her artistic integrity one iota.

Madonna made dance music respectable in the '80s, but perhaps her most important contribution has been to demonstrate that women can direct their sexuality in their public life and performances without fear of losing their self-esteem. Her acting roles in films such as A League Of Their Own have furthered the establishment of women's rights without mounting protest demonstrations.

Aretha Franklin was in a league of her own, a major, major artist in the '60s when she introduced her souled-out gospel approach to rock & roll. She began the decade working with John Hammond at Columbia Records and scored a minor hit in 1961 with Rock-A-Bye Your Baby With A Dixie Melody. When she switched labels from Columbia to Atlantic mid-decade and began to work with Jimmy Drexler, his rocking arrangements of Respect, A Natural Woman, and Chain Of Fools were the perfect vehicle to launch a superstar career. Aretha has been an awesome presence ever since, the all-time Queen of Soul who definitely has her priorities straight. "We are women first, and artists second," she told Cosmopolitan.

Madonna had opened Pandora's box and begun a women's revolution that had turned the music business upside down. Women were selling more records than they ever had before. Worldwide, Celine Dion had sold an impressive 60 million records in a mere 30 months; in the U.S. alone, she had sold 28 million albums. U.S. album sales for Madonna totalled 46 million albums, for Whitney Houston, 45 million, and Mariah Carey, 44 million. Women ruled the pop world.

Nashville represented the final frontier, the last bastion of entrenched patriarchal control. Shania had issued the first challenge. She had breezed by Patsy Cline to become the all-time record-holder for sales of a single country album by a woman. She had begun to rival Garth, as far as selling records went, but she was not seriously considered as a threat to out-do him when it came to touring. Garth had grossed more than $50 million in his first five years. He had staged the largest country concert of all time when he took country to New York City where 250,000 fans had stormed into Central Park one summer night in

1997. (Garth had enthusiastically told his audience, during the show, that there were 900,000 people there, but police estimates were closer to the quarter-million mark.) His 32-month world tour had wound down during 1998 but not before he had sold more than five million tickets.

At the end of 1998, when attendance and ticket sales figures were tabulated, Shania Twain had eclipsed them all — all of the acts that toured during the year, including the hat acts, pop divas, country queens, and teen sensations. She had grossed $35 million ($3 million more than Janet Jackson's Velvet Rope Tour) on ticket sales alone, and entertained more than one million concert-goers. By the time that sales of Shania's COME ON OVER had hit the 17 million mark in North America, she had surpassed sales marks set by Mariah Carey, Alanis Morissette, *and* Garth Brooks. COME ON OVER was now the top-selling album by a woman *and* the top-selling country album of all time. International sales were more than 10 million. She was now tied with the Beatles' *White Album* and the sound track to *The Bodyguard*. Only the Eagles, Michael Jackson, Led Zeppelin, and Fleetwood Mac had sold more copies of a record. She was the first country artist to be listed in the Top 10 on the *Billboard* chart for internet sales. She had performed at the Nobel Peace Prize ceremonies in Sweden and at the Amnesty International Peace Prize Concert in Paris. The most telling incident came a few months before she taped her CBS Special, *Shania's Winter Break*. When Elton John ran into Shania backstage at a radio station, he knew who she was. "He started singing *You're Still The One* to me, right off the bat," she told Brian Mansfield. "I was so flattered that he knew who I was and that he knew my song." If Sir Elton knew your song by memory, there was no doubt about it, you had arrived on the international scene. Only Elvis and the Beatles had been played more on the radio during the modern rock era than the artist previously known as Reggie Dwight. Soon after this, Elton invited Shania to record *Something About The Way You Look Tonight* for his Aida project.

Now that Shania had taken North America (and then Nashville) by storm, she set out to establish her career internationally. When the international mixes of COME ON OVER were released as a separate album, reviewers often took the easy way out and told the readers that Mutt Lange had cut the 'country' elements back or out of Shania's music for this market. There was a little more to it than that. One significant difference between the U.S. release of COME ON OVER, the International release, and the later North American version of the International mixes is the lineup of the tracks. *You're Still The One*, bumped to the lead off position, came into focus at the very time it was being released as a single. The former lead off tracks, *Man! I Feel Like A Woman, I'm Holding On,* and *Love Gets Me Everytime,* were pushed back to make way for upcoming single releases. The overall effect was that you were listening to a new album, and, with some of the re-mixes, you were. Releasing dance mix versions of tracks had given pop artists an edge for several years. Shania and Mercury Nashville were merely taking advantage of this previously unexplored territory for country artists. Country fans were not raising a hue and cry of protest. In fact, Shania's dance mixes were enormously popular in country nightclubs.

Surprisingly, one of the most impartial reviews of the international version of COME ON OVER (when the North American CD of these mixes was released in January 2000) appeared in *Country Weekly,* a country fanzine. "The 16 million fans who purchased Shania's COME ON OVER," wrote Gerry Wood, "will find familiar songs here, but in unfamiliar settings: jived up instrumental surges, boisterously layered background vocals and Euro-tinged production values. One thing that doesn't change is Shania's sensational singing, as she reaches for an even wider audience." Wood's endorsement went right to the heart of the magazine's readership. "Country fans ought not be afraid of venturing into this brave new world of Shania songs," he continued. "That familiar voice is still there. This time it's demonstrating just how flexible and multi-talented she can be. Musically, there's so much going on around the vocals, most singers would get pinned within these walls of sound. Not Shania. She shows the global village something that her country fans have known for seven years. The reigning CMA Entertainer of the Year is one heck of a talent. Country Shania or pop Shania. Take your pick. The Twain meet here."

A poster of Shania soon showed up on a wall in the syndicated comic strip *Nancy* on the same day in March 1999 that CBS aired *Shania Twain's Winter Break* featuring Elton John and the Backstreet Boys. Country comedian Cletus T. Judd had spoofed her with his tribute recording *If Shania Were Mine.* "Shania Twin," a tribute band featuring Shania-look-alike Donna Huber, had been on the road touring the A-club circuit in Canada since 1996, a trivia item that might go down in the *Guinness Book of Records* because it had come far sooner than it had taken for the first Elvis impersonator to show up during the King's illustrious career. When Shania told an interviewer that her secret beauty aid was an animal remedy called "Bag Balm," feed stores and other outlets sold out of the greasy ointment overnight. Sales of Revlon products were not as brisk.

Shania's deal with Revlon came about as a result of her bold appearance on the 1999 Grammys show performing *Man! I Feel Like A Woman!* Revlon Canada General Manager Cynthia Passmore-McLaughlin told a reporter from the *Ottawa Citizen* that "the song fit perfectly with Revlon's message to women." An L.A. photo shoot with famed fashion photographer Herb Ritts would feature her lips for the product pitch of ColorSay Liquid Lip. "She has great lips," Passmore-McLaughlin confided. The working agreement between the singer and the cosmetics firm would run for 12 months. Neither the video for the song nor the television ads that Revlon aired had much to do with Nashville at all, although cross-dressing might be viewed as a rules violation on Music Row where there were so many unwritten rules of conduct that it was difficult for an outsider to know what would offend and what would not.

During the years Eileen Twain emerged from her Canadian heritage to become Shania Twain in Nashville, Eileen, like kd lang before her, began to shed the provincial Canadian country trappings that had shaped her as if they were merely an old wardrobe. When she met and married Mutt Lange, Shania became a player on the international scene and, once again, began to shed the trappings of the Nashville scene. She was "movin' on," as Hank Snow had so aptly put it in song. Snow himself had moved on from his Canadian birthplace in Liverpool, Nova Scotia, to a career as one of country music's top all-time achievers. He had discovered Elvis but was aced out of working with Presley by Colonel Tom Parker who slyly signed the King to a personal services contract that fell outside the mandate of his association with Snow. However, as a recording artist and performer Hank Snow was one of the best — the 20th most-played country artist of all-time. From the moment his breakout single *I'm Movin' On* became a number one smash till his death at the ripe old age of 85 in December 1999, he made his home in Nashville. By the time she packed up her tent and moved on to Lake Geneva, Shania had begun to rival Elvis. She rocked country music's very foundations when she belted out her "Shake, shimmy, make the earth quake" lyrics, the 1990s equivalent of "Shake, rattle and roll." Her *That Don't Impress Me Much* came to be "Don't step on my blue suede shoes" for her '90s audience.

Her record sales alone forced people to compare her with Carole King, Mariah Carey, Celine Dion, Whitney Houston, and Alanis Morissette, the other women who had sold more than 10 million copies of a single album. These top-selling women were rare company indeed, and there were some surprising similarities to be found here, there, and everywhere in their lives and careers. For example, three of the six were born in Canada . . . two were born in

New York State . . . and one in nearby New Jersey.

Long before she became a recording artist, Brooklyn born and raised Carole King was immortalized in song by her teenage heart-throb Neil Sedaka. *Oh Carol* was a Top 10 *Billboard* hit in 1959 for Sedaka, and, of course, a tribute to Carol Klein, King's real life persona. The song has an interesting history, not unlike the songwriting 101 processing that Shania Twain has readily admitted she still applies to this day to the hit records of artists like Elton John and Dolly Parton. She takes their hits apart piece by piece to see what makes them tick.

When Neil Sedaka was in college, already a teen sensation with his break out 1958 RCA hit *The Diary*, he decided to analyze the top three hits of the day on all of the charts. Out of this, he came up with a melody and chord structure that he took to his songwriting partner, Howard Greenfield, who was in residence at the same college across the hall from Sedaka. "I ran out and bought each of the three records," Sedaka recalled in his 1982 autobiography, *My Story*, "listening to them over and over again, analyzing what they had in common. I discovered that they had many similar elements: harmonic rhythm, placement of the chord changes, choice of harmonic progressions, similar instrumentation, vocal phrases, drum fills, content, even the timbre of the lead solo voice. I decided to write a song that incorporated all these elements in one record. It took me two and a half hours to write the rough draft of the melody . . . I called Howie . . . and played him the melody. 'I want this to be an ode to my old highschool girlfriend Carol Klein,' I said. "I like the title 'Carol'. Howie wrote the first draft of the lyrics in 20 minutes. I grabbed the pages out of his hand and said, 'There'll be no re-writing, this time.' I liked it, at once. 'Oh, Carol, I am but a fool. Darling, I love you, though you treat me cruel.' 'Neil,' Howie said, 'you've got to be kidding. Let me polish it.' 'This is exactly what I want,' I said. 'A song can be ruined by too much polishing.' "

After being heralded to the world by Neil Sedaka, Carole King went on to meet lyricist Gerry Goffin, whom she married in 1958. Together, they wrote *Will You Love Me Tomorrow, Go Away Little Girl, Take Good Care Of My Baby*, and *The Locomotion*, all number one hits during the '60s for the artists who recorded them, the Shirelles, Steve Lawrence, Bobby Vee, and Little Eva. Eva was the couple's 13-year-old babysitter. Divorced from Goffin in 1968, Carole King was encouraged by James Taylor to write her own lyrics and record her own songs. She followed his advice and became one of the vanguard artists who kicked off the singer-songwriter era, scoring a few hits on Top 40 radio, cuts like *It's Too Late, So Far Away*, and *Sweet Seasons*, but making her presence felt eternally with her best-selling album TAPESTRY, which, at the time Shania Twain released COME ON OVER, had sold 15 million copies.

Celine Dion, like Eileen Regina Edwards Twain, was born poor, the fourteenth child in a musically talented laboring family in Charlemagne, Quebec, on March 30, 1968. Her mother, Therese Dion, pushed her daughter headlong toward a confrontation with René Angelil, renowned producer-manager of Francophone stars René Simard and Ginette Reno. There is a saying, which has proven true many times, "To become a star you need to have a star manager." This is exactly what Therese Dion found for Celine when she sent a gift-wrapped homespun demo tape of her daughter to Angelil. It was also exactly not what Sharon Twain accomplished when she enlisted Mary Bailey to help her daughter, Eileen, find a public.

With Angelil's help, 13-year old Celine Dion rapidly became a best-selling teenage sensation in Quebec — and an international star before she turned 20. This surrogate father-daughter relationship turned to marriage while Dion was in her early twenties. One hurdle that the young Celine and the fatherly René had been challenged to overcome were her incisors, "fangs," as the cruel Quebec radio people chided. Braces, caps, and success silenced her critics and left Celine relatively unscarred, ready to take on the English-speaking world as a young adult during the 1990s. Shania's teeth were fine, but her nose caused John Derek no end of grief when he was first called upon to photograph her in 1994. "It wasn't funny at the time," she later told Erik Hedegaard. "He said, 'Somebody give me a knife, I've got to cut off that nose!'" Mutt Lange fondly calls his wife 'Woody' in reference to Woody Woodpecker. Where John Derek's concern about the appearance of her nose seems to be accentuated in the footage he shot for the first two videos, subsequent camera angles chosen by Charlie Randazzo, Markus Blunder, Steven Goldmann, and Larry Jordan are not. After the 'Boots' video, shots are clipped before her nose becomes a silhouette, or she is shot full-on from much closer proximity. A digital snip in a video editing suite was seemingly far less painful than a nose job courtesy of the blade of a plastic surgeon, even though at the super-expensive per hour rates post-production facilities charged, it was probably more expensive in the long run.

Like Shania Twain's bio, Celine Dion's story is so remarkable that cynics continually search for a dint in their famous smiles. From the time she first launched herself from Quebec to Paris, France, and captivated the French-speaking world, Celine Dion has savored so many international triumphs that singing for the Pope often gets left out of her bio. As a vocalist, she possesses more power and more range than Shania, but Celine's appeal can be linked with Shania's in one important respect: both singers learned at a very young age just how important their audiences were to their performances. To put yourself across to any audience, no matter how large or how small, you had to open your heart and give freely your deepest feelings. Whether the poverty of their childhood was a factor in all of this or not, both talented provincial Canadian singers went on to join the elite pantheon of women artists who have sold 10 million copies of one record.

Squeezed from the loins of Ottawa, the Canadian capital where the Parliament buildings loom like a benign Kremlin over the daily lives of the city's inhabitants, Alanis Morissette suffered the consequences of an equally ambitious Canadian mother, came to believe in her mother's dream, and as a preteen started hawking her first demo tape. At 10 she was a television star. A self-titled early Canadian album for MCA Records was as timid and predictable as Shania's Nashville debut for Mercury Records, though a second Morissette effort in 1992, NOW IS THE TIME, was better, earning her a Juno award as Best New Female Vocalist. A pop diva before her time, she found her own voice in Los Angeles working with Quincy Jones' protegé Glen Ballard on JAGGED LITTLE PILL. Inspired by the same blood, sweat, and fears that had infused the best angry records of Marianne Faithful, Tina Turner, and Tori Amos, she had also inherited some of the liquid lyricism of Joni Mitchell. Her best cuts like *Ironic* and *You Oughta Know* played on the radio in heavy rotation even before she hit the tour circuit, then on tour she became the leading spokesperson for the women's music revolution almost overnight.

Ironically, Alanis' record label — when people got around to checking out the j-card on her CD — was Madonna's Maverick Records. What was refreshingly different about her angry young women's songs was that when she delivered her lyrics and melodies people felt a positive anger, not a bitter cynicism. She wasn't dumping on anyone. Perhaps her most remarkable achievement was that with the help of Madonna's record label and Glen Ballard's studio magic she had bridged the gap between alternative and mainstream and provided feminism a whole new forum. She was unique. There hadn't really been anyone like her on record before this. Her appearance on the international recording scene was an inspiration for many people. As Madonna once put it, "There's a sense of excitement and giddiness in the air around her — like anything's possible, the sky's the limit."

Mariah Carey's bi-racial heritage complicated her Long Island upbringing but enriched her inner self. She grew up a loner but told *People* magazine that "Singing made me feel special." Like Shania Twain's parents, Mariah's parents divorced when she was only three years old. Mariah's mother, Patricia Carey, was both a vocal coach and a performer with the New York City Opera Company. When Mariah graduated from high school, she began to work as a backup singer in New York studios and soon prepared a demo tape of her own material, which she co-wrote with keyboard player Ben Margulies. Mariah was discovered by Sony Records star maker Tommy Mottola who responded to a demo tape handed to him at a party by dance-music artist Brenda K. Starr as he was making his exit. He returned to the party — once he had heard Mariah's cassette on his car stereo — and sought her out. Carey was working as Starr's backup singer at the time, but Mottola soon had her in a studio recording her own hit records. Teamed with keyboardist/producers Walter Afanasieff and David Cole on her early albums, Carey co-wrote and co-produced her own hits. She won her first Grammy in 1991 for her debut album MARIAH CAREY, which yielded four number one hits, including her radio debut, *Visions Of Love*.

Mariah married her mentor, Mottola, in 1993 and divorced him four years later. This marriage brought criticism along with fame, but her incredible seven octave vocal range was ideally suited to the studio magic of the '90s, and her striking beauty and irresistible sensuality fit the music video era better than all of the other artists vying for recognition. At one time, she was accused of being a studio confection, but put her critics to shame with her tour-de-force performance on an MTV Unplugged show. Touring has not been her thing, although more than a decade after her arrival on the scene, she continues to rule as undisputed champion on the music video channels. By 1999, Mariah had logged more number one hits than any recording artist since the Beatles.

Whitney Houston broke onto the charts in 1985 with *You Give Good Love*, which peaked at number 3. Her next seven singles would hit the top of the charts and propel sales of her self-titled debut album to more than 11 million. Sales of the follow-up WHITNEY rose nearly as high, and, in 1992 the soundtrack album THE BODYGUARD sold more than 13 million. At the peak of her career, Whitney's 1992 recording of Dolly Parton's *I Will Always Love You* sold four million singles and hogged the number one spot on the pop charts for a record-setting 14 weeks. Three years later, Mariah Carey's duet *One Sweet Day* with Boys II Men would eclipse this record achievement.

While critics bemoaned Houston's lite-pop style and content, her fans were solidly loyal no matter what moves she made. Her spectacular sales and wide popularity could be attributed in part to record mogul Clive Davis who had worked with Aretha Franklin and Whitney's cousin, Dionne Warwick, among many other success stories over his long career. However, she came by her liquid vocal style honestly. Her mother is renowned gospel artist Cissy Houston. And Whitney's appeal was clearly more than her sensational good looks because she was embraced by a whole generation of women who saw her as an example of what a woman could accomplish if she put her talent to good use in the entertainment marts of the 1980s.

In the 1990s a dent was perceived in Whitney's seemingly untouchable veneer as personal and marital problems surfaced, rendering her vulnerable to the jackals of the tabloid press. Not surprisingly, many of the mainstream critics who had built her up were also poised to bring her down now that signs of mortality were visible. Such is the life of a diva, although few of the women who had been called divas during the '90s felt comfortable with the designation. The term suggested a certain petulance, a definite arrogance, which had been associated with the Opera stars of yesteryear, as well as a luxury lifestyle beyond most people's wildest dreams.

Few journalists wished to paint portraits of these rich and famous "divas" that suggested they were merely the girl next door. Newspapers and magazines sold because writers built their subjects up into larger than life superpeople. So, while the scribes scribbled their speculations, the lives of the stars themselves were often far more normal than the press would have you believe. No doubt, Whitney would weather this storm no matter what bleak future was prophesied in the realm of mere journalism. She was, she had already proven, rather levelheaded. Plus, she had staying power. The same could be said for Carol, Celine, Alanis, Mariah, and Shania.

When these women changed from being mere singers to divas, the public became increasingly interested in everything about them — their clothes, their diet, you name it. In March 1999, *Cosmopolitan* declared Shania their "Fun Fearless Female of the Year," the first time *Cosmo* had so honored a country artist (and an indication that some folks saw the humor in her music). People were curious about her fitness program. Shania confessed all to *Daily Mirror* reporter Nina Myskow. "I'm a sporty type of shape and figure," she told this British interviewer. "Quick, naturally. I'm a very active person. So, I've never had a weight problem. If I'm really active, for example, when I'm on tour and I'm on stage every night for two hours, I have to eat more. Not just more. I actually have to raise my fat content. I have to add dairy to my diet. Oh yeah, I'll add full cream to my protein shake in the morning."

"I like to keep where my clothes fit comfortably," she continued. "I'm pretty much on 110 lbs all the time. I'm 5'4". Not very tall. I'll go to 112, even 115. And I'll go to, like, 103. That's where I vary. Still, I do feel better when I'm smaller . . . I'm more energetic. And if I'm going to be in front of the cameras, I'll think, 'Well, okay, my video's in a week. I'd better not be bloated. I don't want to be sucking in my gut because I've gained two pounds. I wear very form-fitting things. You can't be lax about your vanity. And it's not even vanity. It's just being professional. I mean, I have a great deal of fun with image, because I like to play dress up." During this final leg of her tour through Europe, Shania must have begun to feel real fatigue. No doubt, her professional attitude toward her health and appearance helped her maintain the stamina she needed to finish out her tour.

Nina Myskow heralded Shania as "the biggest selling female singer on the planet." Shania and her husband were now citizens of the world, not Canada, not Nashville, living in Switzerland at the dawn of the new millennium. In the year 2000, sales of COME ON OVER in the United States would edge over the 17 million mark, putting Shania ahead of nearly everyone who had ever recorded an album. Worldwide sales were more than 25 million. She had become the leader of the pack, the funnest fearless female of all, but she had logged an awesome number of road miles in her bus. Pulling her horse trailer along and getting out in the nearest park on Dancer had helped her keep it all together, but flying off to Australia, to Japan, coming back to criss-cross North America a second time before she took her show to Europe — finally began to take its toll on her. Along the way, there had been some truly memorable moments. In Dallas, a complete show was broadcast to a pay-per-view audience said to number in the millions. Everywhere she went now, people flocked to see her. The stats kept building. An estimated 2.5 million fans had bought tickets to her concerts. By April 1999, the Dallas show had been packaged up into product for the retail market, which would become available to home viewers on May 11th. *Shania Twain Live!* would sell well itself and keep sales of her two best-selling albums brisk for the rest of the millennium.

4
SHANIA SUNDAY

WHEN SHANIA BROUGHT HER TOUR BACK to Canada in 1999, she returned as a conquering heroine, and CMT Canada featured her for 13 continuous hours in their *Shania Sunday* promotion. With her spectacular Grammy performance and two Grammy wins still prominent in people's minds, the video channel felt that it was appropriate to pay homage to the Country Diva by dedicating an entire dawn-to-dusk day of programming to her on March 14th.

"*Shania Sunday*," says Sean Libin, CMT Canada's marketing and public relations manager, "became the most-watched program in the history of CMT Canada, drawing over 2.3 million viewers. *Shania Sunday* eclipsed Garth Brooks' previous record, *Garth Brooks Live In Central Park*, which drew over half a million people in New York. *Shania Sunday* beat that by more than one million viewers."

I had watched the show for several hours, intrigued by the variety of programming, which included Shania's videos, clips of her from interviews speaking about the video shoots called "Shania's Video Bio," a live clip from the first show of her encore tour in Moncton, New Brunswick, and other documentary footage, as well as several call-in-to-win contest opportunities for fans from coast-to-coast to win concert tickets and a special package prize for two which included airfare, hotel rooms, tickets, and a meet-and-greet with Shania backstage at her concert in Quebec City. I had dialed in to win a few times myself. I was not surprised to learn that long distance lines were clogged. For a while that afternoon, you couldn't call out of the 604 exchange at all.

"The incredible reaction we had to CMT's *Shania Sunday* is indicative of the love affair Canadians have for Shania," says CMT Canada Program Director Ted Kennedy. "We knew that it would be a big day for us, but to know that almost one in every 13 Canadians tuned in to the show is amazing."

On Canada Day, July 1, 1999, Shania came home to Timmins for a concert in Hollinger Park. Typically, she came home to controversy. "Timmins city officials have fielded calls from concert-goers this week who feared the Hollinger Park ground may collapse into old underground mine workings from the weight of the crowd in one area," Tony Lofaro reported in *The Ottawa Citizen*. 20,000 people were expected to attend the open-air concert. Timmins' Mayor Vic Power told Lofaro, "We've had architects and engineers looking at the park and we're confident that it's going to go very well. This is the first official concert in Timmins since she made it big. The whole town is excited . . . she's a little girl from Timmins, Ontario, who's become an international star. Her name is synonymous with Timmins."

Daily newspapers featured Shania in six- to eight-page spreads with centerfold posters signed by the artist, and editors scrambled for a new angle. *Ottawa Citizen* food editor Ron Eade came up with one of the most innovative pieces written on Shania during the entire tour. "The Food That Fuels Shania" featured executive chef Orazio La Manna of Palladium Catering Services whose job it was to feed the touring celebrities who staged shows at Ottawa's Corel Center. Orazio often competed at international events as part of Culinary Team Canada. He had crafted tantalizing and nourishing dishes for a varied smorgasbord of celebs and their entourages that ran the gamut from Janet Jackson to Garth Brooks. Aerosmith had thrown him a curve once when they'd requested East Indian food. "Tandori chicken, beef korma, lamb biryani," he told Eade. "That's a lot of spice and flavor, whereas performers usually want low-fat, low-spiced food."

In his five years overseeing the 40 person-staff in the kitchen at the Center, La Manna was used to this new breed of touring star with their grueling schedules, their personal fitness trainers, and specific food requirements. The day when a caterer merely put out a spread of finger food, veggies and dip, deep-fried zucchini, and chicken strips had disappeared with the passing of spandex and party-hardy stars jacked on adrenalin and ego who often forgot to feed themselves at all, more interested in how many kegs of beer the band would have at the ready than good nutrition. He was familiar with vegetarian spreads. Bryan Adams had asked for a meal of "pasta with a tomato garlic sauce, served with freshly grated Parmesan cheese and extra-virgin olive oil. I'll never forget that," he told Eade. "It was opening night at the center and we didn't have extra-virgin olive oil, so I had to run out to Loblaws to get it."

Someone had faxed Orazio Shania's menu earlier in the week. It was not all that different than what he was used to preparing. "They want simple homestyle meals," he related to the food critic, "because they're on the road all the time. They don't want fancy or heavy sauces — just simple, wholesome food." Because Shania is a vegetarian, there would be no meat. Angel hair pasta made with no eggs was specified. La Manna had created "a pasta dish tossed with with fresh yellow corn sauce, drizzled with a light sauce of smoked plum tomato." He had added his own speciality, "Barley Risotto, with the risotto stuffed inside lightly grilled red bell peppers with *ponzu* sauce on top. Sautéed rapini and marinated grilled tofu will be offered on the side. Ms. Twain had also requested arugula salad with shaved Parmesan cheese and a lemon dressing."

If every venue on the tour had a catering service like the Corel Center and a chef like Orazio La Manna, touring would be far less stressful. Some of the arenas were less comfortable and the food less appetizing as Shania told *FHM* magazine feature writer Mike Peake. "They can be awful. Really smelly and dirty. I usually have my bus with me on tour, and that's where I hang out. If I don't have my bus, I shower after the show and I'll put towels on the floor — everywhere — so I don't have to step barefoot on dirty rugs." As she confessed to Peake when he questioned mistakes her bandmembers had made in concert, "I've forgotten words to my songs, too — it usually happens when you see someone singing along in the audience. If they get the words wrong, it can throw you off. And burping is a problem! I have to time when I eat before a show." Shania is always quick to defend her band from criticism and they return the favor. This mutual respect was essential for the success of there tours.

When Jon Landau took over the reigns of Shania's management, he inherited some of the past history from the Mary Bailey Management era as well as half a year of management by Shania's Twain Zone company, based in St. Regis Falls. Part of this inheritance included a loose alignment of musicians put together during 1995 for the anticipated tour that did not occur. These musicians became a talent pool from which players would be enlisted for TV appearances and showcases. From April 1995 until Shania began to record her third Mercury album in 1996, Shania used make-up bands for her showcases.

The players were auditioned by Mutt and Shania during the Mary Bailey Management era, and, although one of the musicians, guitarist David Malachowski, proposed his own dream band lineup, Mutt and Shania made decisions of their own. David made the initial cut along with drummer Gary Burke, fiddle player Allison Cornell, bassist Grahame Maby, slide guitarist-pedal steel player Marc Muller, keyboard player Eric Lambier, and guitarist Shane Fontayne. As it became apparent that there would be no prolonged touring in

1995, players took other gigs when they came along and fill-ins were found. Most of these players were based in or near the Albany, New York area which was relatively close to St. Regis Falls and afforded them an international airport. They were hired guns. Specialists. Often, special configurations were assigned such as the acoustic lineup of Shania, David, and Allison that played the *Regis & Kathie Lee* show at the ABC network studios in New York City. Other times, players like Randy Thomas and Dan Schafer from Nashville were employed.

Once Jon Landau and Barbara Carr were at the helm, team spirit became an important ingredient. Another consideration was the need for multi-tasking in order to present material from both THE WOMAN IN ME and COME ON OVER. One of the first people hired during the days when Sheri Thorn from Mary Bailey Management was making the arrangements was slide guitarist and pedal steel player Marc Muller. Marc came highly recommended. He was from New Jersey and he had played with some heavy people, including Bradford Marsalis, Spencer Davis, and Mark O'Connor. Marc's first gig with Shania was as part of the make-up band for the *Tonight Show with Jay Leno* in the summer of 1995. By the time that Mutt and Shania began to audition musicians for the tour band in 1998, Marc was an old hand at playing Shania's music.

Allison Cornell also survived the unsettled years when there was no regular work for a band. She was a good fiddle player, a decent harmony singer, and could double on keyboards. Plus, she was a woman, which helped to balance the energy on and off stage. The outfit that hit the road in May 1998 was a well rehearsed, fun-loving bunch.

"We spent several months putting the tour together," Shania told Jennifer Gerlock. "I was very particular about who came on the road with me, especially my band. Everyone's made me feel right at home. I am totally comfortable on stage with this show, and it's because everybody around me worked as hard as they did to make it what I always dreamed it would be. . . . The music that we do is very challenging. . . . Every member of my band plays several instruments and they rise to the occasion every single night." By the time that the tour had concluded, some of the bandmembers had become familiar faces through the live shows, live videos, the Direct Pay-TV broadcast, and the home video release of the Dallas show.

Brent Barcus is the blond hunk with the red Strat who played a lot of the lead guitar lines and solos in the touring band. These days, he's hawking a new CD on the web that he put together with his wife Miley. They call their album

Miley & The B.B. Barcus Show. From his shows with Shania, fans know that Brent is a talented, fun loving guy. "What?" one fan wanted to know during an online chat, "was Brent's most embarrassing moment on the tour?"

The band members had kept track of who would fall or stumble on stage throughout their travels. This trivial pursuit had given birth to the band name "The Fabulous Falls." By the end of the tour everybody had fallen except Roddy. Brent's most embarrassing moment came one night when he was wearing a pair of black plastic pants. "During *I'm Outta Here*," he recalled, "they split down my right pant-leg — all the way! So, all you could see was my bare leg! I had to get my guitar tech to wrap my leg with duct tape to finish the show."

Brent was required to work hard during the show, but there were plenty of perks — like his moment in the spotlight riffing a Hendrix-inspired lick into J.D. Blair's kick and snare beat while Shania was held aloft and carried into the audience by the security guys to press a little flesh with her fans. As she came back onto the stage, he and J.D. would be joined by the rest of the band with the fiddlers cutting into the familiar riff from *Any Man Of Mine* and Shania singing a shortened reprise of the hit before they all dug in their heels and kicked off the show finale, *Rock This Country.*

Fiddle player Roddy Chiong came to the band through Brent. Roddy's history included acting roles in films like the Mel Gibson flick *Payback.* He met guitarist Barcus at the Dove Awards in 1997 when he was there as a member of DC Talk's band and Brent was working with Steven Curtis Chapman. Roddy had worked in performance art, too, as a dancer and a choreographer, but when he got a call from Brent in early 1998 he was faking it big time to make it sound like he was a busy guy. Times had been tough, lately. He just had one performance gig on his calendar and it wouldn't last forever. When Brent asked him how his fiddle playing was going, Roddy was intrigued. Brent also wanted to know if Roddy could sing, which was interesting, too. But when he learned that Brent was calling about a band for a country tour, Roddy's enthusiasm sagged. He was, like, more into a rock thing . . . "Do they know that I'm an Asian guy with long hair?" he asked Brent. Brent told him, no problem, they already had a black guy with dreadlocks on the drumkit. "You'd fit right in," he said.

Roddy had been so deeply into his own thing that he didn't have a clue who Shania Twain was, so he did some net-surfing and was surprised to learn that the only country artist more popular than Shania Twain was Garth Brooks. He hustled down to the local record store and picked up Shania's CDs. He listened up, and began spending at least two hours a day rehearsing her material. When he was finished his current commitments, he flew up to Albany where someone picked him up at the airport. While they were driving to Shania's home in St. Regis Falls, Roddy learned that the person at the wheel was Shania's tour director George Travis, whose last three tours had been with Mariah Carey, Madonna, and Bruce Springsteen. Again, he was impressed.

"We had a great time," Roddy relates in his version of things on his website, "talking about everything under the sun — but to be honest, I couldn't help but think about how I wished I had practiced a little more. When we arrived at the very large house, I said hello to everybody and we started playing right away. I almost didn't have time to be nervous. There was a very pleasant man at the front of the room telling us what to do and he was obviously the leader."

Roddy didn't know who the very pleasant man was, yet. "Which," he says, "worked to my advantage because it was legendary producer Mutt Lange, Shania's husband. The first song we played was *Don't Be Stupid*." Roddy's luck was holding out. This was the song that he'd rehearsed the most before coming to the audition, which, in the long run didn't matter, because all of the musicians learned a new international mix version that day. Roddy was still nervous that he'd mess up the new parts, but he was saved from any embarrassment when the power went out and he had time to go off by himself and run through the new parts on his own before the audition got back on track.

Learning just how it had been there on his first day of rehearsal must be a surprise for people who visit Roddy's website because during the shows he comes across as one of the most relaxed, charismatic performers in the band. His background in choreography must have come in handy, too. I'll never forget the sequence where Roddy, with two handfuls of big gourd-shaped shakers two-steps across the stage behind Shania. Most people only saw this once, but Roddy Chiong did it night after night after night and managed to pull it off with a smile. Like most of the musicians in her band, Roddy is a multi-talented guy, capable of strapping on a guitar now and then — when there are no fiddles in the mix. He's got rhythm with those shakers as well. As it would turn out, they were all very motivated players and got along well with each other during the four months of rehearsals.

Prior to singing harmony with Shania at the audition, Roddy took advantage of a lunch break to hop on a stationary bike in the exercise room for some easy pedaling while he warmed up his voice. "That one hour did the trick," he reports, "because when Shania and I got together, my voice was there where it needed to be. That audition took all day long and it was definitely one of the hardest things I have ever been through."

The next day, Roddy flew home to the Chicago area to pack a full suitcase. He had some good news for his home people. He wouldn't be back for a while, he was going on the road with Shania Twain! Their first gig together was the VH1 Special *Divas Live* in the Beacon Theater in New York, where Shania teamed up with Aretha Franklin, Gloria Estefan, Celine Dion, Mariah Carey, and Carole King for the "Save the Music" benefit to raise money for musical instruments for school students in April 1998. Then it was back to St. Regis Falls for several more weeks of rehearsals before they got into full show rehearsals in Lake Placid. "I've been truly blessed," Roddy says, "by this tour with Shania."

There would be many highlights for the band players, like the time they backed Shania and Elton John during the taping of her CBS Special. With the luxury of so many rehearsal hours behind them, the shows were a piece of cake. They were ready. They played the Letterman show, the Jay Leno show, *Good Morning America*, all of the awards shows, and several shows on Australian TV that year.

Drummer J.D. Blair also felt blessed with the gig. He was impressed with the down-to-earth celebs and musicians he encountered, and appreciative of the crew cats and drivers and all of the fans at the shows. But the key guy for J.D. had been his drum tech, Larry Yager, who really knew his stuff. The key guy for Shania, of course, was J.D. Blair who laid out the beat for everyone to lock onto. She called him their "groove regulator."

They were cool even when they were hot, and it *was* sweltering some nights, unbelievably hot under the stage lights with the smoke machines choking up the atmosphere for the lighting guys to paint their patterns of color, and the pyrotechnics exploding right in their faces when they came to the front of the stage. There were breaks designed into the show when they got a chance to towel off. Some of them even had time to slip behind a screen and squirt some water into themselves, or, if the spirit of camaraderie was running particularly high — squirt someone else before the lighting came up and the next production number kicked off. Everybody had a role in each segment of the show. Backing Shania had to be a team effort if they were going to pull it off, night after night, week after week. And the production was so professional from load-in to tear-down that once they found their groove it all came naturally — no matter what city or whatever continent they found themselves in when they woke in the morning.

Their international aspect gave them some perspective on life in the jetstream. They'd all been around the block a time or two. Allison Cornell was from L.A., Cory Churko, from Moose Jaw, Saskatchewan, Hardy Hemphill, from Maine. Randall Waller was from Sydney, Australia, down under, ditto for Andy Cichon who was from Adelaide, which gave them a double edge when they headed for the south Pacific — and when they came back to Canada.

5
IN THE PINK

BECAUSE SHANIA HAD A RECORD DEAL with a Nashville label, she was still tied to these imaginary Music Row rules — at least until she supposedly broke one of them. Nashville artists had to get past country radio to get to their fans. Shania soon learned that she must also get past the Nashville press corp because no matter where she went they interpreted her actions and at least some of the people who read their stories chose to believe the Nashville interpreters more than they believed what she actually said herself.

This tiresome charade was, after all, the real reason that kd lang had moved on, this politicizing of your music into an endless debate as to whether it was country enough, or too country, or whatever. So, more than anything — any of the good, bad or ugly things Nashville writers said about her music — Shania did not break a rule when she issued her international mix of her music — she simply stopped caring at all what Nashville thought about her. Her final statement came with the pink parody outfit she wore to the 1999 CMA Awards, where she was named Entertainer of the Year, at long last. Pink stetson, pink boots, pink long-rider coat, pink halter top and coulottes. She was in the pink, so to speak, a pastel parody of Nashville with her pink belly button exposed for the world to see.

There never was a rule against pink; in fact, Nashville labels had done their best to get artists like Nanci Griffith to wear pink boots in the past. But that was where the parody lay. You could carry the rhinestone philosophy to the extreme but you could not put a lasso around this recording artist. Instead of taking offence to this latest bold fashion statement, Nashville turned it into a fashion trend of their own. Eight months after the awards, an entirely pink page in *Country Weekly* featuring country stars wearing the pastel hue suggested that if the Entertainer of the Year wore pink it must be the secret to success. Pictured were Jessica Andrews, Martina McBride, Lila McAnn, Lee Ann Womack, Lynn Anderson, Shania Twain, Faith Hill, and Shannon Brown.

The country publication, it seemed, now had a regular feature on fashion in every issue. "I write with comic relief," Shania once told Mike Peake. "You can't take it seriously. I don't think hardcore country fans realize it, but everyone else knows that the songs are meant to be humorous and corny." Commenting in *Cosmopolitan* on the female conquest of Nashville symbolized by this media attention, Shania recalled, "there was a time when country radio would never play women back-to-back. It was man-man-man, woman, man-man-man, woman. But I don't think that matters any more. It might be the other way around now!"

Vince Gill could appreciate Shania's point of view. For years Nashville writers had crafted their articles around how he disdained the rhinestone outfits and preferred comfortable clothing, and how he chose the rebel route of preferring to pay more attention to his music than to what he was wearing when he performed it. Vince was such a good-hearted soul that these comments never dampened his spirit. He had also won more CMAs than anyone in the whole history of country music. Significantly, Vince Gill handed Shania her very first CMA award, the newly created International Appreciation Award for her outstanding sales outside of the United States. As he did so, he said, "Well, Shania, that oughta shut everybody up. You did it, baby!"

When it came to handing Shania the most coveted prize, the Entertainer of the Year Award, it was Reba McEntire who opened the envelope. Reba was the last woman honored by this award some 13 years ago. Loretta, Dolly, Barbara Mandrell twice, Reba, and now Shania represented only six Entertainer of the Year wins for women in the 32 year history of the CMA awards show. Reba had made statements in the past defending Shania when her multiple-platinum album was not even nominated for an award. "What does she have to do?" Reba had wondered aloud to a reporter from *USA Today* magazine. "They should have been shouting from the rooftops about what this woman has done for country music." Reba was not the only Nashville artist to defend Shania during those years. "I've been in many arguments about Shania," Faith Hill has told interviewers. "What used to make me very angry was what people said about her. No one would give her credit for being who she is. She's a beautiful, attractive, sexy woman. Anyone who has a problem with that, I feel sorry for."

Reba McEntire, Robert K. Oermann, Tom Roland, Faith Hill — all of these people supported her and most of them were members of the CMA but were unable to overcome the invisible lobby of association members who had opposed giving Shania Twain an award. Now that they had gol' darn gone and lost her to Switzerland, the CMA finally relented. For many performers this would have been far too little and far too late. Shania Twain had been the top-selling country artist for five years. Four times she had come to the Opryland Theater for their awards show with legitimate claim to an award and come away empty handed. Shania proved to be forgiving. On camera, she was in tears, overwhelmed by the honor, but chose to pay tribute to Dolly Parton who was being inducted into the Country Music Hall of Fame that same night. She wanted to meet Dolly. Backstage, Shania fielded questions from the press. "What had Vince been talking about?" they asked. "What had he meant?" Shania smiled and blithely said, "Well, I'm not just a lap dancer, after all." Without much prompting, she told the assembled reporters in the press room that receiving the Entertainer of the Year award from Reba had been special. "I think that meant more to me than the award itself. I think just the fact that Reba presented it, and she's always been so gracious, and been a mentor to me."

Before any reporter could ask her if she was disappointed that Dolly had left the building without meeting with her, Shania kept on speaking. "I was blown away by Dolly Parton's performance. She's my biggest idol of all time. I didn't meet her, she left. I'll meet her someday. I don't hold it against her. My favorite song really is *Coat Of Many Colors*. I sang it for many, many years as a child . . . I think that what Vince said, about not losing sight of the roots of the music, is true . . . My roots are Dolly Parton, Merle Haggard, Waylon Jennings, and that's never going to change. But we change. We evolve. We grow and we create music of our own, we come into our own, and I'm whoever I am right now. I'm enjoying it. I'm happy fans are enjoying it. And I think that this honor comes mostly as a surprise because I sort of convinced myself that I wasn't going to win a thing."

Although there were plenty of journalists present while she was making this coherent and revealing statement, she was not widely quoted in American publications, though Nashville journalist Walt Trott put nearly every impassioned word into his feature story published in the British magazine *Country Music People*. "It's my first CMA," Shania told the reporters at the post-awards show press conference. "I don't resent not winning one before. I've seen many artists who I thought were very deserving who didn't win in the past and I learned from that. I learned not to set myself up for disappointment whether I deserved it or not."

What were her plans for her next album? Would it involve another worldwide tour? "Creatively," she replied, "I write everything that I record, so it takes me so long to put an album together. The fact that my husband is my producer and he takes as long as he does . . . we really have to plan our next album pretty far in advance because I have to set time aside to let me focus on it creatively. I can't be jumping out on the road whenever I feel like it. I will be doing three more weeks of touring in November. That will be the end of this tour for COME ON OVER. I will tour with the next album. I'm looking forward to it. I've had an exciting last year and a half . . . great, great memories."

There were more awards forthcoming before the century ended, from *Billboard* magazine, from the Nashville Songwriters Association, and from BMI (who named her song *You're Still The One* their Song of the Year and Shania herself their Songwriter of the Year). In fact, there were so many awards during late 1999 and the early months of 2000 that she simply could not attend every show.

To escape the award show spotlights and the grind of her tour, Shania occasionally took a few short breaks, flying to Seville, Spain one time with fellow horse-lovers Bo Derek, Daryl Hannah, and Diandra Douglas. Together, they attended an equestrian event. "I had a few days off," Shania told Susan Poharski, "which was a total fluke, so I hopped on a plane and went." During the tour she and Mutt continued to commiserate regularly over long distance lines. As the tour wound down in the fall of 1999, a third version of COME ON OVER was being readied for release.

For her North American fans, who had not heard a lot of the mixes on the international version of COME ON OVER, Mercury Nashville announced they would release a North American edition of the mixes in the early months of the new year. Her fans wanted it. "They wanted to have what the international fans had," Shania told Brian Mansfield in a late fall interview posted by Jayne Twain on a British website. "I thought, 'Well, I think they should get their own thing.' You're talking now fans that probably have the (import) album; let's give them something that's for them. The life of this album just keeps going on and on. People want more versions; they want to hear this, they want to hear that . . . It is fun for me to take my live versions and mix in a little bit of what we've done with the new mixes. On *Honey, I'm Home* the groove is completely different. It's very funky and totally cool."

A ghostly voice from the past showed up that November when JoMaTo Records, a Franklin, Tennessee subsidiary of Renaissance Records, a Nashville area reissue label, packaged up 12 rock demos that Shania had recorded in Toronto in 1989 while she was still appearing at the Deerhurst Lodge in Huntsville, and offered them for sale on CD. While this was seen as a shameless money grab by most people, Renaissance head John Edwards patiently explained the label's position to *Billboard* magazine's Chet Flippo. "We licensed this from Harry Hinde and Paul Sabu back in April of this year. Back in 1989, Harry hired Paul to produce and co-write with Shania. They ended up writing about 14 songs, they cut 12 tracks, and the tape was pitched to A&M Records in Canada for a rock deal. Nothing happened from that." Luke Lewis, President of Mercury Nashville, told Flippo, "It's flattering that consumers would be interested in her early work, but on the other hand, it's a shame that her talent is represented in such a slipshod way, with demos and rehearsal tapes that are not up to her standards."

While the JoMaTo release was titled EILEEN SHANIA TWAIN to forewarn the consumer, some of the European labels that licensed this product from JoMaTo were entirely without scruples. One European label titled their package: SHANIA TWAIN: WILD & WICKED and included a 36 by 48 poster. "We will pay her publishing royalties directly into an escrow account," Edwards told Flippo. "We are also donating a portion of the proceeds to her favorite charities, the Make-a-Wish Foundation and Second Harvest/Kid's Cafe, in her name." Harry Hinde had no comment for *Billboard*.

"It's not the way I want people to hear my music," Shania told Brian Mansfield. "Obviously, I'm not happy that people can take advantage of me this way. It's discouraging to me. Sometimes I get discouraged with human nature. So, that's my personal feeling. I feel like I've been betrayed by a fellow musician. I would never do that to someone else."

Mansfield, however, wanted to know what she thought of the music. "I love the music," Shania replied. "I think it's cool. It's the type of music that I liked to write, that I enjoyed, and that I did do a lot of at the time. There are a lot of people who think that sort of edginess in my music now only came from Mutt and only because of his entry into my world. I try to tell people I've always done all kinds of music, this is not new to me — and this is sort of proof of that."

6
STILL THE ONE

FOR THE FIRST FEW DAYS FOLLOWING THE TOUR, Shania was exhausted. She had been on the road for more than 18 months, entertaining 2.5 million fans. By the end of the tour, some of her shows were spectacularly large. In Dublin, at the very end of the road, she experienced an emotionally overwhelming sense of communion with her audience. Shania had once stated in *Country Music Magazine*, "As a person, I'm very conservative, but when I perform and entertain, I want people to be entertained. I don't want them to feel their aunt is singing to them. I'm one of them. I'm there to get into the music." She had become a conduit for such a spontaneous rush of energy that suddenly, blessedly, she had felt spent, and knew it really was time to go home.

But home had been migrating on her ever since she had left Huntsville and headed for Nashville. Shania had become a celebrity, and celebrity isolated a person. The pleasure of being at home and at peace had become elusive. Instinctively, Shania had reached out and embraced her fans, meeting with as many as was humanly possible, but when she went back to her hotel room, she was alone. Coincidently, while Shania was touring in 1998, the film *Notting Hill* was released which portrayed these problems celebrity poses. Shania's *You've Got A Way* was featured on the soundtrack. In a revealing scene, Julia Roberts' character, a famous film actress, accompanies Hugh Grant, a common bookseller, to his brother's house where family and friends have gathered to celebrate his younger sister's birthday. After a series of awkward moments during which the Notting Hill folks get used to being around someone famous, everyone enjoys the camaraderie of the birthday supper. After the meal is done, the family falls into a ritual competition, telling 'woe-is-me tales'. "I'm going to give the last brownie," the brother says to the others, "for the saddest act here." Several masterfully understated claims are made, several times everyone erupts into spontaneous laughter, and each time a claim is made for the prize brownie. Without meaning to exclude her, they have left Julia Roberts' character out of the loop, but she protests and is granted a chance to "out-woe" the others.

She begins but her audience seems to sense that she's seriously telling the truth rather than gilding the lily, so to speak. They soon learn that her celebrity life, although rewarded by $20 million movie contracts, is surprisingly like their own. She may even be less happy than they are with her lot in life. "I've been on a diet every day since I was 19, which, basically means I've been hungry for a decade. I've had a series of not-nice boyfriends, one of whom hit me. And every time I get my heart broken the newspapers splash it about as if it's entertainment. And, it's taken two rather painful operations to get me to look like this. And one day, not long from now, my looks will go, they will discover I can't act, and I will become some sad, middle-aged woman who looks a bit like someone who was famous for a while."

Finished, she smiles, expectant, waiting for people's opinion, and is grateful when someone says, "Nice try, gorgeous, but you don't fool anyone." They're not buying into believing that she's any worse off than they are, even though what she has said is the bitter truth put across in jest. When Hugh Grant tells his family and friends that he has decided to turn down her offer to live together, perhaps for the rest of their lives, he says, "She said she might be famous as could be, but that she was just a girl standing in front of a boy asking him to love her." As he changes his mind and pursues her at the end of the film, the credits roll to the opening strains of Shania's *You've Got A Way*. The lyrics seem especially appropriate.

Shania knew she would face the challenge that celebrity poses when she took her music to a worldwide audience, but, if she could have it all, she would prefer to be known as a normal person. "What does stardom mean, anyway?" Shania pondered during an interview with *Country Song Roundup* writer Nancy Brooks. "It's just a name that I have. It's like a middle name, 'star' or 'celebrity' or whatever." One of the ways she was able to use this to a positive advantage was to help the less fortunate. "You get calls all the time," she told Brooks, "to visit people who are dying, mostly kids who are dying. . . . Almost all of the kids that I have seen now have died, because they all have just days left by the time they get to talk to you."

"The beauty of being able to reach people, and be able to help people when they are sick or dying," she told Nancy Brooks, was a consequence of celebrity. "If it wasn't 'Shania' . . . it wouldn't be the same." This was what celebrity could be used for. It was necessary to become famous if you wanted to take your music to the people, but fame could also be used to help others in their moment of need. She had used her celebrity in 1997 when she posed with famed NHL coach and *Hockey Night in Canada* broadcaster Don Cherry for a limited edition portrait which was auctioned to raise funds for Special Olympics in Canada. She had created two scholarships for students graduating from Timmins High & Vocational School, and had initiated the building of a Shania Twain Interpretive Center in Timmins scheduled to be opened in 2001.

Now that the touring phase was over, Shania could rest with an unburdened heart. With a good conscience she could put the onslaught of tabloid accusations and doubting Thomases out of her mind. She was still Eileen or "Leeny" to her immediate family members. She was "Woody" to her husband. He was still the one person she shared her life and love and friendship with. And *she* was still the same person she had always been. Celebrity had not hardened her. When she checked herself out in a mirror she did not find herself admiring and embellishing her image like some wicked Queen in a Snow White story. The name on her passport was Eileen Regina Lange, but she had few illusions of grandeur and no pretension to any throne, even though she was sometimes called the Queen of Country Music. Her fans were voting her onto lists of the world's most beautiful women, but Shania didn't see herself in this light. Far from it. Beauty was about inner feeling, not outer gloss.

When Shania called it quits, she went home to Mutt and the dogs and horses to cook a vegetarian Christmas dinner for their relatives and loved ones. In their chateau overlooking Lake Geneva, Mutt and Shania enjoyed a measure of privacy among their neighbors who now included Phil Collins, Sophia Loren, and Tina Turner. Her brothers and sisters came over for the holidays. Life was good. She was happy to be back in her own kitchen. Happy to do her own laundry. Cooking helped her center herself. "The more famous I get, the more I want to do my own laundry," she once told *Country Song Roundup*. Asked what her perfect Sunday would be by a reporter from *Sunday Magazine*, Shania said, "My perfect day would start with breakfast on the terrace, looking at the Alps. I'd wrap a douvet 'round myself, lounge around, then put on a soup or stew. Then, I'd spend time with my horses. I'd come home, have a nice dinner, and then Mutt and I would go to a movie."

She has also said that she and Mutt often write together while he watches sports on television and noodles on his guitar. Shania would be singing in the kitchen, working out melodies and lyrics, and when she had something groovy, she'd share it with Mutt. "He always has a guitar in his hands," she has said. A fuller picture of Mutt and Shania's personal relationship emerged during an interview with Greg Shannon, for which he received an international award.

Born and raised in Saskatoon, Greg had paid his dues working in several rural Alberta radio markets until he ended up in Medicine Hat as the afternoon drive jock and music director. One day, when he was flipping through the Canadian music trade magazine *The Record*, he came across an advertisement that read, "Wanted: Quick-footed personality with love of country music." He sent his resume to the producers of *Craven A's Today's Country* and soon found himself auditioning in a Toronto television studio. The radio show, he learned, would have a live audience, which would turn out to be a great experience when he began interviewing Garth Brooks, Mary Chapin Carpenter, and . . . Shania Twain.

When the radio series got rolling, Greg became known for his lively, off-the-wall interview style. The celebrity artists he interviewed responded with entertaining anecdotes, and *Today's Country* thrived until legislation regulated Craven A out of the picture. By this time, three of Greg's interviews had received international recognition at the New York Festival's International Radio Competition, winning awards over entries from more than 30 countries. So, he walked in to a very good situation with CMT Canada. He was a natural to host the video network's newly created afternoon request show.

When Greg interviewed Shania in November 1997, she had just completed an exhausting encounter with 27,000 fans during her Fan Appreciation Day at Calgary's Southcenter mall. She had spent a lot of time with several of the less fortunate fans, some of them terminally ill cancer patients, before flying to Toronto to appear on *Today's Country*. She was not in a cheery mood when she walked into the studio. "She had a lot of sad things on her mind," Greg remembers. "A lot of sad stories were told to her for a whole day. And she was just not in the mood to do more interviews and talk to more media. But we got her seated, and got started up, and I sort of eased into it, and after about five minutes, all of a sudden she brightened right up and got right into it." One of the first things Greg managed to accomplish was to put a smile on Shania's face. He soon had her laughing.

"I had a kind of an interesting Shania Twain experience the other day," he said, leading off . . . "I was at the clinic to give blood. To drop a pint, as they say . . ." He got laughter from both the audience and his famous guest for this, but kept on, telling the audience that one of the nurses had seen his copy of Shania's new CD in his hands and had said, "She's *ours*." Which referred to the fact that she was Canadian. And then, "I *hate* her." Which, of course, was a compliment. Shania could understand that. It was a love-hate thing that she admitted to Greg she had with some women herself.

Greg asked Shania whose looks she admired the most.

"There's a lot of women I'd like to be," she replied. "Claudia Schiffer is probably my favorite . . ."

"Claudia Schiffer, come on, forget Claudia Schiffer," Shannon quipped. Seated knee to knee with Shania on matching stools before a studio audience, he was obviously overpowered by Shania's immediacy. In his eyes, Claudia Schiffer didn't hold a candle to Shania's beauty. Right away, Shania responded to his compliment by opening up.

"Claudia Schiffer is beautiful," she said, protesting. "She's blonde. She's got beautiful, blonde, long hair. She's tall . . . I think that the key in life anyway is to like who we are . . . But I mean, let's face it, we all have these superficial ideals in our minds of maybe who we would like to be, even if it's only for a day . . . Besides, my husband's really into the supermodel thing. He loves, like, tall women and everything. I'm not at all . . . that. I'm short. I've got brown hair . . ."

Greg began to protest, but Shania kept on going. "Tall blondes are what men really like. All women know these things. Tall, very slim blondes are supposed to be the ideal woman. I don't consider myself the ideal woman. I like myself, don't get me wrong . . ."

"So," Greg said, "He'll be leafing through the fashion catalog and say, 'She turns me on?'"

"No, he doesn't say *that!*"

Greg, always quick on his feet, came back with, "He's more subtle than that . . . He's a smart man . . . How do *you* react?"

"He likes to watch the fashion channel." (Huge laughter) "The men are laughing out there . . ." Shania turned her eyes from Greg to the audience. "But I guarantee, *you* guys out there, you watch the fashion channel. Admit it!" The audience responded, and Shania quipped, "*Don't* they? A lot of men look at the fashion channel. He likes to look at the fashion channel. He wants to see what they're wearing. What's new. Not necessarily for what he's going to *buy* me. He likes to look at beautiful women. All men do. If it's with respect, that doesn't bother me."

"It's kind of, like, a sport?" Greg suggested.

"No, no *that's* not the right attitude," Shania protested. "I mean, I like to look at the good looking guys, too. It's healthy to look. Looking's good . . ."

Greg and his audience broke out into full laughter. When he could speak, he said, "I'm loving this! This is a very honest interview . . ."

Shania finished up her thought. "Looking good is good. And looking is good. So, there you go."

Later, she told Greg that both she and Mutt liked to get out and walk in the bush. They filled up their thermoses and went on long walks and they often came up with ideas for songs during their walks or while they were doing their everyday things around the house. Just to keep Shania on her toes, Greg suggested that nobody had ever seen Mutt. She was probably just making him up. They had fun with this, playing with something other commentators had reduced. Through humor Greg elevated Mutt's involvement in Shania's life to a new level of recognition, showing a refreshing respect for their private lives away from the intense gaze of public scrutiny. From this interview, we also learned that Mutt was more of a fuss-budget when it came to what Shania planned to wear to public appearances than she was. Left to her own devices, she merely tossed a pile of mix-and-match coordinates into a suitcase and made up her mind as to what she wore on the spur of the moment. Shania was very much the girl next door, gregarious and fun-loving, who just happened to be a celebrity. The contrast between the publicly shy Mutt and the outgoing Shania was obviously part of the yin, yang energy of their love for each other.

"Mutt and I come from such different worlds," Shania told *Calgary Herald* music journalist James Muretich. "And in many people's eyes, we were considered unlikely to succeed. But very much to the contrary, we're very happy and very much made for each other in every way — creatively, intimately, and on a friendship level." As with all celebrity marriages, rumors of their break-up continue to be circulated. "I get a call every few days," Luke Lewis told *People Weekly*, "from someone who has heard they have broken up. I would be totally shocked if it happened."

Shania set the record straight during an interview by Nina Myskow in the *Daily Mirror*. "We work together, we write together," she told Myskow. "Musically, we have a great thing going because we share something so intimate, so natural. Mutt's a great guy. I refer to him as Mutt. That's the only name he goes by, but he's 'Love' to me. He's a very deep person, very gentle. He's a very unusual character. When we met, I didn't think of him romantically at all. But he was, like, someone I had known for many years. He became a good friend, fast. One day, we just hugged. We'd hugged before. I mean, goodbye at the airport . . . But that time, we just didn't let go for the longest time. It was so intense. I thought, 'I

really don't want to let go of this person.' At that moment, we knew we had a
lot to talk about. It was great. We met and we were married within six months,
1993. I mean, we were meant to be together. We were so meant to be together.
But he's in the studio working and I'm here, there and everywhere, all over the
place. What's happening to me is a miracle. So many things I would never have
dreamed about. For instance, I'm not a model, but Revlon have asked me to be
a guest for a couple of years. Like, me, the face of Revlon! I was like, 'Wow!'
And lots of free samples."

"Mutt and I are an unlikely pair," Shania told the *Boston Globe*. "There's
been talk in the tabloids that we're divorcing but we are very happy. We love
each other in every way. We have a great relationship. We feel as strong as ever
— and *You're Still The One* is sort of my own personal victory song about the
marriage."

When *FHM* reporter Mike Peake asked what three men Shania would
invite over to dinner, she first chose Nelson Mandela. "I have so many questions
for him . . . I saw a program on him which showed the way he achieved respect
from the guards when he was in prison. He acted like their equal and they had
no choice but to treat him that way." Her second and third choices — Michael
Jackson and Albert Einstein. If they couldn't make it, she'd settle for Jim Carrey
or Steve Martin . . . "Who just make me laugh." Laughing is good, too.

And some of the tabloid articles that appeared with Shania on the cover
about at this time were certainly laughable. Someone leaked details of her
Christmas family gathering and a candid snapshot of them seated at the dinner
table somehow appeared in *The National Enquirer* on March 14, 2000 under the
sensational title, "Shania Joins No-Sex Cult." In one photo, Mutt and Shania
are seated at the head of a long table where everyone is chowing down on the
vegetarian feast she has prepared with Jill and Carrie-Ann; in a second snapshot, they are smiling and holding hands. But the accompanying text states that
all is not bliss in the Twain-Lange household: vegetarian Shania has forced her
guests to miss out on the traditional Christmas turkey dinner; Mutt has stolen
Shania away from her brothers and sisters; they are members of a sinister cult
that practices an ancient yogic practice which, among other things, means that
she doesn't eat meat and she doesn't have sex with her husband. This "strange
sect" is identified as the Sant Mat cult. A picture of Guru Thakar Singh is inset
into the text.

The ascetic practice of *sant mat* does entail restraint, abstention, a vegetarian diet, and daily meditation, but there is no evidence that Shania is a follower

of such Sikh practitioners as the late Guru Kirpal Singh who had thousands of perfectly normal followers at the time of his death a few years ago.

Likewise there is no proof that this exposé came from an interview with Shania's brother Darryl Twain, despite claims by *The National Inquirer*. The story reads like an all-out fabrication . . . or perhaps the Langes and Twains were having a laugh at the tabloid's expense by leaking these photos and pseudo-revelations. Very likely the family life Shania and Mutt enjoy is at least as heart-warming and fun-filled as the interview she taped with Greg Shannon or the film *Notting Hill*. For what it's worth, the character Julia Roberts portrays in *Notting Hill* is a vegan.

Shania began the new millennium having fun, posing for *FHM* (For Him Magazine), squeezed into a black rubber outfit fashioned by The House of Harlot. She looked hot. Shania was now the first female artist to sell more than 10 million copies of two consecutive records, Mike Peake wrote. "Twain is worth a pretty penny," he continued, estimating that she had earned over three million from her Revlon endorsements, "and Lange is thought to be good for 100 million — putting their combined personal wealth on a par with the GNP of Western Samoa, population 170,000. And, with Mutt earning an estimated 10 million a year in royalties . . . $192,000 per week . . . for doing nothing . . ."

"Who's richer these days," Peake asked. "You or Mutt?"

"Ha!" Shania said. She had an answer for that. "We're about equal. I've caught up pretty fast."

Now that Shania Twain had come off the road and largely left public life for a well-deserved period of rest and relaxation at home, her fans could only speculate as to whether she was writing and recording another country album, or whether she would leave country behind, altogether. Considering some of the career moves that Linda Ronstadt made during the 1980s, people should have been keeping their minds wide open. Shania did not announce she was about to take a lead role in a stage production of a Gilbert and Sullivan opera, as Linda did when she played the role of Mabel in the 19th-century light opera *The Pirates of Penzance* in New York City. Shania will probably never record a lushly orchestrated album of pop standards as Linda did when she collaborated with orchestra leader Nelson Riddle for the triple-platinum album WHAT'S NEW. And it's highly unlikely that she will record an album of Mexican folk songs in Spanish, as Ronstadt did while exploring the nuances of her Mexican-German heritage. However, Shania has continued to evolve throughout her career, and it goes without saying that she would not merely repeat what she has already done on THE WOMAN IN ME and COME ON OVER.

Barbara Hager had already speculated in her 1998 biography that Mutt and Shania would record with Bruce Springsteen and a duet would kick off their world tour on December 31, 1999. That intriguing possibility has not come to pass, but Britney Spears has recorded *Don't Let Me Be The Last To Know*, one of Shania's original songs, for her latest album. As Britney told *Top Of The Pops* in May 2000, "I worked with Mutt Lange and Shania Twain . . . so, I spent some time in Europe recording. It's a really powerful ballad and I get to showcase my vocal range." Perhaps, a duet for a blockbuster movie theme will follow with someone like Elton John . . . or a cool recording like *That's What Friends Are For*, which Sir Elton made with Dionne Warwick, Gladys Knight, and Stevie Wonder, might be on her calendar. Not many people were willing to bet Shania and Mutt would return to Music Row to lay down the bed tracks for her next album on it. With a state-of-the-art recording studio on their own property and no troublesome helicopter flybys to distract them, it is far more likely that Nashville musicians will visit them.

A possibility scarcely mentioned in the media at all has been whether there would be a period of time devoted to making little Mutts and little Shanias. Belly-button-counting videophile Shaniamaniacs cringed at the very thought, but family life is central to Shania. During the final months of her tour, interviewers like Nina Myskow had found her reflective and resolute that she was going to take life a whole lot easier once she stopped touring. "The escape from the stress of not having enough money for so long in my life is wonderful," she told Myskow. "But I don't get to see Mutt enough. When I'm away for long periods, it's always difficult reuniting. We're constantly making readjustments. But I think we're past that now because I'm not planning on ever going away from home for any length of time anymore. I don't have to. I think maybe we're finally going to start living our life together. I'm thinking about babies, but anytime over the next few years will be fine."

Would she try her hand at a film role? Perhaps Shania Twain and Bo Derek will make a film about the real cowgirls of the late 19th century? A spaghetti western filmed in Spain and directed by an Italian filmmaker? Such speculation simply underscores the freedom Shania has achieved. Freedom of expression. Freedom to grow. Shania no longer woke up to find herself a 'girl singer' in a Music Row stable of hat acts, and, for that alone, she surely must have been thankful. Her fans had made that possible. She was still the one.

There were also rumors that Shania would release a Christmas album, yet her very makeup foreshadowed a different Christmas album, perhaps more to do with Jesus than merely a Hollywood *White Christmas*, more to do with the spirit of giving and the rebirth of hope and light at the darkest time of the year than the capitalist extravaganza and consumer shopping frenzy that the holy day has become associated with in recent times. Giving was good. Some of the results of Shania's generosity were already beginning to manifest. Lana Floen, cured of her stagefright, had begun to record. Tianna Lefevbre had completed her album with Tony Rudner and it was being released to record stores. Bobbi Smith's album had drawn rave reviews. Her singles were flying up the Canadian country charts. In June 2000 she scored her first cover story when she was featured on the cover of Canada's national country newspaper, *Country Music News*. Shania's fans continue to grow in number, in part because of her music, in part because of her generous spirit.

Despite her 'pop' popularity, Shania is still a country singer in her heart. On the April 4, 2000 cover of *Country Weekly* magazine Shania is portrayed back-to-back with Alan Jackson. Emblazoned across the two superstars like a brand are the words: "Country vs Pop: The Battle's On! And stars like Alan Jackson and Shania Twain find themselves on opposing sides." Alan Jackson had teamed up with George Strait to record *Murder On Music Row*, an anthem for traditionalists in a rear-guard effort to fight off the power of women artists like Shania. While the country music media tries to exile Shania from the country music ranks, claiming she has gone pop, she disagrees.

"It's really cool to see that both audiences are enjoying what I'm doing," Shania told "Country vs Pop" author Bob Paxman. "There are a lot of country fans and pop fans out there. I enjoy that my music reaches so many different types of fans." To further his argument, Paxman quotes Martina McBride as saying, "I always thought that the idea was to reach as many people as possible." He adds Faith Hill's observation, "There are a lot of people who did not listen to country radio, but do now. They heard me on a pop station, but now they've tuned into country, and that's *really* cool." Paxman reminds his magazine readers that in the '60s the "Nashville Sound" was considered too pop. The most absurd example of posturing Paxman can dig up is the time that Charlie Rich burned the CMA Awards show envelope bearing John Denver's name on stage during the televised awards show as a protest against the association voting Denver their Entertainer of the Year. Rich, you might remember, is the countrypolitan dude who crooned such country pop as *Behind Closed Doors, The Most Beautiful Girl,* and *A Very Special Love Song*. In retrospect, Denver's 1975 hit, *Thank God I'm A Country Boy,* seems so much more "country" than Rich's hits.

"What I think I'm bringing to country isn't something that's new to country," Shania stated in the *Seattle Post Intelligencer*, "but something that's left country. People used to write songs with more direct lyrics, like Johnny Paycheck's *Take This Job And Shove It*. Country used to be much more conservative than it is now. We've gone into this serious, politically correct stage that artistically I find very restrictive."

Politicizing country music may no longer be necessary, but, as George Jones pointed out to Bob Paxman, "Most of it now is this happy-go-lucky positive kind of music that draws in the young audience. I think that is great. But at the same time, they are leaving out the traditional fans, the people who made country music what it is. And that's wrong!" If the Possum could have his way, country radio would be diversified. It would have something for everyone who loves country music. Lee Ann Womack concurs. "Putting some pop in your country doesn't spell *traitor*. I really like the artists that *can* do it all."

"I don't think I'll ever be able to crossover like Shania," Toby Keith told Bob Paxman. "I'm definitely country all the way. But the big numbers come when you get some pop play along with country." Bryan White summed up the open-minded side of the argument with a statement from the younger generation. "The audience today is different," Bryan told Paxman. "Younger people like myself did not grow up listening to only one kind of music. So there will always be rock and pop mixed in with my music. That's what audiences want." "Country music is obviously my home," Faith Hill added, "I just think great music should be universal."

"Honestly, I would be disappointed if I was not being recognized by the country world," Shania has stated. Shania told *Country Weekly* writer Nick Krewen for a June 1999 article he called "Country Music Still the One Shania Twain Loves" that her music "goes from country to new traditional country to a very pop country. People want something different. Something fresh." Reams and reams of copy have been generated declaring that Shania changed country music but hearing it from her point of view, you come to realize she did not set out to revolutionize the industry or change the music. She merely followed her spirit. "Maybe it's changed as a result of what I've done," she told *Edmonton Sun* pop/rock critic Mike Ross. "I don't know. A lot of people say that. But that's not my goal. I guess the beauty of that is that I've been able to be myself and country has embraced it. And by doing that, they've had to loosen up a bit and widen their margin of what they support. What made that happen is the fact that fan support was there. That's all that the industry needed. That's all that counts. I think fans don't even really care if it's labeled country or not, to be honest. They just want to be entertained. They want great music. They want something cool to party with. I consider my music somewhat of a free spirit. Let it just land where it lands."

A free spirit. "I was called Eileen after my Irish grandmother," Shania reminds us in a recent interview in *The Daily Mirror*. "By chance I met an Ojibwa girl called 'Shania.' So, I became Shania. It means 'on my way,' and I think I am, now. Finally I really am on my way. Life is good. I feel that the worst is over and the best is yet to come."

The Bard once wrote, "Let me not to the marriage of true minds admit impediments . . . Love is not love which alters when it altercation finds." So, I say to Shania fans, wherever you find yourselves, "We have received music nurtured by true love and a union of great talents, and this surely tells us that our world is blessed." Our Juliet and Romeo have overcome the antagonistic forces that would not admit the marriage of their two worlds, country and pop. Though years ago Kipling wrote, "East is east, and west is west," in Shania's world the twain *does* meet. Our story's ending has no poison-potion, no dagger thrust, and is — after all is said and done — a midsummer night's dream.

Sweet dreams, dear reader, and to all a good night.

REFERENCES

Books

Alden, Grant and Peter Blackstock, eds. *No Depression: An Introduction to Alternative Country Music (whatever that is)*. Nashville, TN: Dowling Press, 1998.

Anderson, Christopher. *Madonna Unauthorized*. New York, NY: Island Books, 1992.

Bedwell, Randall, ed. *Unbroken Circle: A Quotable History Of The Grand Ole Opry*. Nashville, TN: Cumberland House, 1999.

Bego, Mark. *Country Gals: The Superstars of Today's Country Music*. New York, NY: Pinnacle Books, Windsor Publishing Corp., 1994.

Brown, Jim. *Country Women in Music*. Kingston, ON: Quarry Music Books, 1999.

Crouse, Richard. *A Voice and A Dream: The Celine Dion Story*. New York, NY and Toronto, ON: Ballantine Books, 1996.

Cohen, Leonard. *Beautiful Losers*. New York, NY: Bantam Books, 1967.

Dickerson, James. *Women On Top: The Quiet Revolution That's Rocking the American Music Industry*. New York, NY: Billboard Books, 1998.

Feiler, Bruce. *Dreaming Out Loud*. New York, NY: Avon Books, 1998.

Gray, Scott. *On Her Way: The Shania Twain Story*. New York, NY and Toronto, ON: Ballantine Books, 1998.

Hager, Barbara. *Honour Song*. Vancouver, BC: Raincoast Books, 1996.

Hager, Barbara. *On Her Way: The Life and Music of Shania Twain*. New York, NY: Berkley Boulevard Books, 1998.

Jennings, Nicolas. *After The Goldrush: Flashbacks to the Dawn of the Canadian Sound)*. Toronto, ON: Viking Penguin Books, 1998.

Jones, George (with Tom Carter). *I Lived To Tell It All*. New York, NY: Bantam, Doubleday, Dell, 1997.

Leamer, Laurence. *Three Chords and the Truth: Behind the Scenes with those Who Make and Shape Country Music)*. New York, NY: HarperPaperbacks, 1997.

Marsh, Dave. *Born To Run: The Bruce Springsteen Story*. New York, NY: Dell Publishing Co. Inc., 1981.

Nadel, Ira B. *Various Positions: A Life of Leonard Cohen*. Toronto, ON: Random House of Canada Ltd., 1996.

Radner, Gilda. *It's Always Something*. New York, NY: Avon Books, 1990.

Romanowski, Patricia and Holly George-Warren, eds. *The New Rolling Stone Encyclopedia of Rock & Roll*. New York, NY: Fireside, A Rolling Stone Press Book, 1995.

Sedaka, Neil. *Laughter in the Rain: My Own Story*. New York, NY: G.P. Putnam's Sons, 1982.

Thomas, Dave (with Robert Crane and Susan Carney). *SCTV Behind the Scenes*. Toronto, ON: McClelland & Stewart, 1997.

Tosches, Nick. *Country: The Twisted Roots of Rock 'n' Roll*. New York, NY: Da Capo Press, 1998.

Whitburn, Joel. *The Billboard Book of Top 40 Albums*. New York, NY: Billboard Books, 1995.

Whitburn, Joel. *The Billboard Book of Top Country Albums*. New York, NY: Billboard Books, 1996.

Whitburn, Joel. *The Billboard Book of Top 40 Country Hits*. New York, NY: Billboard Books, 1996.

Whitburn, Joel. *The Billboard Book of Top 40 Hits*. New York, NY: Billboard Books, 1996.

Newspaper & Magazine Articles

Anonymous. "Controversy Over Country Music Studio." *The Buffalo News*, November, 1995.

Anonymous. "Shania Twain." *CMA Closeup*, April, 1995.

Anonymous. "Shania Twain Is on Her Way with Second Album." Mercury Polydor Canada Press Release. 1995.

Anonymous. "CMT Names Shania Twain Its February Showcase Artist." *CMT* Press Release, December 14, 1995.

Anonymous. "Twain Plays Down Fuss over Native Heritage." *Ottawa Sun*, April, 1996.

Anonymous. "Twain's Story Draws Tears." Thomson News Service.

Anonymous. "Twain Not Truthful on Heritage, Paper Says." *The Toronto Star*, April 6, 1996.

Anonymous. "Twain Has Family Trouble." *Ottawa Sun*, April 7, 1996.

Anonymous. "Canadian Shania Twain Named Best New Female Singer." *Ottawa Citizen*, April 25, 1996.

Anonymous. "Twain Meets Hometown Fans." Canadian Press, 1996.

Anonymous. "Twain Comes On Over to Bloomington to Promote CD." *Star Tribune*, November 5, 1997.

Anonymous. "Fans Crowd Mall to Greet Shania." *Windsor Star*, November 11, 1997.

Anonymous. "Shania Twain Record Review." *Windsor Star*, November 13, 1997.

Anonymous. "Not to Disappoint Mutt ..." Ft. Lauderdale *Sun-Sentinel*, February 20, 1998.

Anonymous. "Country Guru Heaps Praise on Shania." Canadian Press, *Winnipeg Sun*, June 1, 1998.

Anonymous. "Teen Choir Thrilled to Join Twain Tour." *Detroit News*, August 24, 1998.

Anonymous. "Shania Twain: Sweet Country Girl or Die-Hard Feminist?" *Playgirl*, October, 1998.

Anonymous. "CMT Announces 'Shania Sunday'." *CMT* Press Release. March 4, 1999.

Anonymous. "Faith in the Grammys." *National Post*, February 25, 1999.

Anonymous. "If You Were a Canadian

Female in L.A. Last Night, You Probably Won a Grammy." *National Post*, February 25, 1999.

Anonymous. "Crying the Blues over Shania Show. $3,000 loss." *Ottawa Sun*, October 20, 1999.

Anonymous. "Shania's Holiday." *National Enquirer*, March 14, 2000.

Anonymous. "Oh, those Divas!" *The Province*, April 11, 2000.

Anonymous. "Celine Dion Buys $7.8 mil Quebec Mansion." *The Province*, April 11, 2000.

Anonymous. "In the Pink." *Country Weekly*, May 30, 2000.

Anonymous. "Country's 25 Sexiest Stars." *Country Weekly*, May 30, 2000.

Bane, Michael. "Shania Twain: After The Gold Rush." *Country Music*, November, 1997.

Barnes, Deborah, with Wendy Newcomer and Tamara Saviano. "A Tale of Two Cities on a Night to Remember." *Country Weekly*, October 13, 1997.

Barnes, Deborah. "For Shania Twain . . . It's All About the Music." *Country Weekly*, October 16, 1998.

Bell, Pat. "Girl, 8, to Sing with Shania." *Ottawa Citizen*, March 17, 1999.

Betts, Stephen L. (with Sebastian Chen and Sandra Schulman). "Video Vixen, Shania Twain's Reel Life Story." *Country Music Today*, June/July 2000.

Bliss, Karen. "Shania Twain." *Canadian Musician*, April, 1998.

Bliss, Karen. "The Tracking of Come On Over." *Canadian Musician*, April, 1998.

Blosser, John (with Sherry Cremona and Bennet Bolton). "Shania Twain's Lonely Marriage. The Bizarre Truth about Why She Doesn't like Sex and Sleeps with Her Dog." *National Enquirer*, June 8, 1999.

Blosser, John. "Shania Joins No-sex Cult." *National Enquirer*, March 14, 2000.

Bouw, Brenda. "Twain Peaks: Singer Is Best-selling Woman Ever in U.S. Album Even Surpasses Garth." *National Post*, March 17, 2000.

Breithaupt, Jeff. "Twain Explained." *National Post*, March 20, 2000.

Brooks, Nancy. "Shania Twain: Intimate Sessions." *Country Song Roundup*, April, 2000.

Brown, Jim. "Twainmania." *Country Music News*, October, 1998.

Chiong, Roddy. "Getting the Shania Twain Gig." *www.roddy.com*.

Chodan, Lucinda. "Twain Turns Quebecers on to La Belle Country." *Ottawa Citizen*, May 8, 1996.

Chomin, Neva. "Twain Makes Mark on Adoring Fans: Country Diva Genuine but Frothy at Shoreline." *San Francisco Chronicle*, June 20, 1998.

Christgau, Robert. "Review: COME ON OVER." *The Village Voice*, January 27, 1998.

Churko, Cory. "Cory Churko's Musical Background." *www.corychurko.com*.

Clark, Michael D. "Twain Pleases Cowboys with Two Hours of Country Rock." *San Jose Mercury News*, June 20, 1998.

Colurso, Mary. "Shania's Star Zooms as

Mutt's Trophy Wife." *Birmingham News*, December 5, 1997.

Coulson, Sandra. "Shania Look-a-like Riding the Wave." *London Free Press*, November 6, 1997.

Cromwell, Richard. "Come On Over and Eat Some Moose!" *Sunday Magazine*, August 27, 1999.

Dafoe, Chris. "Diva, Diva on the Wall. What's Their Diva Quotient?" *The Globe & Mail*, February 20, 1999.

Delaney, Larry. "Producer Stan Campbell Brings New Artists into Recording Studios." *Country Music News*, December, 1984.

Delaney, Larry. "Canadian Ladies: Hitmakers of the 90s." *Country Music News*, February, 1992.

Delaney, Larry. "Canadian included in Mercury's Triple Play U.S. Record Launch: Ontario Singer Shania Twain 'Hit Bound'." *Country Music News*, March, 1993.

Delaney, Larry. "Shania Twain: What Made Her Do That." *Country Music News*, May, 1993.

Delaney, Larry. "Canuck Connections at Fan Fair Week." *Country Music News*, July, 1994.

Delaney, Larry. "Shania Twain Is on the Right Track." *Country Music News*, July, 1995.

Delaney, Larry. "Shania Twain ... The Metamorphosis of a Star." *Country Music News*, September, 1995.

Delaney, Larry. "CISS-FM 1st Annual 'FAN FEST' at Canada's Wonderland, August 6th." *Country Music News*, September, 1995.

Delaney, Larry. "Nashville Columnist Dumps on Cancountry (an editiorial response)." *Country Music News*, October, 1995.

Delaney, Larry. "George Fox TV Special Ratings Winner. Canadian Ladies a Featured Attraction. *Country Music News*, November, 1995.

Delaney, Larry. "The Twain Keeps on Chuggin' ... Canadian Star Shania Twain Now Country's Hottest Chart & Video Artist." *Country Music News*, February, 1996.

Delaney, Larry. "Cancountry Stars at Fan Fair '96." *Country Music News*, July 1996.

Delaney, Larry. "Standing Tall, Cancountry Circles the World: Shania Twain Leads the Way." *Country Music News*, August, 1996.

Delaney, Larry. "Songwriting Awards to Shania Twain." *Country Music News*, September, 1996.

Delaney, Larry. "Shania Twain." *Country Music News*, February, 1997.

Delaney, Larry. "'The Coach' Meets Country's 'Star Player'." *Country Music News*, August 1997.

Delaney, Larry. "Shania Twain." *Country Music News*, December, 1997.

Delaney, Larry. "Let the Tour Begin! Shania Twain Tour Dates Announced." *Country Music News*, April, 1998.

Delaney, Larry. "1998 CCMA Nominees Announced. Shania Twain Leads the Way with Eight." *Country Music News*, August, 1998.

Delaney, Larry. "The Glitter of It All." *Country Music News*, June, 1999.

Delaney, Larry. "Shania Twain ... Awards

e!" *Country Music News*, March, 2000.

ey, Larry. "Cover Story Flashback." *try Music News*, April 2000.

ey, Larry. "Shania Twain Wins ACM rtainer of the Year Award ...Canadian To Sponsor Hometown Scholarship l." *Country Music News*, June, 2000.

uca, Dan. "Twain's 'Come On Over' a ghty Inviting Album." *Philadelphia uirer*, November 4, 1997.

le, Ron. "The Foods that Fuel Shania." *tawa Citizen*, March 17, 1999.

rle, Charles. "Grammy Schmammy." ashville's Country Weekly *In Review*, larch 2, 1999.

Edwards, Trent. "Twain Defends Life Story of Poverty." *Ottawa Citizen*, June 6, 1999.

Farber, Jim. "New Twain CD Light, Frothy, Entertaining." *London Free Press*, November 6, 1997.

Fazari, Lori. "Shania Takes Revlon's Fancy." *Ottawa Citizen*, 1999.

Feiler, Bruce. "Country's New Women Find Fans Who Get It." *The New York Times*, November 2, 1997.

Feiler, Bruce. "Twain's World." *Live*, May, 1998.

Flippo, Chet. "Twain Branches Out on New Set." *Billboard*, October 18, 1997.

Flippo, Chet. "JoMaTo Bows with Early Twain Demos." *Billboard*, November 20, 1999.

Flohill, Richard. "Shania Scores in Run-Up to Juno Awards." *Country Canada: CCMA Official Newsletter*, February, 1996.

Flohill, Richard. "Shania Sweeps Canadian Country Music Awards." Official Media Information Release, 1998 CCMA Awards Show, Calgary, Alberta.

Flynn, Andrew. "Superstar Shania Touring — At Last." *Calgary Herald*, March 18, 1998.

Flynn, Andrew. "Northern Lights Shine: Canada's Stars, Twain, Dion and Morissette, Come Out Winners in Grammy Awards Ladies' Night Out." *The Province*, February 25, 1999.

Ford, Don. "Shania Twain." *Country Music People*, February, 1996.

French, Serena. "The Woman in These. Fashion Editor Surveys the Eclectic Wardrobe that Has Helped Twain Rise to the Top." *National Post*, March 20, 2000.

Gardner, Elysa. "Throwing Nashville a Curve." *Los Angeles Times*, November 2, 1997.

Gerlock, Jennifer. "Portrait of a Lady." *Country Song Roundup*, July, 1999.

Gerlock, Jennifer. "Portrait of a Lady Part 2." *Country Song Roundup*, Sept 1999.

Goodman, John. "The Buzz on Bobbi." *North Shore News*, March 10, 2000.

Graff, Gary. "A Country Woman: Twain Has Some Fun with Success." *Boston Herald*, November 15, 1997.

Grey, Colin (with Lynn Saxberg). "Glamour Girl Graces Capital. Shania Twain Squeezes in Photo Shoot in Little Italy. *Ottawa Citizen*, March 17, 1999.

Gunderson, Edna. "Unsinkable Celine Dion." *Calgary Sun*, September 27, 1998.

Gunderson, Edna. "Dion Bitten by Golf Bug." *Calgary Sun*, September 15, 1998.

Harbrecht, Gene. "Shania Rocks, a Little Over the Top." *The Orange County Register*, June 23, 1998.

Harrington, Richard. "Finally, Time to Meet Twain." *Washington Post*, August 17, 1998.

Harris, Kelly. "Shania Sparkles." *Calgary Sun*, November 9, 1997.

Hedegaard, Erik. "Shania Twain the Triumph of the Girl Next Door." *Rolling Stone*, September 3, 1998.

Helligar, Jeremy (with Natasha Stoynoff, Jennifer Longley, Beverly Keel, Julie Jordan, Helena Bachmann and Josie Bailenger). "Against All Odds." *People Weekly*, June 14, 1999.

Hepner, Lisa. "Snaps from a Concert." *Edmonton Journal*, June 6, 1998.

Hilburn, Robert. "Lots of Sizzle. Not Much Heat." *Los Angeles Times*, June 23, 1998.

Hunt, Dennis. "The Story: Woman Meets Man ..." *Los Angeles Times*, July, 1995.

Jinkins, Shirley. "Shania Twain Follows Up Top-selling 'Woman In Me'." *Range County Register*, November 10, 1997.

Johnson, Brian D. "Shania Revealed." *Macleans*, March 23, 1998.

Johnson, Kevin C. "Shania Twain's Riverport Visit has Rough Edges." *St. Louis Post Dispatch*, July 20, 1998.

Kauffman, Bill. "Shania Shares Spotlight: Local Performer Wins Chance to Sing with Superstar." *Calgary Sun*, June 5, 1998.

Kellogg, Alan. "Women in Country Music / Real Country Music Alive and Well." (Based on an interview with Robert K. Oermann). *Calgary Herald*, June 5, 1998.

Kennedy, Paul. "Come On Over Concert Review, Moncton, NB." *Country Music News*, April, 1999.

Klotz, Hattie. "The Beauty of Bag Balm." *Ottawa Citizen*, November 24, 1999.

Kovach, Joelle. "Shania Twain ... Gets Her 'Day'." *Country Music News*, Oct., 1996.

Krewen, Nick, and Tamara Saviano. "Shania's Other World." *Country Weekly*, April 25, 1998.

Krewen, Nick. "Country Music Still The One Shania Loves." *Country Weekly*, June 22, 1999.

LePage, Mark. "Superstars on the Skids: Demise of the Divas?" *Vancouver Sun*, April 15, 2000.

Lofaro, Tony. "Shania Homecoming to Go Ahead. Timmins Dispels Fears of Concert Park Collapse." *Ottawa Citizen*, June 11, 1999.

MacNeil, Ian. "A Night With Shania." *TV Week*, April 3, 1999.

McRae, Earl. "Beefing up Shania's Country Star Image." *Ottawa Sun*, June 8, 1999.

McLaughlin, John P. "Looking Back and Ahead." *The Province*, December 1998.

McLaughlin, John P. "That Dress! Shania Twain's Videos and Marc Bouwer's Fashion Sense Have Altered the Look of Country Music Forever." *The Province*, April 1, 1999.

McLaughlin, John P. "Life's Good on Shania's Road." *The Province*, April 1, 1998.

McLaughlin, John P. "It's Fun First with Shania." *The Province*, April 4, 1999.

McLeod, Tyler. "20,000 Greet Shania!" *Calgary Sun*, November 5, 1997.

McLeod, Tyler. "The Camera Loves Her." *Calgary Sun*, November 6, 1997.

Mansfield, Brian. "She's the One: Country Sees a Future in Shania's Pop Appeal." *The Province*, February 17, 1999.

Mansfield, Brian. "Come on Over, Again and Again." CDNow Interview with Shania posted by Jayne Twayne (aka Jayne Spears) on British website. November, 1999.

Mansfield, Stephanie. "Shania Twain." *USA Today*, February 21, 1999.

Miller, Sue (with Eve Heyn, Todd Gold, Cindy Dampier, Don Sider, and Joanna Blonska). *People Weekly*, January 18, 1999.

Mitchell, Rick. "Country Carpetbagger. Looks Aren't Everything. What about Talent, Passion, Depth?" *Houston Chronicle*, November 2, 1997.

Moon, Tom. "Shania Twain at CoreStates." *Philadelphia Inquirer*, August 17, 1998.

Morse, Steve. "Shania Twain Sings with Deeper Soul on New Album." Reprinted from original *Boston Globe* article, in *The Oregonian*, November 7, 1997.

Muller, Marc. "Marc Muller's Bio / History." *www.home.hyperworx.com.*

Myskow, Nina. "The Real, Real Me ... Shania Twain Reveals All." *The Daily Mirror*, August 27, 1999.

Muretich, James. "The Mall ... Where Fans and Twain Can Meet." *Calgary Herald*, November 9, 1997.

Muretich, James. "Sophomore Album for Shania." *Windsor Star*, November 10, 1997.

Muretich, James. "Twain Removes Any Doubts." *Calgary Herald*, May 30, 1998.

Muretich, James. "Shania Relaxed before Concert." *Calgary Herald*, May 30, 1998.

Muretich, James. "Shania! Twain Hits Town." *Calgary Herald*, June 6, 1998.

Muretich, James. "Singer Wins Contest to Perform with Star." *Calgary Herald*, June 6, 1998.

Muretich, James. "Shania! Twain Hits Town." *Calgary Herald*, June 6, 1998.

O'Connor, James. "Review: Shania Twain COME ON OVER." *The Winnipeg Sun*, Nov 14, 1997.

Oermann, Robert K. "I'm On My Way: Shania Twain Rock's Canada's Country Awards." *The Tennessean*, September 30, 1995.

Oermann, Robert K. "Shania Twain: More Than Meets the Eye." *The Tennessean*, February 28, 1996.

Oermann, Robert K. "Twain's Kin Questioning the Indian in Her / Twain Defends Native American Heritage as Her Own." Syndicated in North America, 1996.

Orr, Jay. "Canadian Country Star Twain Primed to Take Hot New Album on the Road." *Nashville Banner*, November 7, 1997.

Overall, Rick. "Music City Love-in: Fan Fair for Country Music." *Ottawa Sun*, June 11, 1996.

Overall, Rick. "Shania Twain's Wake-up Call." *Ottawa Sun*, September 14, 1997.

Pagan, Ken. "Shania Twain's Hometown to Explain Concert Costs." *National Post*, December 27, 1999.

Parsons, Clark. "Shania Twain's Lessons for Music Row, Twain of Command." *The Journal Of Country Music*, Volume No. 18:3.

Pareles, John. "Sure, She's a Rebel. And, Make No Mistake, A One-Man Woman." *New York Times*, August 24, 1998.

Patterson, Jim. "Elusive Honor: Shania Twain Has Won Every Award in The Book — Except One." *Ottawa Sun*, October 1, 1996.

Paxman, Bob. "Martina McBride: Theory of Evolution." *Country Song Roundup*, January, 1998.

Paxman, Bob. "Country vs Pop." *Country Weekly*, April 4, 2000.

Peake, Mike. "Shania." *FHM*, May/June 2000.

Pocharski, Susan. "Filly." *Cosmopolitan*, March, 1998.

Pond, Neil. "Shania Twain: Most Likely to Succeed." *Country America*, March, 1993.

Powell, Betsy. "Bottom Line Is Music, Twain Says." *Ottawa Citizen*, February 8, 1996.

Provencher, Norman. "Twain a-comin'." *Ottawa Citizen*, May 27, 1998.

Provencher, Norman. "Southbound for Shania: Timmins Empties as Singer's Fans Head to Sudbury." *Ottawa Citizen*, May 28, 1998.

Provencher, Norman. "Shaniamania: Sudbury Backup Singers Pumped for Tonight's Concert." *Ottawa Citizen*, May 29, 1998.

Reiner, Eric L. "Twain's Performance at Fiddler's Worthy of a Star." *Denver Post*, July 17, 1998.

Roberts, Mike. "She's Still the One!" *The Province*, April 4, 1999.

Roberts, Mike. "All Dressed Up." *The Province*, April 4, 1999.

Rohrer, Trish Deitch. "Twain's World." Cover story, for "Fun, Fearless Female Awards." *Cosmopolitan*, March, 1999.

Roland, Tom. "Get a Taste of Shania Twain's Mix of Rock, Country." *The Tennessean*, February 13, 1995.

Roland, Tom. "CMA Show Launch Pad for Twain." *The Tennessean*, September 23, 1997.

Roland, Tom. "Twain Rocks in 'Come On Over.'" *The Tennessean*, November 3, 1997.

Roland, Tom. "At Long Last, Shania Twain Ready to Roll Out Major Tour." *The Tennessean*, March 3, 1998.

Roland, Tom. "A Critical Gaze." *The Tennessean*, May 23, 1998.

Roland, Tom. "Twain Concert: 'The Singer in Me.'" *The Tennessean*, May 31, 1998.

Roland, Tom. "Shimmy, Shake, Make the Earth Quake. Any Audience of Shania's Will Walk the Line, Pulled in by Her Energetic Delivery." *The Tennessean*, September 25,1998.

Roland, Tom. "Shania Twain's Songs Net Writer-artist Award." *The Tennessean*, April 17, 1999.

Ross, Mike. "Sweetheart of the Rodeo: Shania Twain Pushes All of the Right Buttons." *Edmonton Sun*, May 31, 1998.

Rottenberg, Josh. "Leap of Faith." *US Weekly*, May 15, 2000.

Sardi, Liza. "Let's Talk about Multiplying Love ... Chanteuse Celine Dion Says She'd Like to Have a Baby ... What's the Hold Up?" *Calgary Sun*, October 8, 1998.

Saxberg, Lynn. "Shania Shines on Ottawa." *Ottawa Citizen*, March 18, 1999.

Schneller, Johanna. "The Unstoppable

Shania Twain: Runaway Twain." *Chatelaine*, May 1996.

Schoemer, Karen. "The Malling of Shania." *Newsweek*, February, 1996.

Schoemer, Karen. "The Girl Problem." *Newsweek*, November 17, 1997.

Simons, Stephanie. "Some Kind of Diva." The Tacoma *News Tribune*, June 12, 1998.

Skinner, Ron. "Choosing a Recording Studio. Advice from Bryan Adams, Moist, Econoline Crush and Marc Jordan." *Canadian Musician*, March-April 2000.

Starnes, Richard. "Twain Covers Cosmo Mag." *The Province*, March, 1999.

Stevenson, Jane. "Sweet Smell of Success: Canadian Shania Twain Riding High." *Ottawa Sun*, February 6, 1996.

Stout, Gene. "Twain Shall Meet Her Legions of Fans on First National Tour." *Seattle Post Intelligencer*, June 12, 1998.

Sweetland, Phil. "Country Insider Faces Off with Terri Clark." *Country Music News*, April 2000.

Taradell, Mario. "Her Way. Why Tour? Shania Twain Finds Success without the Stage." *Dallas Morning News*; reprinted in *The Buffalo News*, April 6, 1996.

Tianen, Dave. "Shania Won't Be Death of Country ..." *Milwaukee Journal Sentinel*, November 9, 1997."

Tianen, Dave. "Twain Sets a New Tone. There's Nothing Submissive about This Country Babe." *Milwaukee Journal Sentinel*, June 28, 1998.

Trott, Walt. "Shania Twain Voted Entertainer of the Year." *Country Music*

People, November, 1999.

Twayne, Jayne (aka Jayne Spears). "Interview with J.D. Blair." *www.shania-twain.co.uk.*

Twayne, Jayne (host). "Online chat with Brent Barcus." *www.shania-twain.co.uk.*

Van Wyk, Anika. "Shania Wants You to Come On Over." *Calgary Sun*, November 3, 1997.

Van Wyk, Anika. "Shania's Learning Curves: Canada's Sexy Country Singer Recalls Her Awkward Years." *Edmonton Sun*, November 4, 1997.

Van Wyk, Anika. "Emotional Meeting." *Calgary Sun*, November 9, 1997.

Van Wyk, Anika. "Queen of Sudbury: Twain's Confident, Excited as Tour Begins." *Calgary Sun*, May 30, 1998.

Van Wyk, Anika. "Shania Soars! First Concert of the Tour a Real World-beater." *Calgary Sun*, May 30, 1998.

Van Wyk, Anika. "Vindication!" *Calgary Sun*, May 31, 1998.

Van Wyk, Anika. "Twain Alone." *Calgary Sun*, August 5, 1998.

Van Wyk, Anika. "Sweet Six for Shania. CCMA Sweep for Queen of Country." *Calgary Sun*, September 15, 1998.

Van Wyk, Anika. "Calgary's Big Night: Twain Savors Her Triumph Backstage." *Calgary Sun*, September 15, 1998.

Van Wyk, Anika. "Country Talent Gets in Groove. Rehearsal Part Business, Part Pleasure." *Calgary Sun*, September 15, 1998.

Van Wyk, Anika. "Terri Clark Has the Last

Laugh as Shania Twain Sweeps Awards." *Country Weekly*, October 13, 1998.

Veitch, David. "Short 'n' Snappy." *Calgary Sun*, September 15, 1998.

Victor, Allen F. "Mercury's Triple Play Tour Charts New Territory." *Performance*, May 7, 1993.

Victor, Allen F. "Triple Exposure for Toby Keith, Shania Twain and John Brannen." *Performance*, May 7, 1993.

Walsh, Jim. "Go Figure…Country Superstar Shania Twain Bares the Facts about Her Revealing Wardrobe, Feminism and the Business of Being a Talented Beauty." *Saint Paul Pioneer Press*, November 4, 1997.

Waring, Michael. "The Shania Storm." *Just Betwain Friends: "The Official Shania Twain Fan Club Newsletter"*, Volume 1, Issue 4.

Weikle, Brandie. "Twain's Got a Heart. Gives Tickets and Backstage Pass to Cancer Survivor." *The Province*, April 1, 1999.

Wild, David. "Interview with Joni Mitchell." *Rolling Stone*, May 30, 1991.

Williams, Janet E. "Shania Twain on the Road at Last." *Country Song Roundup*, June, 1998.

Wood, Gerry. "Record Review: COME ON OVER (International Version). *Country Weekly*, February 8, 2000.

Woods, Judith. "The Spiritual Girl. Madonna 'a typical pitta.'" *The Province*, April 24, 2000.

Zimmerman, David. "Daddy's Little Girl." *Ottawa Sun*, June 20, 1996.

Zimmerman, David. "Super Slick Pop Follow-up Misses Country by a Mile." *USA Today*, November 3, 1997.

Zimmerman, David. "Twain Le224ts Fans Be Her Guide for 'Come On Over'." *USA Today*, November 3, 1997.

Videos & Films

Behind the Music: Shania Twain. Polygram Video, VH1 Music First, 1999.

The Complete Woman in Me Video Collection. Polygram Video, 1996.

Come On Over Video Collection. Mercury Records, Universal Music, 1999.

Shania Twain Live. Mercury Records, Universal Music, 1999.

Notting Hill. A Roger Michell Film. Polygram Films, 1998.

ACKNOWLEDGMENTS

THE AUTHOR WOULD LIKE TO THANK THE FOLLOWING people, without whose help this book could not have been written. Larry Delaney at *Country Music News* for the research, support, and for believing in Shania from that first story in 1984. (For subscription information, call 613-745-6006.) Cathy Taylor. Greg Shannon. Ken Ashdown. Curry King at CMT: *Country Music Today*. And Lauren Bufferd at the Country Music Foundation Library and Media Center.

LYRICS

Oh Carol. By Neil Sedaka and Howard Greenfield. Screen Gems — EMI Music Inc.
Half-Breed. By John D. Loudermilk. Cedarwood Publishing (BMI).
Man! I Feel Like A Woman!; *Love Get's Me Every Time*; *Don't Be Stupid (You Know I Love You)*; *If You Wanna Touch Her Ask*; *You're Still the One*; *Honey I'm Home*; *That Don't Impress Me Much*; *Rock This Country!* By Shania Twain and Robert John 'Mutt' Lange. Songs of Polygram Int. Inc. / Loon Echo Music, Inc. (BMI) / Out of Pocket Productions Ltd. Controlled by Zomba Enterprises, Inc. (ASCAP) for Canada and the United States of America.

PHOTOGRAPHS

Front Cover: Reuters/Jeff Christensen/Archive Photos
Back Cover: Maggie Scherf

p. 2   Mercury/PolyGram
p. 6   Mercury/PolyGram (Timothy White)
p. 35   Mercury/PolyGram (Barry Hollywood)
p. 36   Country Image/Barb Blanchard
p. 37   Myron Zabol (photography)/Virginia Team (art direction)